D1109714

Half Moon

By the same author

God's Mercies: Rivalry, Betrayal, and the Dream of Discovery
Molson: The Birth of a Business Empire
Yacht Design Explained (coauthor)
The Bubble and the Bear: How Nortel Burst the Canadian Dream

HALF MOON

*Henry Hudson and
the Voyage That Redrew the
Map of the New World*

DOUGLAS HUNTER

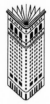

BLOOMSBURY PRESS
New York • Berlin • London

Published by Bloomsbury Press, New York

All papers used by Bloomsbury Press are natural, recyclable products made from
wood grown in well-managed forests. The manufacturing processes conform
to the environmental regulations of the country of origin.

LIBRARY OF CONGRESS CATALOGING-IN-PUBLICATION DATA

Hunter, Doug, 1959–
Half moon: Henry Hudson and the voyage that redrew the map of the
New World / Douglas Hunter.—1st U.S. ed.
p. cm.
Includes bibliographical references.
ISBN-13: 978-1-59691-680-7 (alk. paper)
ISBN-10: 1-59691-680-X (alk. paper)
1. Hudson, Henry, d. 1611. 2. America—Discovery and exploration—Dutch.
3. Half Moon (Ship) 4. Explorers—America—History—17th century.
5. Nederlandsche Oost-Indische Compagnie. 6. Hudson River Valley (N.Y. and N.J.)—
Discovery and exploration. I. Title. II. Title: Henry Hudson and the voyage that
redrew the map of the New World.
E129.H8H866 2009
910.92—dc22
2009000642

First U.S. Edition 2009

1 3 5 7 9 10 8 6 4 2

Typeset by Westchester Book Group
Printed in the United States of America by Quebecor World Fairfield

To voyagers everywhere

Introduction

THIS BOOK BEGAN TAKING SHAPE IN 2003 and followed a course almost as circuitous as Henry Hudson's in the *Half Moon*.

I was planning to write about the Laurentian Shield and its role in the history and culture of Canada. One chapter would deal with early exploration, and I decided to use as a thematic rallying point the lost astrolabe of Samuel de Champlain, a showcase holding of the Canadian Museum of Civilization. Researching the history of that astrolabe produced the first of many unexpected turns. The provenance of the device where Champlain was concerned was iffy at best, and I ended up writing a cover feature for the *Beaver*, Canada's national history magazine, on why Jesuit missionaries were a much better fit as its owners.

Explaining the provenance issue also required me to investigate why Champlain was traveling on the Ottawa River in the summer of 1613, when he supposedly lost the astrolabe. It turned out he was making a harrowing journey into uncharted territory, in hope of both reaching the Northern Sea and collecting from an Algonquin people called the Nebicerini an English boy they were holding captive. The *Discovery* mutiny of 1611 on James Bay was the only possible source of the boy, as John Hudson had been cast away in a shallop with his father, Henry, and seven other Englishmen and had never been seen since.

While Champlain did not find the boy (and it's never been entirely clear that the captive youth ever existed), the story was irresistible. The book about the Laurentian Shield was itself cast away, as I wrote instead the story of the traumatic convergence in the careers of Hudson and Champlain. Three years of research and writing produced *God's Mercies*, which was published by Doubleday Canada in 2007.

Along the way, I conducted more than enough research to write an entire biography of Hudson, covering all four of his known voyages. Before *God's Mercies* was published I began making plans to that end. But it was the "prequel" voyage to the final, fatal one of 1610–11, which I wrote about in detail in *God's Mercies*, that especially intrigued me. The 1609 *Half Moon* voyage was as strange and at times as tragic as the *Discovery* venture. And it also had the distinction of laying the groundwork for the founding of the great city of New York. Early in 2008, I telescoped the plan to write a full biography and began writing the book you now have in your hands. I had dealt with the 1609 voyage tangentially in *God's Mercies*, which meant that in some aspects of the story, I would be revisiting familiar terrain. I expected some amount of retelling of what I had covered—the basic facts about Sir Thomas Smythe and Robert Juet, for example. But it soon became clear that, as much research as I had performed in the previous three years, there was still more to do, in digesting new materials, revisiting the sources I already had, and deciding what it all meant.

When I lecture on the craft of narrative nonfiction, I stress that writing history requires an imagination. By that I do not mean the skill or nerve to make things up. Rather, it is the ability to sift through available evidence, however thin at times, and see patterns, connections, and possibilities. And the new book provided a fresh opportunity to think hard about what the evidence was trying to tell me. That was especially true of the remarkable letter written by Thomas Holland, mayor of Dartmouth, to Sir Robert Cecil after Holland met Hudson and debriefed him on where he had just been on the *Half Moon* voyage and what he was planning to do next. That encounter was a prelude to events in *God's Mercies*. Now, it was both an aftermath to the *Half Moon* voyage and a crucial bit of evidence in fathoming Hudson's motivations. I had pondered those motivations in *God's Mercies*, but for this new work I was able to bring the evidence into much clearer focus.

I also changed my mind about something I'd already written in *God's Mercies*, which thankfully was a minor fact in that work, but a major one in the new book. I had accepted the conclusions of earlier writers that Hudson's first landfall in the *Half Moon* was around the Georges River in what is now Maine. Viewed in isolation, the Georges River did seem a good fit. But as I now had the time and the writing space to properly dissect the

1609 voyage and the journal entries of Robert Juet, I realized that his account was impossible to reconcile with a passage from the Georges River to the *Half Moon*'s next landfall, Cape Cod. The evidence instead clearly was pointing back from Cape Cod to Nova Scotia's south shore, to the area around Liverpool and La Have—something I believe my friend the scholar Conrad Heidenreich tried to tell me while I was researching *God's Mercies*, but it had failed to sink in.

The deductive process was an interesting lesson in working with historical narrative and required a slew of hydrographic charts with soundings to compare to those recorded by Juet in order to come to a satisfactory answer. The voyage essentially had to be reverse-engineered, starting with a known landfall, at Cape Cod, and working backward to see where the trail of evidence led. Having settled on La Have as Hudson's first landfall, I was then able to trace the voyage back to an uncomfortably close encounter with Sable Island. The voyage record for that leg, from the first encounter with the Grand Banks to the arrival at La Have, is at times confusing and difficult to reconcile with cartographic references, but this only underscored for me what a confusing and difficult time Hudson was having in making his way safely through substantially uncharted waters.

My research already had led me to propose a new theory of how the French initially colonized eastern North America at the dawn of the seventeenth century. I was able to show striking parallels in the writings of Champlain and the midcontinental passage theory of Englishman Edward Hayes, published in 1602, which strongly suggested that Champlain and his cohorts had taken their cue from Hayes's writings, to the point that Champlain had fudged some of his evidence for what lay upstream of the rapids at present-day Montréal in order to agree with what Hayes had committed to print. I published an article to this effect in the *Beaver*. I was unable to make full use of the evidence in the course of telling the essential story of *God's Mercies*, but I've now been able to employ it more completely, as it is so critical to understanding what Hudson was up to during his at times bewildering 1609 voyage. (Champlain is also back, in a noteworthy supporting role.) I've also been able to employ additional evidence of Spanish ideas about a midcontinental passage that were in circulation in the 1560s. The notion that there was a route right through North America to the Orient's riches was a highly influential one, and its importance in the motivations and justifications of the early colonization period is in my mind underappreciated, when appreciated at all.

A FAIR-SIZED CHALLENGE in telling the story of the 1609 *Half Moon* voyage, as my struggles with his initial landfall indicate, lay in figuring out where Henry Hudson was on any given day. As the narrative explains, above and beyond the considerable problems of accuracy in surviving navigational data for the voyage, one has to contend with significant changes in terrain, shorelines, and water depths.

I set out to create the maps in this book for two reasons. One was to help me figure out where Hudson was and what he would have seen. The other was to help the reader follow the story.

The *Half Moon*'s reported daily position fixes and dead-reckoning results were far too incomplete and error-prone for me to dare plot a course for the entire voyage that a reader might construe as definitive. With a few exceptions, I've opted instead to draw regions visited with sufficient detail to allow the reader to appreciate where the ship (probably) was. In the cases of Rockaway Inlet, Chesapeake Bay, and Delaware Bay, I have used historic navigation charts as base maps. These are old enough that significant modern changes (by and large man-made) are avoided, but not so old that their accuracy is an issue. It would be wrong to assume that any places in these charts from the nineteenth and early twentieth centuries were exactly as presented when Hudson came calling. But they give a more informative picture than an up-to-date navigation chart.

The real cartographic challenges arose in the greater New York area and along the length of the Hudson River to Albany. The man-made changes to coastlines and depth contours have been enormous since Hudson's time, and working back to a reasonable portrait of what these waters might have been like circa 1609 is no easy matter. I consulted many maps and charts (technically, a chart is a map used for marine navigation) dating back to the seventeenth century, but their plotting accuracy is often suspect, and depth soundings do not start to become both detailed and authoritative until the nineteenth century.

For the maps of the New York area in chapters 13 and 16, I began with the lovely *Map of New-York Bay and Harbor and Environs*, a tour de force of hydrography and topography published by the Survey of the Coast of the

United States in 1845. Its soundings serve as the main basis for my depth contours. The map also provided the essential shape of the shore, but for some details, especially in Upper New York Bay and particularly Manhattan, I consulted maps and charts dating back to the era of New Netherland. I would not presume my efforts to be definitive, as we can never know exactly what was there, four hundred years ago.

The Hudson River turned out to be a much bigger challenge to draw than I first imagined. The river has seen many changes in its depths and shorelines. Railway construction in particular has "hardened" many miles of shore. I began with a series of nineteenth-century nautical charts for some 150 miles of river from New York to Albany, which gave soundings as well as contours of where the river began to shoal, at the three-fathom line. To help the reader appreciate where the river was particularly challenging, I made a tracing of these shoaling waters. For the shoreline (and a more accurate plotting of the river's course), I turned to U.S. Geological Survey topographic maps that were generally the result of fieldwork in the 1890s. These had a major advantage of being fairly accurate in plotting while preserving many natural shoreline contours that existed before the railways were completed.

When I finished plotting, I realized I had created a series of digital illustration files totaling some fifteen feet in length, which was a little more detail than a book warrants. The river was then broken into six sections and greatly scaled down to fit the printed page.

After all that, I cannot guarantee that the river looked exactly like this to Hudson. Shoals (and islands) come and go and shift over time in any river. Some of the areas described as shoaling waters still would have been navigable to a vessel that drew eight or nine feet of water like the *Half Moon*; other areas would have been dry at low tide. As with the maps of the New York area, the ones describing the Hudson River are a best effort by me to give the reader a sense of the landscape and seascape Hudson encountered, and an appreciation of the obstacles he faced.

Some final notes on style: To make the story more digestible by the general reader, I have used English translations for titles of seventeenth-century Dutch publications and the names of trading companies. To the same end I have "translated" quotes from contemporary English documents into modern English. In that regard, little more has been done than adopt modern spelling, without which many passages can be difficult for nonscholars to follow.

CHAPTER 1

O N TUESDAY, SEPTEMBER 1, 1609, seventeen of the most powerful
and affluent merchants in the world gathered in Amsterdam. They
were the directors of the Generaale Vereenigde Geoctroijeerde Oost-
indische Compagnie—the General United Chartered East-Indian Company, better known by its initials as the VOC, and to the English as the
Dutch East India Company. However one referred to it, the VOC was the
most powerful and profitable commercial entity in the world, the main engine of prosperity for the United Northern Provinces, or Dutch Republic. It
held the country's monopoly on trade to the Far East on the proven ocean
trade routes: around Africa, and through the Strait of Magellan at the tip of
South America.

The enormous profits from porcelain, textiles, coffee, tea, and spices
made the little nation a colossus of global trade. Perpetuating that wealth
was the responsibility of the VOC's board, the Here Sewentien, or Lords
Seventeen. All attention at this board meeting was on the members from
Amsterdam, who represented the largest of the company's six regional
chambers of investors, which ran individual shipping operations in the name
of the greater company. Having contributed about half the investment capital when the world's first joint-stock company was formed in 1602, Amsterdam's chamber dominated the company's affairs, but was still answerable
to the rest of the investors. The company's charter limited Amsterdam to
eight of seventeen board seats. They had been able to have their way on a
pet project with a bit of boardroom arm twisting, but now it was time for

the other nine directors from Hoorn, Rotterdam, Enkhuizen, Delft, and Zeeland to hold them to account.

The Amsterdam directors were asked to distribute copies of two critical documents. One was the sailing instructions for a voyage of discovery dispatched the previous April. The other was the contract of the Englishman hired to command it.

A single vessel, the *Half Moon*,* had been sent out at the initiative of the Amsterdam investors. Her master, or commanding officer, was Henry Hudson, an Englishman who had made two arctic voyages aboard a little ship called the *Hopewell* for commercial interests in his own country in 1607 and 1608. The first voyage had tried and failed to prove the feasibility of a midsummer passage to the Orient over the North Pole. The second had tried and failed to prove the feasibility of a midsummer passage to the Orient over the top of Russia. Thanks to the Amsterdam chamber, Hudson had been hired to again try the route over Russia, this time for the VOC.

The *Hopewell* voyages, despite their failure, had made Henry Hudson the leading international figure in efforts, however sporadic and unproductive, to prove a northerly passage to the Orient. Interest had been falling in and out of fashion among merchant adventurers for decades. The English had not attempted the Northeast Passage, over the top of Russia, since 1580 when Hudson again tested it in 1608. But the possibility of a northern route, like the prospect of turning lead into gold, or of perpetual motion, continued to entice.

A viable route would reduce a round-trip trading voyage to the Far East from two years or more to about six months. Returns on capital would be far quicker, and risks could be greatly reduced. About one ship in five never came back from the round-Africa route. A northern passage could avoid, among other hazards, battles with the Spanish and Portuguese, devastating diseases, hulls that rotted during lengthy stays in tropical waters, and the mysterious, debilitating scourge of scurvy, which cut down men by the score on lengthy ocean passages.

Dutch merchants had made a concerted effort to prove a northern route on three voyages in the 1590s associated with the pilot Willem Barentsz.

---

* Spelling of the ship's name varies in Dutch documents and accounts. It is commonly rendered as *Halve Maen* or *Halve Maan*. The anglicized version of the name is used in this book.

The death of Barentsz on the final voyage, in 1597, had brought an end to that phase of the quest, but the idea of pursuing the passage search had never entirely gone away. Any possible solution to the bottom-line problem of a transportation pipeline that tended to consume one fifth of the delivery vehicles—and about one third of the employees—was going to merit a second, third, or fourth look.

The VOC had been grappling not only with the potential of a Northeast route but with the consequences of some other group of Dutch merchants discovering it and securing the applicable monopoly from the government, the States-General. A new Oriental trade that could be conducted in six months would vaporize the value of investments in a VOC monopoly on a route that took far longer and involved myriad hazards and losses. At a meeting in August 1603, the VOC's directors had resolved not to mount an arctic expedition but had also rather grimly decided that "if this navigation should be undertaken by any private persons, it ought to be by all means prevented."

The renewed Amsterdam interest in the autumn of 1608 that had led to Henry Hudson's hiring was born of daunting geopolitics. The northern provinces of the Netherlands had formally become independent from Spanish rule in 1581, in a rebellion that had launched the Eighty Years' War in 1568. While the new republic was supported by England and France, its former Spanish overlords of the Hapsburg empire long refused to recognize its independence. Peace negotiations had begun in 1607 at The Hague (Den Haag) but had just collapsed. The Spanish were insisting that the Dutch give up the East Indies trade as a condition of peace, a nonstarter. The Spanish delegation had gone home, and the prospect of outright war on the main southern trade route, around Africa, was high. It was time to consider, once again, the possibility that there was an alternate route to the Orient's riches through arctic waters.

Henry Hudson was considered to be the best man for the job when the Amsterdam merchants decided that the VOC should have another look at the hypothetical route over the top of Russia. Hudson's previous ventures for his English employers had amounted to an extended fact-checking of the arctic voyages made by Barentsz on the same routes in the 1590s.

Hudson might have been forty years old when he received his invitation in the autumn of 1608 to come to Amsterdam and chat about arctic passage-making. A speculative portrait would later show him with close-cropped hair and beard, slightly bulbous eyes, and a ruff collar almost as wide as his shoulders, but there is no evidence he actually looked anything like this. He would have been well weathered by his arctic adventures, and while his connections at the court of England's James I would prove to be considerable, he was not a courtier or a noble but a professional mariner, as the positions of master and pilot attributed to him in the 1608 voyage journal were licensed by Trinity House on Deptford Strand. We know he was married to a woman named Katherine and that he had three sons. But because we don't know when they were married, we can't say whether all of his dependents were their shared offspring or were the products of an early Hudson marriage to a different woman. There was a toddler, Richard, and a young man, Oliver, who was about to make him a grandfather. Finally there was John, who had been the ship's boy on the 1607 *Hopewell* voyage. While he was listed as a general member of the 1608 crew, Hudson nevertheless called him "my boy" in his journal. John might have been in his early teens when his father entered into negotiations with the Amsterdam merchants.

The Amsterdam chamber liked what it heard from him about the feasibility of the northeast route. On December 27, 1608, according to the chamber's minutes, three members were tasked "to draft the contracts with the Englishman and the letters to be written to the Chambers." These letters were to solicit the other chambers' support for sending out Hudson on a voyage backed by the entire company, as opposed to what would have been a "private" venture by the Amsterdam chamber. A simple majority vote of the seventeen directors would be required. At the same time, two directors were commissioned "to look out, in conjunction with Dirck Gerritsz, the chief boatswain, for a suitable vessel . . . wherein the Englishman may sail."

THE EMPLOYMENT CONTRACT called for Hudson to depart around April 1 and sail to a northern latitude that would allow him to clear the tip of Novaya Zemlya, the great Russian archipelago known as the "belt of stone," as Barentsz twice had. He was then to proceed east until he was able to sail at least as far south as latitude 60—a physical impossibility, as the Asian landmass reached into far higher latitudes than geographers thought. "He shall obtain as much knowledge of the lands as can be done without any

Europe/Arctic.

considerable loss of time, and if it is possible, return immediately in order to make a faithful report and relation of the voyage to the Directors, and to deliver over his journals, log books and charts, together with an account of everything whatsoever which shall happen to him during the voyage, without keeping anything back."

Should Hudson be successful in reaching latitude 60 beyond Novaya Zemlya—and in returning alive—the directors pledged, they would "reward the before named Hudson for his dangers, trouble and knowledge, in their discretion, with which the before mentioned Hudson is content." Further, if the directors thought it "proper to prosecute and continue the same voyage"—in other words, to have another try—"it is stipulated and agreed with the before named Hudson that he shall make his residence in this country, with his wife and children, and shall enter into employment of no other than the Company, and this at the discretion of the Directors who also promise to make him satisfied and content for such further service in all justice and equity, all without fraud or evil intent."

The Amsterdam chamber had hired Hudson for a basic reconnaissance mission with a narrowly defined set of objectives. The contract, in modern parlance, was significantly back-loaded, with promises of ample rewards, lengthy employment, and security for Hudson and his family, should the Englishman prove his skills and worth on the initial voyage.

The Amsterdam chamber was able to have Hudson's voyage anointed as an official VOC undertaking, and he departed the city on April 4, sailing north up the inland sea, the Zuiderzee. The *Half Moon* negotiated the shifting sands at Texel, the island marking the entrance to the North Sea, on April 6. Three days later, the Twelve Year Truce between Spain and the Dutch Republic was signed at Antwerp. While it was not an outright indefinite peace, it did promise safe passage for unescorted and unarmed merchant ships. And there was no requirement that the Dutch abandon the East India trade. Any concerns the VOC might have had about being forced to relinquish its fabulously profitable trade via the southern routes vanished right after sending out Hudson to find a replacement route to the northeast.

Hudson cleared Norway's North Cape on May 5. The little ship and crew of sixteen were very much alone: no report would survive of a sighting or a "parlay," an exchange of greetings and news between ships on the high seas. The Saami, or Lapps, who traded with Europeans along the Kola Peninsula, likely watched her pass. Instead of calling on them or bearing southward for the Russian trade port of Arkhangel'sk on the White Sea, Hudson had forged eastward across the Barents Sea, toward Novaya Zemlya, beyond anyone's sight or knowledge.

Five months after the *Half Moon* left Amsterdam, the VOC board requested the copies of Hudson's sailing instructions and contract. The directors wanted to review exactly what they'd gotten themselves into at the Amsterdam contingent's urging: above all, where they had explicitly told him to go and when they might expect him back with their ship and crew.

THE LORDS SEVENTEEN plainly had become restive as they convened on September 1, 1609. If Hudson had succeeded, he should have been in China by then. If he had failed, any number of things could have happened. And failure was the greatest likelihood. Only Barentsz had ever succeeded in sailing above Novaya Zemlya, and in 1596–97 that had gotten him trapped in ice for the winter, which cost him his ship and ultimately his life. Before Barentsz, the English had hammered away at the Northeast Passage for decades without coming close to success, and Hudson had not even matched Barentsz's progress on his 1608 voyage.

If Hudson wasn't actually in China, the best that could be hoped was that he had put in at Arkhangel'sk for repairs, or that he was on his way back to Amsterdam, having been thwarted by pack ice. At worst, the *Half Moon* by now had been crushed by ice, Hudson was dead, and the VOC would be contractually obligated to pay Hudson's widow, Katherine, a death benefit of two hundred guilders. And there would be an entire ship to write off on the company ledgers.

The truth about the *Half Moon*'s circumstances would have astonished and enraged the VOC's highly pragmatic directors.

The *Half Moon* that day was steering north-northwest, with the lead line tickling the plunge of the continental shelf as crewmember Robert Juet, one of four Englishmen aboard, noted in his journal: "fair weather, the wind variable between east and south." They took a noon fix of the sun and calculated their latitude: 39 degrees, 3 minutes. Henry Hudson was in command of a Dutch ship he had effectively stolen and was skirting the east coast of North America, about a hundred miles off present-day Atlantic City, New Jersey.

Hudson had turned a basic assignment to assess the Northeast Passage route into a rogue voyage of discovery. He had wandered thousands of miles in defiance of his employers across the northern hemisphere, commanding a voyage whose exact purpose defied explanation.

The *Half Moon* voyage seemingly had become an end unto itself, answerable only to its own momentum, without any fixed goal or termination point. Most of it so far had been a waste of time and effort, with little new knowledge to show for the thousands of sea miles logged. But having just recorded what may have been a European first in probing Delaware Bay, Hudson was about to confront a complex tidal estuary and an unexplored river that would fix his name to the charts.

His impending discoveries would change the geopolitical momentum of North America and lead to the founding of a new locus of global economic and political power. But so many aspects of the *Half Moon* voyage—who Hudson thought he was actually working for, what he thought he would find, when (if ever) he was prepared to show his face in Amsterdam again, and why he had chosen to so egregiously defy the most powerful merchants in the world—would remain enigmas for centuries. The answers are far from definitive, but Hudson's motivations and aspirations can at least be proposed, with good evidence leading in extraordinary directions.

CHAPTER 2

THE WEATHER ON THE MORNING OF September 2, 1609, Robert Juet recorded, was "close"—humid and stifling, as a lazy southerly wind delivered warm tropical air above latitude 39. The *Half Moon*'s yards were set square to the wind as she ran before it at little more than a brisk walking pace. Somewhere to the west, to their left, to port, was land. They had lost sight of shore in the haze but could see smoke from a great fire, which meant *terra firma* could not be far off.

Hudson may have been watching for some fresh sign of it with a telescope: the first commercial models had gone on sale in Amsterdam in 1608. He continued to feel his way forward along the seafloor, as the lead line was endlessly heaved and retrieved, the fathoms called out with every fresh contact. The shore, when they could see it, was comprised of beaches, barrier islands, and tidewater embayments that stretched for tens of miles, and Hudson gave it a wide berth. It was a dangerous stretch of coast, running north and east from what would be named Cape May. Nineteenth-century pilot's guides would advise mariners to sound regularly and come no closer than ten fathoms, or sixty feet of depth.

When their soundings retreated steadily from twenty to ten fathoms, Hudson prudently steered east-southeast, directly out to sea. The yards swung as the sails were trimmed more parallel to their course and the ship moved onto a reach, its fastest point of sail. But the wind was light, and the little ship likely was leaving only gentle ripples for a wake.

Juet eyed the half-hour glass, which was kept at hand to mark time and help estimate distance sailed. Four times the glass was flipped as the *Half Moon* stood out to sea. And so they sailed for two hours away from the shoaling water, enough to gain some easterly advantage on the shore's northeasterly trend.*

The sun then broke through the haze, a change in weather that would have been faintly noticeable to the helmsman as he peered out of a hutch-like opening beneath the poop deck. Protected from the elements, he could scarcely see where he was directing the ship. The mainmast was smack in the center of his field of vision, the boots of the men on the quarterdeck tromped through the view, and the rise of the forecastle at the bow further impeded his sight lines. A man gawking out of a curbside storm sewer was only slightly more impaired in his perceptions.

The helmsman directed the vessel in one of two ways. By craning his neck to take in the mainsail, he could adjust his course to keep the sail in proper trim as the wind direction varied. Otherwise he blindly heeded commands shouted at him by whoever was deciding the ship's course (called conning) on a particular watch. Commands were made according to the thirty-two "winds," or points of the compass—east-northeast, southwest by south, and so on—or by giving course alterations in so many points and half-points.

The strategy of providing the course for the helmsman to steer was the one preferred by Hudson, as it was important to keep a running tab on direction in order to estimate their progress and to aid in charting. This meant that the trim of the sails had to be regularly adjusted as the ship's course remained fixed for long periods while the wind shifted back and forth. It made the *Half Moon*, a preindustrial machine of wood, hemp, canvas, and iron, a busy vessel.

A new course was shouted out. In front of the helmsman was a compass

---

* Juet only tells us in his journal that "four glasses" were marked; he says nothing about the glass itself. A watch glass marked four hours, but ships of the early seventeenth century kept a half-hour glass at the helm, and this seems to be what Juet was referring to. Elsewhere in his journal he mentions sailing half a league (1.5 nautical miles) in "two glasses," which reinforces the likelihood that his references to glasses were to the half-hour glass. (It also indicates in that instance that the *Half Moon* was moving at a ponderous 1.5 knots, or nautical miles per hour.) An alternative is that he was referring to the sand glass used in estimating speed in conjunction with a log line, but as these were only glasses of thirty seconds or one minute, the reference is unlikely.

housed in a protective cabinet called a binnacle, which could be illumi-
nated by a candle. The compass card, which had a magnetized wire fixed to
its back, was marked with the thirty-two winds (bearings in degrees had
not yet come into use). Minding the rotating card, the helmsman leaned on
the whipstaff, a sort of vertical tiller that emerged from the interior deck on
which he stood and swung the true tiller beneath it, which changed the
alignment of the great rudder mounted on the tall, narrow stern.

Beyond the fact that the helmsman had little sense of where the vessel
was actually headed, the *Half Moon* would not have been easy to steer. The
rudder probably could only swing through about forty degrees, perhaps less,
and the helmsman was called upon mainly to make adjustments that kept
the ship on a particular course. The ship otherwise was coaxed in a fresh
direction by manipulating the trim of the sails, to make the bow swing toward or away from the wind, and to do likewise with the stern. Bearing
away from the light southerly, the *Half Moon* settled back onto a ponderous
run, pointed north.

Now they could see land, strung along the horizon from roughly the west
to the northwest. They closed with the shore, and when seven fathoms of
water were marked, Hudson was satisfied to turn parallel to it and follow
along, northeast-by-north, the lead line constantly probing for further signs
of threatening shallows.

Juet called this shore "drowned land, which made it to rise like islands."
They were running along the east side of Sandy Hook, the low-lying spit
that extends the beaches of New Jersey north of the three-hundred-foot
hump of the Navesink Highlands. Clumps of trees on the spit likely suggested islands and flooding. The *Half Moon* was approaching the New York
bight, the broad definition of the estuary from Sandy Hook northeast to Jamaica Bay on the Long Island shore. Beyond Sandy Hook was Lower New
York Bay, and behind the Hook, to the west, was Raritan Bay.

Thomas Pownall, who would be appointed lieutenant governor of New
Jersey in 1755 and governor of Massachusetts in 1757, arrived at New York
from the sea in 1753, as the thirty-one-year-old private secretary to New
York's governor, Sir Danvers Osborne. As he would describe the experience
in 1755, "This was the first land of America that I saw & here I first landed.
My Eye was upon the watch, and everything struck it. My imagination was
all suspense & every thing made a vivid impression on my mind."

We can imagine that Hudson and Juet looked upon the same vista with their attentions as seized as Pownall's would be. The *Half Moon*'s men could see beyond Sandy Hook, in Juet's words, "a great lake of water, as we could judge it to be." The "mouth," the gap between Sandy Hook and the lands to the north, he went on to explain, "hath many shoals, and the sea breaketh on them as it is cast out of the mouth of it. And from that lake or bay the land lyeth north by east, and we had a great stream out of the bay."

For passage seekers, few clues were thought to be more vital than the strength and direction of a tidal stream. Such a volume of water had to have a greater source than the bay they could see. There was more to the landscape than first met the eye. Hudson needed time, and patience, to sort it all out.

All along the coast, Hudson would have been consulting a working chart with the plotting grid of latitude and longitude ruled and labeled, and known landfalls already recorded to the best of the chartmaker's ability. Hudson could have made it himself, consulting published and unpublished sources to fashion a guide to what was known or suspected about the eastern seaboard of the New World. He would have filled in the blanks as the voyage progressed: marking in discoveries, taking note of errors in source materials, and recording his ship's progress.

Whatever chart Hudson consulted and elaborated would not survive, and only fragments of his voyage journal would endure, in paraphrases and direct quotes. Juet's journal narrative, the most complete record of the voyage, would provide clues to the *Half Moon*'s location at any given time, but exactitude was an impossible expectation. Mariners at this time had no reliable way to determine their longitude, the component of the global position grid composed of lines running from pole to pole that divide the world into 360 degrees. They relied substantially on the highly unreliable tool of dead reckoning, which used a ship's estimated speed (calculated with a log line, which was a board and a marked piece of rope that would be played out astern) and elapsed time measured with a sand glass to arrive at distances covered. Latitude, which is described by degree lines drawn parallel to the equator (marking out 90 degrees above it and 90 below), could be calculated by measuring the angular elevation of the sun at noon as well as of certain stars in concert with an almanac. In actual practice, the limitations of instruments and the myriad challenges of making precise observations meant that a navigator did well to produce a latitude fix that was in error by no more than a quarter to a half of a degree, which translated into fifteen to thirty nautical miles, north to south.*

And so determining where the *Half Moon* was when Hudson arrived in the general environs of Sandy Hook on the afternoon of September 2, 1609, is a matter of informed speculation. Juet recorded that they had ten fathoms of water, two leagues (six nautical miles) from land: too many fathoms for the *Half Moon* to have moved west of Sandy Hook and into Raritan Bay. Those waters to the west, as he had noted, were confounded by breaking shoals. Hudson and his men would have watched the waves smear across the shallows of the Hook and the bank just to the north that would be called Dry Romer, which was immersed beneath only two to three feet of water at low tide in the nineteenth century. Nor would Hudson have dared to move the *Half Moon* directly into Lower New York Bay. For now, they held back. At five o'clock, with the southerly wind having all but expired, Hudson anchored in eight fathoms to the east of the Hook, with Long Island and Jamaica Bay to the north.

Concluded Juet, "The night was fair. This is a very good land to fall with, and a pleasant land to see." No European had seen it for certain since 1524, and briefly at that. And only Hudson really knew why he was even here, as the directors of the VOC back in Amsterdam studied his sailing directions and his employment contract and wondered what had become of him and of their ship.

Dissenting and chiding voices doubtless were being heard, airing suspicions that something other than high-seas tragedy might be responsible for the lack of news. Indeed, long before the *Half Moon* had sailed, the VOC

---

* Nautical miles are used commonly in this narrative because of their relationship to leagues, the measure employed by Juet. There were twenty English leagues to every degree of longitude as measured at the equator, which for our purposes is equivalent to any degree of latitude. One English league thus was the equivalent of three nautical miles. A modern nautical mile is 6,076 feet, versus 5,280 feet in a modern statute mile; speed of vessels is still given in nautical miles per hour, or knots. While the nautical mile thus is about 15 percent longer than a statute mile, the difference in this story is not critical, in part because the earth's circumference hadn't been correctly determined. The English considered a degree of longitude at the equator to be divided into sixty miles of five thousand feet each. As well, Juet's expressed distances in leagues are often rough guesses or the results of dead reckoning. Juet also could use the latitude fixes from day to day to arrive at progress over the past twenty-four hours, but these distances were subject to the error margins of those fixes.

had good reason to suspect that Henry Hudson would be all but impossible to control.

The plan to send out Hudson had spawned a confusion of rumor and chicanery, with one blatant episode of insubordination by the English hireling that could have or should have terminated the voyage before it even left Amsterdam. But the controversies had gone far beyond Hudson's own disobedience, and it's not clear that Hudson himself was ever fully aware of all the maneuverings. They had involved not only different groups within the VOC but the king of France, the French ambassador to The Hague, and a duplicitous VOC investor. But then, Hudson had conducted some fairly clever maneuvering of his own. It had all begun with his return from his 1608 voyage to the northeast.

THE ARRIVAL OF the *Hopewell* at Gravesend on the lower reaches of the Thames on August 26, 1608, launched the chain of events that led to Henry Hudson's strange and vexatious spell in command of the VOC's *Half Moon*, which a little more than a year later would find him setting an anchor in a dying breeze off Sandy Hook.

The *Hopewell* had just been above the arctic circle, where polar bears on ice floes had roared at her passing, and two crewmembers had witnessed a pair of mermaids frolicking along the ship's side. Observed her master and pilot, Henry Hudson, of one of them: "from the navel upward, her back and breasts were like a woman's, as they say that saw her; her body was as big as one of us; her skin very white; and long hair hanging down behind, of colour black: in her going down they saw her tail, which was like the tail of a porpoise, and speckled like a mackerel."

As marvelous as this report was, Hudson had not been sent north to find mermaids. Hudson's second voyage of discovery in as many years aboard the *Hopewell* was ending at Gravesend much the same as the first: in resounding failure.

Merchants from the East India and Muscovy companies had dispatched him from London on April 22, 1608, to prove the Northeast Passage over the top of Asia to the lucre of the Orient. Hudson had been rebuffed by ice, and by the impassible archipelago of Novaya Zemlya. His first voyage of discovery in 1607 had been an audacious attempt to sail the *Hopewell* to

China's riches by steering over the North Pole. While he had not been seized by the "sucking sea" believed to plunge into the center of the earth at the pole, where a lodestone mountain one hundred miles in diameter held compass needles in a mysterious thrall, neither had he been able to penetrate the polar ice that proponents of the theory of a temperate arctic argued wasn't there at the height of summer. He could at least claim to have sailed to a higher latitude on that voyage than anyone before him (80 degrees, 23 minutes, to be precise), higher than even Willem Barentsz, in whose historic wake he had been sailing the *Hopewell* these last two voyages.

Swinging at anchor off the west coast of Novaya Zemlya on the morning of July 6, 1608, watching the wind drive an ice field to the east of him, Hudson had realized he would never see China by the northeast route, either. He set sail that evening, "being out of hope to find passage by the northeast." Negotiating the crowded traffic on the lower reaches of the Thames seven weeks later, Hudson knew he would have to answer for this latest misadventure.

Already, rather than return to London from Novaya Zemlya without any useful result, Hudson had proposed to the *Hopewell*'s 1608 crew that they sail west and have a go at the final possible northern route: the Northwest Passage, over the top of North America. As he recorded in the voyage journal: "I therefore resolved to use all means I could to sail to the north-west; considering the time and means we had, if the wind should friend us, as in the first part of the voyage it had done." But the crew had rejected his plan, which entailed sailing at least 2,500 nautical miles across the top of the world, in a vessel that did well to move at four knots, just to reach the purported entrance to that passage and begin the really hard slogging. The crew moreover secured from Hudson "a certificate under my hand, of my free and willing return, without persuasion or force of anyone or more of them."

The *Hopewell* soon moved upriver from Gravesend to conclusively end the 1608 voyage where it had begun, at London's St. Katherine's Docks. Hudson's home was in the adjoining St. Katherine precinct, a suburb that had erupted as the city of some two hundred thousand spilled beyond its medieval walls. Immediately downriver was Wapping, "the usual place of execution for pirates and sea rovers," as John Stowe remarked circa 1600. Moving upriver from St. Katherine, a visitor encountered the looming Tower of London, a multifaceted palace cum prison containing only the highest class of enemies of state, whose prisoners at that moment included Sir Walter Raleigh. Once Elizabeth I's favorite sea dog and long the chief English figure in colonizing the New World, Raleigh was now indefinitely incarcerated after being found guilty of treason on thin evidence after James VI of Scotland became James I of England on Elizabeth's death in 1603. Raleigh had been taking in the river traffic long before Henry Hudson had made his historical debut, and would continue to gaze upon it long after Hudson had vanished from the pell-mell arrivals and departures at the docks and water gates beyond the tower's twelfth-century curtain wall and moat.

The tower property marked the waterside limits of the old city walls. Next stop of note upstream was the Custom House, where 90 percent of the nation's foreign trade was processed and tithed. Just ahead, before river navigation was interrupted by London Bridge and the gruesome display of severed heads on Traitor's Gate, was Butolph Wharf. Butolph Lane ran north from here, turning into Philpot Lane after crossing Little East Cheap.

The Philpot Lane residence of Sir Thomas Smythe assuredly was where Hudson headed to account for his 1608 effort aboard the *Hopewell*. Its great hall, in which an Inuit kayak hung from the ceiling beams, was where the East India Company conducted its business, and it was also a point of convergence for sailors seeking work and a resolution to wage disputes. Wives loitered there while ships sent out by his various ventures were at sea; Hudson's wife, Katherine, would have contributed to the daily throng while her husband and younger son, John, who was along for both *Hopewell* voyages, were off probing ice-strewn latitudes.

Smythe dominated England's commerce-driven exploration in the early years of James's reign. He had narrowly escaped ruin through his implication in the Essex plot against Elizabeth in 1601. He was fined heavily and incarcerated in the Tower of London but was liberated by James I when he came to power. As a parliamentarian, he was a favorite of the new king. In commerce, he was a ubiquitous power: a merchant adventurer, a member of the skinner's and haberdasher's guilds, and "customer" of the port of London, which gave him a cut of the value of all the foreign trade landing on London's docks. He was about fifty years old when Hudson began his exploration career in 1607, and there was scarcely an overseas trade venture in which he didn't have some interest. He negotiated trade terms for England with the Dutch Republic, and his governorships included the

London as seen from Southwark, in a circa 1616 engraving by Claes Jansz Visscher. Heads of traitors are displayed on the south gate of London Bridge. To the right of the bridge is the anchorage of St. Katherine's Pool.

Muscovy, Levant, and East India companies. These gave him a prominent role in English trade to and from Russia, the Mediterranean, and the Orient. Although its exclusivity was at times challenged, the Muscovy Company had been granted in its charter from Elizabeth the sole right to exploit any northern passage to the Orient. Smythe was also one of four patentees of the London wing of the original Virginia Company of 1606, which established the Jamestown colony on the Chesapeake the following year.

Although Hudson's first *Hopewell* voyage of 1607 had failed as a transpolar venture, it had nevertheless paid dividends to Smythe's Muscovy Company in revealing an eminently exploitable whale and walrus fishery in and around Spitsbergen, for which it secured a monopoly. Hudson would have been keen to demonstrate a similar positive result from the second voyage as he called on Smythe. He would have presented not only his ship's papers and chart with course plots and landfalls but also his evidence of the resources and alleged temperate nature of Novaya Zemlya. There was a severed walrus head (harvested on the day Hudson ruefully rode at anchor, and by then probably reduced to tusks), bits of scavenged whalebone, samples of plant life ("green things"), and reindeer dung. Hudson unloaded these lustrous offerings before a man who understood the coarse value of essential commodities like train oil and rope cordage but for whom true treasure was porcelain, cinnamon, silk, and mace, and whose New World ambitions were concerned at least as much with discovering gold as with establishing a colony on the Chesapeake.

Hudson wasn't interested in returning to the northeast, however much he might have tried to buff the significance of his aromatic offerings from Novaya Zemlya. It was the northwest that was drawing him in. Of three possible arctic routes to the Orient—to the northwest, the northeast, and over the pole—it was the only one yet untested by him.

While Hudson's voyage to Novaya Zemlya wasn't entirely without merit—it would be cited by the Muscovy Company in attempting to defend its northern fishery monopoly against Dutch incursions in 1614—this was the wrong time for Hudson to be seeking another round of financing for a northern passage search. The available pool of venture capital was rapidly being drained. A third East India Company trading expedition had been sent out in 1608. (It would prove to have been a complete disaster. One ship was wrecked near Diu, north of Bombay, and the other was abandoned off Brittany within reach of home, most of her crew having perished.)

Smythe's home meanwhile would have been busy with preparation for the company's fifth voyage. More important, Smythe was leading the effort to reorganize the struggling Jamestown venture under a new royal charter. Smythe would serve as the treasurer (the de facto governor) of this "second" Virginia Company when it was chartered in May 1609. The Virginia venture would send out an unprecedented nine-vessel relief flotilla to Jamestown that summer, and it evidently was consuming the lion's share of available capital: the fifth voyage of the East India Company would consist of a single ship, the 150-ton *Constant*, which left Tilbury Hope on March 12, 1609.

Having now coasted Spitsbergen and Novaya Zemlya in two successive voyages, Hudson had drained the Barentsz expeditions of interest for English merchants like Smythe. And the Northwest Passage wasn't on anyone's current agenda. There was nowhere Hudson was next proposing to go that investors were prepared to send him, at least in 1609.

Men were fortunate to reach forty in this day and age, particularly in Hudson's disaster-prone profession. His brief moment in the exploratory limelight may have come and gone at this point. The march of time moved to quickstep pace on September 18, 1608, when Hudson attended the christening of his granddaughter Alice at St. Mary Aldermary, a fine London church on Bow Lane in the heart of the city that was still waiting to receive the steeple designed for it in 1511. But whatever discouragement Hudson felt was short-lived. His ambitions would not be hemmed in. Hudson was soon back on the Thames, outbound from James's realm, answering a fortuitous invitation by members of the VOC's Amsterdam chamber to discuss the feasibility of the Northeast Passage.

CHAPTER 3

THE VOC PROBABLY HAD BEEN ALERTED to Hudson's availability by the Dutch consul in London, Emanuel Van Meteren, who had moved there as a teenager and knew everyone worth knowing in the City. On arriving in Amsterdam, Hudson would have met with Petrus Plancius, the VOC's chief hydrographer and a long-standing advocate of the Northeast Passage search. By the end of December, the Amsterdam merchants were sufficiently impressed with Hudson to draft an employment contract and begin looking for a ship for him. On January 8 they sent out the letters to the other chambers, soliciting the directors' votes necessary to turn the voyage into an official one of the VOC. The effort seems to have focused on Zeeland, home to the port of Middelburg. As the second-largest chamber, Zeeland held four votes and so could deliver the necessary majority approval from the Lords Seventeen if they were cast with Amsterdam's eight.

The Zeeland chamber took a few days to consider the Amsterdam missive. It was unenthusiastic, replying that the proposed voyage "was considered by the majority to be connected with much difficulty." Zeeland pointed out that according to the company charter, the VOC was restricted to trade around the Cape of Good Hope and through the Strait of Magellan, and that it could not expand into a northern passage, even if one proved to be viable. Thus the Hudson voyage "is more an affair for private individuals than for our Company." And Zeeland was not comfortable providing the votes that would allow Amsterdam to ignore the opinions of the other chambers, pointing out that "upon such weighty matters an opinion should be given by all the Chambers in order that it may be seen in common what is deemed most expedient and advisable for the Company."

Finally, Zeeland declared that "we cannot see that it is useful or practicable for the Company and feel certain that it will be so much money thrown away; should it, however, be undertaken by private individuals we do not believe it would be prejudicial to the Company, and if there were such prospects as the person [Hudson] holds out, the Company which has already twice equipped him"—the English investors of 1607 and 1608—"would not leave him short of a thousand pounds for the sake of getting a third prize, since they have already borne the cost of two voyages." The Zeelanders had a point: if Hudson's new scheme was so promising, why were his English backers refusing to send him out again?

Amsterdam must have replied with some urgency. We don't know what was said, but Zeeland fell into line, albeit with unenthusiastic assent, on January 14: "we have no objection thereto except our belief that it will be

One of many variations on the logo of the Dutch East India Company. (Illustration by author.)

but so much more lost expense"—a reference to the fact that Zeeland merchants had bowed out entirely from the Dutch efforts to the northeast after
the second of three voyages in the 1590s, leaving it to Amsterdam interests
alone to fund the final (failed) Barentsz voyage of 1596–97. "And even if it
were undertaken by other private individuals," Zeeland reiterated, "we do
not believe it would be prejudicial to the company." Nevertheless, Amsterdam evidently had secured the support required to make Hudson's third
voyage an official VOC venture, and to get it off the dock that spring. Amsterdam may have asked Zeeland simply for its vote of approval, while promising to fund the venture itself.

In the meantime, the effort to secure Hudson's services had become im-
pressively complicated. A new player had surfaced: a disenchanted VOC investor who also happened to be a stock market manipulator of incredible
ambition and cunning.

ISAAC LEMAIRE WAS wealthy, conniving, and unhappy.

The Fleming had come to Amsterdam after the Spanish blockade of
Antwerp crushed the economic life of the leading port of the Low Countries, and he had prospered. Lemaire was the single most important investor in the VOC's Amsterdam chamber when the company was formed
in 1602, but by the winter of 1608–9, he had seriously fallen out with the
VOC. Despite all the guilders (some eighty-five thousand) he had invested,
Lemaire could not get the VOC board to abandon its policy of retaining all
profits within the company until the end of its initial charter term in 1612,
and instead begin paying its investors a dividend. When the VOC directors
rebuffed his dividend proposal, Lemaire reacted in a way that was very
clever and very ruthless.

By the time Henry Hudson arrived in Amsterdam to discuss another
voyage to the northeast, the hyperkinetic capitalism of the Dutch Republic
had invented many of the forms of tradeable security known to modern
Wall Street brokers and investment bankers. Trading shares in the joint-
stock VOC was only the beginning. There were futures contracts, options
to buy and sell, and even "derivatives" that allowed speculation in the
volatile value of options. Trading of securities (as well as commodities) was
also about to acquire a formal space. Hudson would have walked past more

than once the foundations of the new bourse, or exchange, that began to take shape in Amsterdam in May 1608 and would be completed in 1611.*

Lemaire decided that he would form a secret "bear" syndicate that would conspire to manipulate trading in VOC shares. When their price fell, investors would no longer be able to accept appreciation of share value in lieu of a dividend. The investing masses would rise up and demand from the directors a dividend, which is all that Lemaire claimed to want. But Lemaire and his co-conspirators could make a tidy fortune if they also "shorted" the stock, profiting hugely by entering into options and derivatives that paid off when the share price fell rather than rose. It's impossible not to imagine that this, in no small part, was what Lemaire was actually up to in his so-called shareholder revolt.

Lemaire also had grand ambitions to secure his own Dutch trade monopoly for the Orient. He couldn't challenge the VOC directly on the southern routes protected by their charter. He needed an alternate route, and the only ones inviting serious consideration were in the Arctic. He didn't want to publicly mount the effort himself. He could contribute a ship and crew, but someone else would have to come up with the operating costs and front the enterprise.

Lemaire did not work in half measures. The investor he had in mind was Henry IV, the king of France. As for the man who could actually attempt to prove the alternate route, Lemaire understood there was an English pilot, footloose in Amsterdam, whom the VOC had just turned down for an arctic voyage in 1609.

DISCUSSIONS BETWEEN LEMAIRE and the Fontainebleau court of Henry IV had already begun in early 1608 through a French overture that dropped the king and his financial resources into Lemaire's lap. The channel had been opened with Lemaire through Pierre Jeannin, Henry's ambassador to the Dutch government, the States-General (Staten-Generaal), in The Hague,

---

* Once the Spanish delegates to the truce negotiations had indicated they could accept the division of the Netherlands into the northern and southern provinces, the risk of trade conducted by immigrant merchants like Lemaire returning to Antwerp greatly declined, which encouraged the construction of the Amsterdam trading facility. Actually a roofless square, this open-air market had been modeled on the Royal Exchange in London and Antwerp's Bourse.

about thirty miles southwest of Amsterdam in the province of Holland.*
While brokering the hoped-for peace between Spain and the Dutch Republic, Jeannin had opened a file on a secret scheme to steal away the greatest
economic asset of the Dutch. It was to Lemaire that Jeannin turned in early
1608 for help in establishing a French version of the VOC.

Lemaire was receptive but, according to correspondence of Jeannin's
from February and March 1608, advised delaying until after peace was secured between Spain and the northern provinces. Lemaire believed that as
a condition of peace, the Dutch might indeed relinquish the Indies trade,
and that could open the door for Dutch capital to move to a French company devoted to the Indies. But in early 1609, Lemaire was suddenly in a
hurry to get the French to agree to a new venture. He wanted Henry IV to
hire Henry Hudson and send him to the northeast, before the VOC did.

Jeannin begged off making any firm arrangement for Hudson until the
peace negotiations were concluded, a position that Lemaire initially appeared
to accept, since this had been his own advice a year earlier. But when Lemaire
sensed a snag in the negotiations between the VOC and Hudson that January,
he pressed hard for the French to secure Hudson's services through him.

As the ambassador informed his king, Lemaire "sent to me his brother,
to inform me that an English pilot, who has been twice by sea in search of
the northern passage, has been called to Amsterdam by the East India
Company [VOC], to tell them what he had found, and if he hoped to discover that passage. They had been well satisfied with his answer, and had
thought they might succeed in the scheme." But as Jeannin explained, the
VOC was not prepared to send out Hudson until 1610.

Lemaire understood that the Amsterdam chamber could not move
quickly enough to secure approval for a voyage backed by the entire company for 1609. A window of opportunity had opened that could bring together Hudson, Lemaire, and Henry IV.

Since taking his leave of discussions with the Amsterdam chamber, Hudson (according to Jeannin) had met with Lemaire, as well as with Petrus
Plancius, although there is no indication that Hudson understood that
Lemaire was trying to set up a French rival to the VOC, or even wanted to
employ Hudson on behalf of Henry IV. Two days after receiving Lemaire's

---

*The southern provinces, which remained under the Hapsburgs, had their own States-
General in Brussels. Most of them would form modern Belgium.

brother, Jeannin too met with Plancius, who happened to be in The Hague. Jeannin assured Henry IV that he had not let Plancius know "that Lemaire had made overtures to me, for Lemaire wishes nobody to be aware of it." From Plancius, Jeannin absorbed the essential arguments in favor of a northern route to the Orient, some of it secondhand from Hudson. The French ambassador was hooked.

Lemaire offered to supply the ship and crew for a French voyage employing Hudson, unless the king wished to use men of his own. Lemaire assured Jeannin he required only three or four thousand crowns at the most, which he requested that the king provide because as a common or private person (*un particulier*), he claimed, he would not be able to deploy such a large sum. Lemaire said he also did not want anyone to know of his involvement, because the VOC feared above all to be forestalled in its plan to return to the northeast with Hudson. For this reason, Lemaire avowed, he had conducted his discussions with Hudson in great secrecy.

Nevertheless, Lemaire suspected word had leaked to the VOC of his discussions with Hudson. The breach was probably Jeannin, who somehow thought he could engage Plancius in discussions of the feasibility of the Northeast Passage and the opinions of Henry Hudson without suggesting that Henry IV might be interested in employing Hudson to discover the route.

Jeannin was unable to complete his lengthy January 1609 letter to his king before he was further informed by Lemaire that directors of the Amsterdam chamber were so concerned that Hudson might be hired to make the voyage for the French that they had written their counterparts at the other chambers, seeking approval to send out Hudson in 1609 on an official VOC voyage.

It's not clear that Lemaire knew Hudson's name was already on an Amsterdam chamber contract. He had signed it on January 8, the same day on which Amsterdam wrote the other chambers seeking their approval for an official company voyage. But Lemaire appeared to think that there might be a window of opportunity: if a Hudson voyage for the VOC could not be mounted until 1610 because of approval delays, then there would be an opening to secure Hudson's services for 1609. Hope was slim, though: Jeannin advised Henry IV that it would not matter if the other chambers withheld their approval, as Lemaire suspected the Amsterdam chamber was prepared to employ Hudson on its own.

Jeannin's letter finally was sent to Henry IV on January 25 from The Hague. The French ambassador did not know it yet, but he had lost the race for Henry Hudson's services, as Zeeland had assented to grant its support on January 14. Henry IV sent a draft for the four thousand crowns Lemaire had requested through Jeannin on February 28—far too late to engage Hudson.

The VOC had beaten Lemaire and the French to the most ironic prize: the services of Hudson for an undertaking that the explorer assuredly thought was impossible, and that he would subvert at the earliest opportunity.

HENRY HUDSON DID not appear to drive a hard bargain in his contract of January 8 with the Amsterdam chamber. His fee of eight hundred guilders might seem to have been handsome, as a master in the Dutch navy earned a monthly salary of fifty guilders. But Hudson's fee not only served to compensate him for his services for the duration of the voyage and months of preparation and to provide for his wife and children but also had to fund "his outfit of the said voyage." Purchasing powers of currencies across centuries are difficult to assess, but conversion rates suggest the contract was worth only about eleven thousand U.S. dollars in today's money. While that sum did not cover the entire investment in the *Half Moon* voyage, it was still a relatively inexpensive venture for the Dutch, since the voyage of a single merchant ship in the Asia trade, fully manned and victualed for a voyage of two years or more and stocked with trade wares, required an investment of about one hundred thousand guilders, or about $1.4 million U.S. today.

As we have seen, Hudson's contract promised ample rewards, lengthy employment, and security for Hudson and his family, should the Englishman prove his skills and worth on the initial voyage. Which makes Hudson's subsequent behavior all the more baffling. Why did he agree to a contract that paid him so little up front, and whose true worth depended on Hudson proving the Northeast Passage, when he had so little hope, or intention, of doing so?

He may not have had a choice, as the VOC would have dictated the terms most advantageous to itself. And it may well have been Hudson's realization that he was almost certain to fail in the northeast that provoked him into hijacking the whole enterprise in hopes of achieving a genuine and spectacular success.

But first he'd had to convince the VOC that he was the right man for the job. The correspondence between Pierre Jeannin and Henry IV with respect to the Lemaire scheme proved to be highly revealing about the relationship between Henry Hudson and Petrus Plancius—about the way Hudson charmed Plancius by telling him whatever he wanted to hear about the feasibility of the Northeast Passage in order to secure the *Half Moon* assignment.

The fifty-six-year-old chief hydrographer of the VOC and firebrand minister in the Dutch Reformed Church had been a leading figure in mounting expeditions to the northeast in the 1590s that were best associated with his protégé, the pilot Willem Barentsz. Plancius well knew the skills of English pilots, having hired some when he founded a navigation school at Enkhuizen in 1593; the arctic explorer John Davis had also been recruited as the pilot of the first Dutch trading voyage to the Far East, in 1598. Plancius held considerable sway in Amsterdam and was still championing the possibilities of the northeast route.

Plancius had long hoped that a renewed push on the northeast route could be made under Jacob van Heemskerck, who had commanded the final Barentsz voyage. But the possibility evaporated on April 25, 1607, two days after Henry Hudson departed London on his first *Hopewell* voyage. Heemskerck was by then an admiral in the Dutch navy, and he led a devastating attack on the Spanish fleet at Gibraltar. He destroyed twenty-one enemy ships in the harbor and killed four thousand Spaniards in an action that largely forced the Spanish to the peace table at The Hague. But as Heemskerck engaged the Spanish flagship, a cannonball decapitated a Dutch sailor and carried away one of Heemskerck's legs. Plancius's best hope for his country's return to Novaya Zemlya promptly bled to death.

For Plancius, Hudson had become the logical successor to Barentsz, whose explorations he had just finished fact-checking for English backers. Hudson ensured this by catering to Plancius's notions of a temperate arctic. The idea dated back to an English merchant, Robert Thorne, in the 1520s. Because the sun does not set above the arctic circle at the height of summer, it was argued that its low, weak warming rays would create an ice-free zone at the top of the world for at least part of the season. To exploit this phenomenon in reaching the Orient, one would have to sail as far north as possible, which is how Hudson came to make his transpolar attempt of 1607.

The idea was far from eccentric in Hudson's time. John Davis had argued in its favor in his 1595 book *The World's Hydrographical Description*, and in Hudson's journal account of the 1607 *Hopewell* voyage, not even persistent encounters with massive ice fields and bitter cold could dissuade him. Hudson regularly commented on a favorable climate in one of the world's most inhospitable environments. After passing along the Greenland shore above latitude 70 in the *Hopewell*, he observed that the land "was very temperate to our feeling." Such a conviction also required Spitsbergen to be warm and welcoming. So when the *Hopewell* first came upon this high-latitude archipelago,* Hudson wrote: "here it is to be noted, that although we ran along near the shore, we found no great cold; which made us think that if we had been on shore the place is temperate." When Hudson's crewmembers did go ashore at the top of Spitsbergen, above latitude 80, he insisted "we found it hot" and further emphasized, "Here they found it hot on the shore, and drank water to cool their thirst." And at Novaya Zemlya in 1608, crewmembers sent ashore also reported the land to be "hot."

It is impossible to know how much Hudson sincerely believed and how much of his reportage was torqued to satisfy the theoretical biases of his audience, so that further commissions would come his way. In the case of the 1609 *Half Moon* commission, Hudson knew how to play to Plancius's interests. He told the aging VOC hydrographer things he already knew and believed about the possibilities of the northeast route. For Plancius (according to Jeannin), Hudson blamed his failure in 1608 on inexperience: instead of keeping to the open sea, which was held to be ice-free because of its great depths and the action of waves and currents, he had clung to the shoreline.

But his voyage journal indicated otherwise. Hudson had tried to approach Novaya Zemlya from higher latitudes and was persistently forced southward by pack ice in the open ocean. Only when the high-latitude course was denied him did he find himself coasting the western shore of the archipelago, working southward in search of an alternate route. As for the climate, in his 1608 voyage journal Novaya Zemlya abounded with evidence of its temperate nature and plant and animal life: "generally, all the land of Nova Zembla that yet we have seen, is to man's eye a pleasant

---

* Today "Spitsbergen" refers to one island in the archipelago known as Svalbard, which belongs to Norway. For the purposes of this story I have retained the historic label.

land . . . looking in some places green, and deer feeding thereon." But in his discussions with Plancius, Hudson (again, according to Jeannin) stated that the archipelago was "barren" and populated only by "carnivorous animals." The deer and greenery, Hudson avowed, were to be found much farther north, at Spitsbergen, thereby agreeing with Plancius that the world became warmer closer to the pole.

Having convinced the Dutch of his fitness for their service and signed the contract before Lemaire and the king of France could get to him, Hudson then all but ruined his standing with them. VOC records capture the Zeeland chamber responding almost immediately to a March 11, 1609, letter from their Amsterdam counterparts (since lost), detailing alarming difficulties with Hudson in the voyage preparations. The Amsterdam communiqué's missing content is not difficult to infer, and could be summed up as: "Henry Hudson has left the project in a huff, taking with him 150 guilders we advanced him on his wages on January 19. What do you think we should do?"

Zeeland wrote Amsterdam on March 14, following a meeting of its own directors that day. "We are much surprised at Mr. Hudson's strange behavior and consider it inadvisable to let him undertake the voyage, for if he begins to rebel here under our eyes what will he do if he is away from us?" They could not possibly know how perceptive that would prove to be. "We therefore consider it advisable that Your Honors cancel his voyage and demand from him the £25 Flemish given him and that, if he will not repay these amicably, Your Honors shall compel him thereunto by law."

The planned sailing date was less than three weeks away, and would come a week after the Lords Seventeen were scheduled to meet. Zeeland further advised that the voyage still be pursued, under the command of a "competent and sensible person, experienced in such voyages, engaging him with the advice of Plantius [sic] so that the expense and trouble incurred may, if possible, not remain fruitless."

Having already concluded that Henry Hudson was neither competent nor sensible, the Zeeland chamber made a further reply that day to another frantic message (also lost) from Amsterdam, acknowledging that it had "learned therefrom that the Englishman, Mr. Hutson [sic], had great dispute with Dierck Gerritss [sic], the chief boatswain, concerning the wages of the

Englishmen who were to sail with him and such other matters as Your Honors write of."

The nature of those "other matters" went unrecorded. Zeeland reiterated its position on how Hudson should be dealt with: "Whereas the said Hutson [*sic*] has taken his departure he shall remain dismissed; and even if he came to change his mind with respect to performing the journey Your Honors shall in no wise engage him but leave him dismissed. And whereas there was advanced to him certain monies to the amount of twenty-five pounds more or less, Your Honors shall compel the said Hutson, by law or arrest, to repay the aforesaid monies which the Company has advanced him."

Where Hudson went with his wage advance while the Amsterdam and Zeeland chambers debated what to do about him is unknown. While it's possible he tried to strike a belated deal with Lemaire, now that the money had arrived from Henry IV, there's no mention of this in Lemaire's subsequent letters to Jeannin. More likely is that he went home to London. The mouth of the Thames was only 170 nautical miles from Texel, and he could have been in London in a few days. And Hudson had vanished at a conspicuous moment in the annals of England's overseas ventures.

The City was aboil with more than the typical amount of intrigue, as Sir Thomas Smythe worked frenetically to create a new, unified Virginia Company. Although the new company's charter would not be ratified by James I until May 23, its plans were well advanced. On March 15, the Spanish ambassador to the court of James, Pedro de Zúñiga, was able to send to Philip III a Spanish translation of an announcement detailing the new company's activities, with the admission, "They have collected in twenty days an amount of money for this voyage that frightens me." Smythe had attracted about 650 investors, of whom twenty were nobles and one hundred were knights.

The announcement secured by the Spanish ambassador was *Nova Britannia*, a "broadside," or bit of propaganda, written in support of Smythe's initiative by his son-in-law, Robert Johnson, which had been published in February. It surely reached Amsterdam as well in short order and may have propelled Hudson back to London, to learn more.

Preparations were being made for the relief flotilla of the Jamestown colony. The Zeelanders' mention of an argument between Hudson and the chief boatswain over the wages to be paid his English crewmembers may have arisen from trouble Hudson was having in competing with Smythe's new venture for the services of the better men. In returning to London, Hudson also would have hoped to find out for himself what was going on with the handsomely capitalized Virginia venture and whether the new company Smythe was organizing presented a better opportunity than a northeast voyage for the VOC, which he had taken on as a stopgap measure in his career.

Hudson obviously did not find himself a formal role in Smythe's new Virginia venture, and he resurfaced in Amsterdam in time, and with sufficient good grace, to retain his command of the *Half Moon* expedition. The VOC had declined, as the Zeeland chamber repeatedly insisted, to consider him dismissed and sue or have him arrested for the return of his advance. Instead, the company chose the predictable course of merchants who were fond of paperwork: they would put in writing what was expected of him, and would naturally expect him to obey it to the letter. Hudson was issued a severe set of sailing directions, which would have been drafted by Plancius and been approved at the meeting of the Lords Seventeen on March 25.

Hudson was now ordered to be back in Amsterdam before winter, and "to think of discovering no other routes or passages, except the route around by the North and Northeast above Nova Zembla; with this additional provision, that if it could not be accomplished at that time, another route would be the subject of consideration for another voyage." In addition to the lingering disquiet over Hudson's insubordination in March, there now seemed to be well-founded concern that he might be tempted to pursue a passage other than the one in which the VOC was interested.

After he departed Amsterdam on April 4, 1609, Hudson's ambitions indeed soon proved to be directed anywhere but to the northeast. What possessed him to defy his employers' orders and sail for the eastern seaboard of North America would confound the Dutch. How he even managed to do it was another matter.

CHAPTER 4

WHILE ISAAC LEMAIRE RIGHTLY SUSPECTED in early 1609 that he had missed his chance to secure Hudson's services for a Northeast Passage search, he still pressed the French ambassador, Pierre Jeannin, to mount an expedition through him. Lemaire informed the ambassador "that he has at his disposal a pilot, who has already made this same voyage, and is more experienced and capable than the Englishman." This may have been one of the participants in the 1590s efforts of the Dutch such as Cornelis Nai, who had commanded an Enkhuizen vessel in 1594. Jeannin, for his part, had also been speaking with other unnamed men about opportunities to make voyages to the East or West Indies. "There are also many rich merchants who will join in the trade with the East Indies, and yet more willingly if this northern passage be found," Jeannin explained to Henry IV.

A Dutch ship, financed by Henry IV and organized by Lemaire, did sail north about one month after Hudson in 1609, commanded by a man named Melchior van den Kerckhoven. He was no more successful in proving the Northeast Passage than Hudson. Hudson, at least, harbored no illusions about actually succeeding. Around the time Kerckhoven set out under the French flag, Hudson and the *Half Moon* were turning back from Novaya Zemlya. But not, of course, returning to Amsterdam.

HUDSON'S DECISION NOT to report back promptly to the VOC was on the surface utterly perplexing. Why would he risk angering the most powerful merchants in the world? Surely defying his orders would only compound his problems. Returning obediently to Amsterdam seemed the most sensible course of action.

But then he would have to convince the VOC to send him out again, to test a different passage possibility. And Hudson already would have understood that his chances of gaining company approval weren't much better than nil. Beyond the fact that he was fortunate to have been allowed to even begin this voyage, having so annoyed the VOC with his behavior in March, it must have been clear, from his pre-voyage discussions with Petrus Plancius, that the VOC had little interest in pursuing any of the alternative routes—particularly as those alternatives were of no interest to Plancius himself, on whose learned opinion the company relied.

If Hudson thought he was facing the end of his exploration career, he could well have decided that defying his sailing directions was worth the risk, if there was any possibility of returning with results so promising or spectacular that the VOC could not help but reward him in some way. According to historiographer and cartographer Hessel Gerritsz, who would succeed Plancius as the VOC's chief hydrographer in 1617, Hudson had discussed the feasibility of the Northwest Passage route as last probed by George Waymouth in 1602 with Plancius, but Plancius "had proved to him the impossibility of success, from the accounts of a man who had reached the western shore of that sea." It was a cryptic observation that suggested Plancius was relying on intelligence from the Pacific that the Northwest Passage was unfeasible. If Plancius did not believe there was any other route to the Orient in the northern hemisphere worth pursuing, then Hudson would have to change his mind with actual results. And if the VOC was not impressed with his findings, he could shop them to merchant adventurers in his own country.

WHEN HENRY HUDSON turned the *Half Moon* around in the Barents Sea and steered for eastern North America, the geopolitical situation awaiting him could not have been more fluid, more saturated with dispute. Rival European nations, all nominally at peace, thought they had an exclusive right to most or all of it. Within England, merchants and nobles had just failed to agree on a unified approach to colonizing its lands and exploiting its many resources, real and imagined.

The original Virginia Company of 1606 had been an odd assemblage, with two different investment groups, or wings. The London wing, which featured Sir Thomas Smythe as one of four patentees, was granted rights to the coast from latitude 34 north to latitude 41. The Plymouth (or West Country) wing, with investors in Plymouth, Exeter, and other locales in southwestern England, was granted overlapping rights, from latitude 45 south to latitude 38. Both wings agreed not to establish a colony within a hundred miles of each other. The London wing founded Jamestown in 1607; by 1609 it was barely hanging on. The Plymouth wing built Fort St. George at the mouth of the Kennebec River in what is now Maine. This Sagadahoc colony struggled through the winter of 1607–8 and was then abandoned.

Smythe was a signatory of a February 17, 1609, letter inviting the mayor and aldermen of Plymouth to have West Country investors join forces with London interests in focusing exclusively on the Jamestown colony under a new company charter. The invitation was declined. Colonization was not a priority for the West Country interests, but they hadn't given up on the northern part of the company territory as a potential fishery. James I could not justify handing over to Smythe's London-based group the territory bestowed on the Plymouth wing in 1606. The company's exclusive realm under the new charter was limited to the lands from Point Comfort at the mouth of the river James to a parallel two hundred miles north, about halfway up the New Jersey shore, which was the equivalent of between latitudes 37 and 40. Everything north of that line arguably had no specific commercial claim in England, although Sir Ferdinando Gorges of Plymouth felt that the West Country wing's rights had never been extinguished.

But internal English arrangements concerning the seaboard were of no concern to any country that thought England had no right to claim the lands in question as her own in the first place. England relied on the poorly documented voyages of John Cabot (Giovanni Caboto) in the late fifteenth century and those of his son Sebastian in the early sixteenth for its claims to eastern North America. The French leaned on Giovanni da Verrazzano's 1524 voyage for Francis I in arguing that the entire coast from the Carolinas to modern Nova Scotia qualified as New France, with further claims in the Gulf of St. Lawrence and the St. Lawrence River secured by the subsequent explorations of Jacques Cartier. The Portuguese made their own claims to

Newfoundland and Labrador (at the very least) based on the explorations of the Corte-Real brothers in 1501 and 1502, and the abundance of place-names with Portuguese roots underscored the pioneering work of its explorers and fishermen. Spain favored the weight of the Treaty of Tordesillas of 1494, which had encoded a 1493 papal bull from Alexander VI that divvied up the New World along a meridian that gave to the Portuguese the easternmost part of modern Brazil and Newfoundland and Labrador, and to Spain everything else west. With the crowns of Portugal and Spain having united under Philip II in 1580, Spain could lay claim essentially to all of the Americas, including the Caribbean.

But any claim to sovereignty was impossible to defend without a physical presence. In 1609, Jamestown, struggling with internal frictions, famine, and hostile natives, was the only European settlement on the entire seaboard, north of Spain's humble outpost at San Agustín, Florida. Only the French post, Port Royal, in the Annapolis Basin on Nova Scotia's Bay of Fundy coast, was a potential rival, but it had been unoccupied since the summer of 1607. (The French habitation at Québec, established on the St. Lawrence River in 1608, was too far removed to be an issue and was more of a fortified trading post, or factory, along the Dutch model, than a true colony.)

What is more, the coast scarcely had been charted. Regardless of their presumptions of ownership, the Spanish had little experience of it north of Cape Fear. The English had made several visits since 1602 to Norumbega, an area north of Cape Cod equivalent to modern Maine and Massachusetts. It was claimed as part of New France but would become known as New England after Captain John Smith's explorations in 1614. The English also had an emerging understanding of the Chesapeake Bay area through the Jamestown settlement. The French (specifically Samuel de Champlain) had made a concerted effort to chart the coast north of Martha's Vineyard between 1604 and 1607. But most everything from Chesapeake Bay north and east to Martha's Vineyard was a conceptual fog. Men and nations were arguing over lands they hadn't even defined.

In May 1609, Henry Hudson set a course that would help define them.

HENRY HUDSON WANTED to find routes through or around impediments to the Orient. Charting coastlines was a good use of his time if the exercise indicated where a passage was or wasn't. He also fundamentally was a fact-

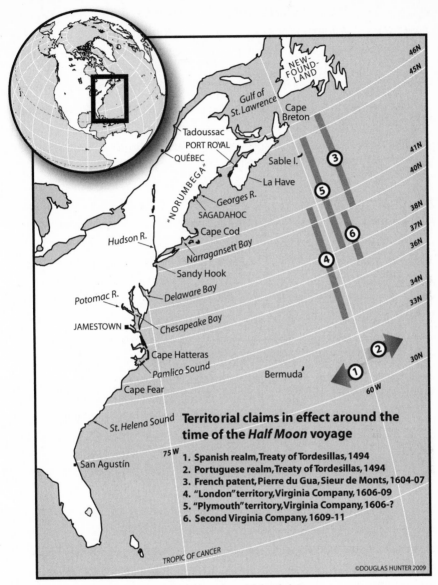

Eastern North America with land claims.

checker rather than a trailblazer, as his 1607 and 1608 voyages in the wake of Barentsz's discoveries already indicated. There was no sailing off the edge of the known world with him. He never went anywhere that he didn't already understand at some fundamental level. Cosmographers, cartographers, and theoreticians of passage possibilities had filled in the blank parts of the globe before explorers like Hudson even got there. They relied on Ptolemy's *Geographia* and a mishmash of genuine discovery, fraudulent claims, highly confused reportage, quasi-mythical accounts, and a fair amount of wishful thinking in locating great slabs of geography in places no European, living or dead, had actually visited.

Hudson was indefatigably curious about places others had already been, wanting to verify for himself (and for those who employed him) what was actually there. Even where discoveries had been genuine, navigational tools (and key elements of navigational theory) were so limited in their accuracy that the evidence from a particular voyage, set down in journals and charts or carried on the winds of rumor and anecdote, could only be believed if that evidence was investigated firsthand, if necessary over and over again.

Pressing farther than the adventurers who inspired him was an achievement that had thus far eluded Hudson, if only because these extraordinary accomplishments were unlikely to be easily surpassed. (And Hudson's claim to have sailed farther north than Barentsz in 1607, above Spitsbergen, was so marginal as to be well within the norms of observational error.) But even his ambition to investigate the Northwest Passage, as stated at the end of his 1608 *Hopewell* journal, was implicitly limited to seeing for himself no more than what English explorer George Waymouth had accomplished in 1602.

Waymouth had commanded a two-ship expedition backed by the Muscovy and East India companies in search of the Northwest Passage. So confident was Waymouth of success that he carried a letter of greeting from Elizabeth I to the emperor of China and had agreed to be paid one hundred pounds if he succeeded, nothing if he failed. Hudson's desire, as expressed at the end of his 1608 voyage journal, "to make trial of that place called Lumleys Inlet, and the furious over-fall by Captain Davis, hoping to run into it 100 leagues, and to return as God should enable me," was a clear reference to Waymouth's claim to have sailed a hundred leagues beyond the tidal rip around latitude 61 at the eastern entrance of what we now call Hudson Strait, which had been called the Furious Overfall by John Davis on his final voyage to the northwest in 1587.

Hudson knew the records of previous voyages to waters he probed, and the published charts they inspired. He also had plainly gathered confidential, unpublished information, both charts and journals, from these earlier voyages. Many if not most would have come to him from England's leading historiographer, Richard Hakluyt, author of the landmark *The Principall Navigations, Voiages, Traffiques and Discoveries of the English Nation*, issued as a second edition in three volumes from 1598 to 1600 (and best known today simply as *Principal Navigations*). More than a scholar and an editor, Hakluyt had become a promoter of English overseas ventures and even an active participant, serving as a patentee alongside Sir Thomas Smythe in the London wing of the 1606 Virginia Company and joining the new Virginia effort of 1609.

Hakluyt continued to amass voyage documents and would share his unpublished items (generally judged too sensitive to make public) with anyone who could further the causes of English colonization and passage-seeking. Hudson honored Hakluyt on his 1607 voyage by giving the name Hakluyt's Headland to a promontory at Spitsbergen, and the journal accounts of Hudson's English voyages were made available to Hakluyt by Smythe. Hudson's personal papers from the 1609 voyage (as opposed to the ship's log and summary journal) would come into Hakluyt's possession. There can be little doubt that Hakluyt and Hudson knew each other and shared in their hoarding of documents.

The preparations for the *Half Moon* voyage provided a sparkling opportunity for Hudson to expand his private collection of confidential papers. Hudson engaged in a shrewd game of show-and-tell in his negotiations with the Dutch. By telling Petrus Plancius things he wanted to hear about the arctic realm, he harvested in return precious items from the papers of the VOC hydrographer, as well as from the renowned cartographer Jodocus Hondius (Joost de Hondt), who according to Hudson's VOC contract served as his adviser during the negotiations and probably provided translation services.

Hondius had fled to London as a twenty-year-old Protestant refugee in 1583 after Spanish troops captured Ghent, having earlier made the personally hazardous decision to decline to work for Alexander Farnese, Duke of Parma, commander of Spanish forces in the Low Countries. Hondius spent ten years in London in the service of the chart publisher Edward Wright, through whom he met the explorer/adventurers Drake, Raleigh, and Cavendish and participated in some of the most important cartographic work of his adopted home. Hondius and Plancius were well known to each other: Hondius executed the engraving for Plancius's celestial globe of 1599, on which Plancius introduced new constellations of his own devising for the southern hemisphere, based on observations collected by VOC navigators.

Hudson gathered from Plancius and Hondius items that had nothing to do with his duty to probe the Northeast Passage aboard the *Half Moon*, and everything to do with his interest in alternate routes to the Orient. Hondius possessed a copy of a set of sixteenth-century sailing directions for the east coast of Greenland (which Hudson had cruised in 1607 but had scarcely seen in inclement weather). Hudson had Hondius's copy translated into English by a merchant named William Stere. But Hudson's most remarkable acquisitions came from Plancius.

Hessel Gerritsz revealed in 1612 that Hudson secured from Plancius copies of journals of George Waymouth. Gerritsz asserted that Plancius had gotten his copies from his own incomparable sources, noting that he "pays most diligent attention to such new discoveries, chiefly when they may be of advantage to our country." Gerritsz's Latin account used the plural *diaria*, suggesting that Plancius had acquired more than one set of records. Gerritsz assumed they were from Waymouth's 1602 voyage in search of the Northwest Passage. And Hudson, having declared in the conclusion of his 1608 voyage journal that he next wished to match Waymouth's achievements in that direction, would have been delighted to secure a personal copy of Waymouth's official record.

But as Waymouth had been sponsored in 1602 by the East India and Muscovy companies—the same companies that then sent out Hudson in the *Hopewell* in 1607 and 1608—the voyage details should not have been difficult for Hudson to secure on his own in England. And his stated ambition to sail a hundred leagues beyond the Furious Overfall, as only Waymouth had, indicates he already knew at least the basic unpublished facts when he made the 1608 *Hopewell* voyage.

The Waymouth journal that Hudson would have been especially pleased to secure from Plancius was from an entirely different voyage. It was made in 1605 to eastern North America and was backed by people beyond the circle of London merchants that had previously employed Hudson. Gerritsz appeared to be unaware of this voyage, even though there had been an official published account, *A True Relation*, written by participant James Rosier.

All the same, there didn't seem to be much about the 1605 Waymouth voyage to pique Hudson's interest, or to warrant its details being shared with him by someone like Hakluyt, who certainly was aware of it and may have had a hand in editing the published account. Hudson was associated exclusively with arctic passage-making. Waymouth's 1605 voyage was one of several English probings of Norumbega that were made between 1602 and 1606, before the first Virginia Company was formed and the territory they explored was assigned to the Plymouth wing.

Waymouth was a Devon mariner and shipwright whose father, also a shipwright, had invested in Sir Humphrey Gilbert's ill-fated 1583 venture to the New World. In 1605 Waymouth was sent out by West Country interests that wanted to establish a Catholic colony in North America. Waymouth himself wasn't Catholic, but he assessed the potential of a site on the Georges River in Maine. Rosier's report, rushed into print on their return, was meant to incite investor interest in the proposed colony. The venture's Catholic slant was glossed over, but the religious sentiments of one of the voyage's main sponsors, Lord Arundell, were well known, and the colonization cause was not helped by the exposure of the Catholic "Gunpowder Plot" to blow up Parliament (and the king with it) that November. Waymouth had struck an agreement mere weeks before the Gunpowder Plot with a West Country nobleman, Sir John Zouche, for a 1606 voyage that would fish the Norumbega shore and trade with the natives. But the Zouche-Waymouth initiative never sailed, as it was quickly superseded by the formation of the 1606 Virginia Company, with its separate London and Plymouth wings.

The 1605 Waymouth voyage might have remained a minor footnote in the English explorations of Norumbega, were it not for what was left out of the published version of Rosier's account. Book publishing was the purview of the stationers' company, and guild members could not print anything until a license for it was issued, which required any new offering to pass inspection with state censors. However it occurred, one remarkable observation by Rosier of what Waymouth claimed to have found was struck. The surviving manuscript (which would be published intact in 1625 by Samuel Purchas) stated: "And our Captain verily thought (though he concealed it) [that the Georges River] might possibly make a passage into (or very nigh) the South Sea; which he neither had commission nor time now to search."

Now that was the sort of geographic intelligence that could hold Henry

Hudson's attention. And given how the quixotic *Half Moon* voyage unfolded, it most certainly did.

WAYMOUTH'S 1605 VOYAGE was a weird imbroglio that even Rosier's official published account was compelled to at least partly address. While Rosier omitted the idea that the Georges River was the entrance to a passage to the South Sea—the Pacific Ocean—it made extraordinary assertions about nefarious designs on the voyage's leading participants and the geographic intelligence they had gained. Rosier asserted that "some foreign Nation (being fully assured of the fruitfulness of the country) have hoped hereby to gain some knowledge of the place, seeing they could not allure our Captain or any special man of our Company to combine with them for their direction." This foreign nation also allegedly tried to make off with five natives Waymouth had brought home. To keep this foreign power in the dark, Rosier stated, he had "neither written of the latitude or [compass] variation most exactly observed by our Captain with sundry instruments, which together with his perfect Geographical Map of the country, he intendeth hereafter to set forth."

Rosier had scrubbed his manuscript clean of useful navigational information, leaving it all for Waymouth to publish (along with a map) in his own good time. But no map or geographic data ever appeared, nor has ever been found in manuscript form. Waymouth's work vanished. As for the foreign nation with purported designs on Waymouth's findings, and which attempted to hire away Waymouth and others and to steal the natives brought back to England, its identity remains unknown. But Waymouth was soon being detained on suspicion of spying for the Spanish, who were intensely interested in what the English were up to in eastern North America.

On August 12, 1607, Sir Robert Cecil, Earl of Salisbury, England's secretary of state—a position that made him the country's spymaster—received a letter from his right-hand man, Sir Walter Cope, who was close to Waymouth. Cope expressed his concern that Waymouth—"a man best experienced in these coasts"—was defecting to Spain with a Captain Hazell to betray the Virginia effort and might not be stopped in time. Cope believed the pair had made it as far as Deal Castle, a coastal fort that belonged to the crown in Kent, on the lower Thames. But within days—if not by the time Cope wrote to Cecil—Waymouth had been apprehended.

On August 18, Dudley Carleton, a thirty-three-year-old parliamentarian and diplomat who had traveled to Spain in 1605 as part of the ratification of the Treaty of London that brought peace between Spain and England, wrote to a regular correspondent, John Chamberlain, who was something of a highly placed gossip who liked to keep abreast of the news of the day by loitering in St. Paul's Cathedral. Carleton's subject was a ship captain named Waiman, a name sometimes given to Waymouth in contemporary records. Carleton observed that "one Captain Waiman[,] a special favourite of Sir Walter Copes[,] was taken the last week in a port in Kent[,] shipping himself to Spain with intent as is thought to have betrayed his friends and shown the Spaniards a means how to defeat this Virginia attempt."

Given that Waymouth was awarded a pension by James I that October, hardly something a traitor would deserve, and that he continued to work as a shipwright and surveyor with the Royal Navy and later as a military engineer, it's very likely that something else entirely was going on. Historian David B. Quinn wondered if Waymouth was a double agent. If so, the arrest may have been staged to recall Waymouth from an assignment to expose Spanish spies in England in a way that would mislead the Spanish network. The Carleton letter, then, was part of the disinformation campaign, deliberately engaging Chamberlain's fondness for gossip in order to spread the story. But the earlier letter from Cope to Cecil is problematic, as Cope's concerns appear genuine and there was no obvious reason for him to engage in such disinformation with Cecil, unless Cope somehow had been left out of the loop by the chief spymaster. More likely—if anything in this strange episode could be called likely—was that Cope's letter to Cecil was also part of the disinformation game, intended for hostile eyes that might intercept and read it, or with whom Cecil might deliberately share it.

And there was a further complication where Henry Hudson was concerned. When Hudson concluded the 1609 *Half Moon* voyage by holing up in the West Country port of Dartmouth while trying to figure out his next move, he was chatted up by the mayor, Thomas Holland, who happened to be part of Cecil's domestic spy network. Hudson boasted to Cecil's coast watcher of being close to two prominent figures at the court of James I. One of the names he judiciously dropped was that of Sir Walter Cope.

CHAPTER 5

H ENRY HUDSON'S CLAIM TO THOMAS HOLLAND at the end of the *Half Moon* voyage of being "well known (as he told me)" to Sir Walter Cope inevitably fuels speculation over what Hudson might have been up to at the beginning. After all, he asserted to Holland a personal relationship with one of the country's most prominent figures in politics and overseas ventures. Cope was a parliamentarian who assiduously curried favor with James I. As early as 1593, he had been called a secretary of Sir Robert Cecil, who became Elizabeth I's secretary of state in 1596.

Cope and Cecil were close friends, and partners in politics and commerce. Sir Robert was a dwarfish, hunchbacked character whom Elizabeth I called her "elf" and James I "my little beagle," and who has long been condemned by historians for corrupt practices. (Among his less noble acts was accepting a pension from the king of Spain. When Don Pedro de Zúñiga arrived in London as the new Spanish ambassador in the autumn of 1605, he allegedly discovered Cecil's name on a list of six prominent English citizens who were on Philip III's payroll. The arrangement only further confuses the Waymouth episode of 1607.) Cecil secured the additional post of Lord High Treasurer in 1608, and by January 1609, it was becoming common knowledge that Cope would soon secure the second highest financial position in the realm, chancellor of the exchequer—an appointment that came through in June, while Hudson was about-facing in the *Half Moon* and heading for North America.

Cope and Cecil also were prominent in the Virginia Company initiative. Cecil had been a patron (and a possible silent partner) of the London wing of the 1606 company and was participating directly as an investor in the "second" company taking shape in early 1609. Cope had served on the fourteen-man governing council of the original 1606 company and joined Cecil in the investor ranks of the new company being organized by Sir Thomas Smythe, when Hudson was preparing to begin the *Half Moon* voyage.

And Cope, as we have seen, was directly linked to George Waymouth during the espionage affair of 1607. The previous passage-making efforts of Waymouth in 1602 and 1605 were now prime motivators for Hudson's change of course in the *Half Moon*. That course change would also mean that Hudson was about to use a VOC ship to enter, if not transgress upon, the territory of the Virginia Company, in which Cope and Cecil were prominent investors.

And there was more. Hudson's boast to Thomas Holland of knowing Sir Walter Cope was impressive enough, but the second name he dropped was that of Sir Thomas Challener (or Challoner). Challener had been added to an expanded Virginia Company council in 1607 and figured prominently alongside Cope and Cecil in the new 1609 company. Challener was also close to James I's eldest son, Henry, who would be vested as Prince of Wales in 1610. Challener served as governor of the prince's household and advised the young man on scientific matters, including a particular passion of the prince: the search for the Northwest Passage. When Hudson was said on his 1610 voyage to promise a participant a position in the "prince's guard," it was his connection to Challener that he was intending to exploit.

Hudson thus was close to some of the most important figures in the Virginia Company, who also occupied positions in the highest echelons of power at court. When Francis Perkins wrote home from Jamestown in March 1608 to ask a friend to lobby for his appointment to the colony's council, he advised him to approach five people on the matter. Three of them were Smythe, Cope, and Challener.

It seemed that Hudson was playing a very dangerous game with the *Half Moon*: defying his VOC employers while risking giving grave offense to Cope, Challener, and Smythe (not to mention Cecil) in planning to trespass on the Virginia Company's territory with a VOC ship. It appeared to be impossible for Hudson to complete the rogue voyage without making serious enemies on both sides of the English Channel. Unless, of course, he had secured tacit approval, or even active support, from the English side before the *Half Moon* departed Amsterdam.

English ambitions toward eastern North America were riven by rivalries and factions, some within the Virginia Company itself. The company's objectives were so multifold that there were heated disagreements on priorities: Establish a profitable plantation? Find a passage through the continent to the Orient? Secure cargoes of medicinal herbs? Seek out rumored mineral riches, especially gold? With more than six hundred active investors, some would likely have accepted an opportunity to surreptitiously employ a freelancing Hudson to further their own aims. And all to the better that the VOC was unwittingly putting up the ship and crew. If Hudson was in fact in London in March 1609, it might have made sense to one or more unknown patrons to have him make the illicit voyage to the Virginia territory, to pursue their own interests, when the new company hadn't yet coalesced.

Already, something of an independent voyage had been commissioned for 1609. Samuel Argall, a cousin by marriage of Sir Thomas Smythe, was being sent out in a ship called the *Mary and John*. He was to research a more northerly route to the Chesapeake, as English mariners were still relying on a sweeping route south to the Azores so as to ride the trade winds to America, which usually meant an initial landfall in the Caribbean. Emanuel Van Meteren, whose London intelligence was impeccable, wrote about the Argall voyage in his wide-ranging *History of the Netherland*, stating that Argall was sent out "to discover a more convenient route or passage there [so as] to shun the worrisome route of the southern indies course and quarrels with the Spaniards over [their] express command nowhere to touch Spanish territory, and to fix a course away from the roadsteads frequented by pirates, who lie just offshore and in narrow passages."

Although Smythe was to serve as head of the new Virginia Company, Argall seems to have sailed on Smythe's private account when he departed Portsmouth in May, less than three weeks before the new company's charter was ratified by James I. Argall fished for sturgeon to help defray the voyage costs, and also traded with Jamestown (rather than directly supplying it) once he arrived.* Argall had sailed an alternate trade winds passage on the outbound journey, initially steering even farther south than the Azores, to the Canaries, but then turned directly west to cross the Atlantic and worked north to the Chesapeake. While he avoided altogether the Spanish Caribbean in the process, he left a fully northern route for the voyage home. It would fall to Henry Hudson, in a VOC ship, to actually prove that same summer an outbound route to the colony via the North Atlantic.

Was this an accident of history, or did someone, even Smythe himself, put Hudson up to it? Had Argall not bothered with testing a true northerly approach on the outbound leg because he had been told someone else would be taking care of it?

BEYOND HUDSON'S ASSERTION of high-placed connections at court, the true scope of his social and political reach is an enigma. His statement to Thomas Holland may have been little more than dockside boasting. Cope could have known Hudson simply because the new chancellor of the exchequer was a private collector of exploration exotica, and after Hudson's disappearance in 1611, the mariner seemed to rapidly fade in stature. When the Muscovy Company petitioned the High Court of the Admiralty in 1614 to defend its exclusive rights to the northern fishery and trade in the face of incursions from the Dutch, it cited Hudson's 1608 voyage to Novaya Zemlya but erroneously referred to him as *William* Hudson.

Many heads of English exploration ventures, like Sir Humphrey Gilbert, were nobles or knights, or men with the right family connections to those dispensing favors. Hudson could have been a privileged dilettante, of the sort who were fascinated with theoretical advances in navigation theory and infamously managed to secure commissions from a corrupt naval administration despite having absolutely no sea sense. While on his own word Hudson was well connected at court, on balance he seems to have

---

* Writing home from Jamestown on August 31, 1609, Gabriel Archer, who had encountered Argall—"a good Mariner, and a very civil Gentleman"—on his own arrival about one month earlier, was more ambiguous about who was employing Argall. Archer allowed that the *Mary and John* had been "sent out of England by our Counsel's leave and authority, to fish for Sturgeon, and to go the ready way, without tracing through the Torrid Zone, and she performed it."

been a professional mariner who was training his son John to follow in his footsteps.

Nothing is known about Hudson's life before he walked into the historical record on April 19, 1607. Four days before the first *Hopewell* voyage, Hudson and his eleven fellow crewmembers had squeezed into the fifty-six-foot by thirty-foot interior of St. Ethelburga's church on Bishopsgate to receive communion alongside the other Church of England parishioners. The view astern of his life from that point was unbroken sea. Only the scattered appearances of the Hudson family name (with spelling variants typical of the era) in earlier Muscovy Company records suggests a deeper, multigenerational obsession with profitable passage-making and connections in a web of like-minded men influential in commerce and exploration.

The Muscovy Company arose from a 1553 venture to prove the Northeast Passage, which ended in disaster (two of three ships in the original expedition were frozen in for the winter on the Kola Peninsula, costing the lives of both crews) but led to the establishment of the lucrative Russia trade. The company secured the exclusive right to exploit any northern passage to the Orient in its 1555 charter, thus placing it at the heart of arctic exploration as well as northern trade into Henry Hudson's time.

London was, by modern standards, a small city in a small nation, but it was home to a disproportionate number of players in the global exploration and colonization game, due to the concentration of power and wealth in the capital, particularly through overseas merchants who belonged to the Company of Merchant Adventurers and their influence at court. The fraternity of investors, theoreticians, mariners, and explorers in the late sixteenth and early seventeenth centuries was accordingly tight, and membership inevitably drew connections among most of the significant figures.

One of those key figures was Christopher Hoddesdon, a tough old bird who was associated with the Muscovy Company almost from its beginning. Named a Muscovy agent in Russia in 1560, he had also been called "Hudson" in company documents dating back to the 1550s. He sat on a committee struck by the company to listen to Sir Humphrey Gilbert advocate colonization of North America and recommended that it invest therein. He invested personally in Martin Frobisher's expeditions to the northwest in the 1570s and may have been the Christopher Hudson involved in an English trade scheme in Brazil in 1580. He was also probably the "Master Hoddesden" who sat on a Muscovy Company committee that agreed in 1583 to underwrite a North American colonization scheme by Christopher Carleill, whose distracted expedition in 1584 never made it beyond Ireland. And he was completing a term as governor of the powerful Company of Merchant Adventurers in the year that Henry Hudson took command of the *Hopewell*. He may have been from the same Hudson family as Henry Herdson, one of the twenty-four original "associates" of the 1553 trade venture, a city alderman and merchant from London's tanning guild, whose letters to Edward VI survive.

Because Henry Herdson succumbed to fever in 1555, the explorer Henry Hudson would never have known him, whatever their actual relationship. But there were more Hudsons, beyond Henry Herdson and Christopher Hoddesdon, who were intimately involved with England's exploration initiatives and formed possible connections to and around the explorer from within the Muscovy ranks.

Henry Herdson's eldest son, Thomas Hudson, resided up the Thames from London, at Mortlake, in Surrey, where Dr. John Dee also lived. The two men knew each other, and this placed Thomas in the company of one of the most informed, if eccentric, of English exploration advocates. An astrologer to Elizabeth I, from about 1560 to 1583 Dee was a focal point of planning for English voyages in search of an arctic route to the Orient, all of which, because of its monopoly in northern trade and exploration, naturally required some level of involvement from the Muscovy Company. Dr. Dee taught Martin Frobisher and his pilot, Christopher Hall, the latest mathematical concepts in navigation, and loaded them down with books, charts, and instruments, before they set off on their first voyage to the northwest in 1576. Dee then advised Arthur Pet and Charles Jackman (who had been involved with the Frobisher expeditions) before they attempted the Northeast Passage for the company in 1580, the last such confirmed effort by Muscovy men before Henry Hudson entered the picture. Dee was also closely allied with the Digges family, publishers of successive editions of a mariner's almanac, the *Prognostication*. One prominent Digges, Sir Dudley, would become an investor in Henry Hudson's final voyage in 1610.

Dee's last act on the exploration front, before heading to continental Europe and immersing himself in several years of occult activities (which ultimately saw him flee Poland to avoid charges of necromancy), was to meet, according to his diary, in 1583 with John Davis, Adrian Gilbert (a close childhood friend of Davis, younger brother of Humphrey Gilbert, and half brother of Walter Raleigh), and a "Mr. Hudson." Dee, Adrian Gilbert, and Davis had formed the Fellowship of New Navigations Atlanticall and Septentrionall, which advocated colonization of North America. They had gathered with "Mr. Hudson" to help Davis plan his resumption of England's Northwest Passage search in 1585.

This "Mr. Hudson" was probably another Thomas Hudson, a captain in the Muscovy Company service who lived at Limehouse. His exact relationship with the other Hudsons is unknown, but he had recently participated in an epic Muscovy expedition to Persia, which traveled through the Russian river system all the way to the Caspian Sea. Departing London in the spring of 1579, the expedition did not return until the autumn of 1581, and only after numerous narrow escapes from shipwreck, hostile locals, disease, and starvation.

Captain Thomas Hudson's journey reinforced the Hudson name's relationship with the brothers William and Stephen Borough.* They were aboard the *Edward Bonaventure*, the sole ship to survive the 1553 expedition to the northeast, and had also made an extraordinary passage for the company in 1566, a round-trip of some 4,600 miles into the Russian arctic in pursuit of the Northeast Passage, before joining Thomas Hudson in the 1579–81 Persia venture. A line could also be drawn from the Boroughs to Christopher Hoddesdon. William Borough sat with Hoddesdon on the Muscovy committee that recommended investing in Humphrey Gilbert's colonization proposal for North America, after the company initially stood in Gilbert's way, in defense of its charter rights, when he wanted to seek the Northwest Passage in the 1560s. While serving as the Muscovy Company's Russia agent in 1570, Hoddesdon wrote to London to complain about Danish freebooters who were horning in on the Russia trade through the Baltic port of Narva. Hoddesdon requisitioned a nautical strike force against the

---

* William Borough was one of the most respected figures in the Elizabethan drive to turn England into a maritime power. He served as a Muscovy agent in 1574–75 and in 1581 became Elizabeth's controller of the navy, serving until his death in 1599. He accompanied Dee in providing advice to Martin Frobisher for his Northwest Passage search that turned into a misguided northwest mining venture on Baffin Island, in addition to sinking his own money into the third voyage, every pence of which was lost. One of Borough's most significant contributions to the Frobisher enterprise was the plane chart he drew for him (which still survives), with known lands inked into place, so that Frobisher could fill in the blanks. William also promoted mathematical literacy in navigation.

pesky Danes, and it was William Borough who delivered it and then joined him in laying waste to the company's competitors.

The Hudsons were also close to the prominent Barne (or Barns/Barnes) family. It was Sir William Barne to whom Christopher Hoddesdon wrote in 1570, requesting the ships he needed to roust the Danish freebooters from Narva. (And Christopher Carleill, the financing of whose inept voyage to America was approved by Hoddesdon, was a Barnes on his mother's side.) The crew list for Henry Hudson's 1608 *Hopewell* voyage included a man named John Barnes, who could have been a member of the esteemed family. And another crewmember of Hudson's 1608 voyage, Humfrey Gilby, could have been a member of the Gilbert family.

But beyond these many impressive connections to the Hudson name in the passage-search business, Henry Hudson's life and career prior to the 1607 *Hopewell* voyage remain a mystery. Historians and popular writers would stretch to make connections to John Davis, proposing that Hudson might have sailed with him to the northwest in the 1580s, or that he fought alongside him in repelling the Spanish Armada of 1588. There is no evidence for any of that. But Hudson may have sailed with Davis much later, in 1602, when Davis was the pilot for the East India Company's inaugural trade expedition under Sir James Lancaster. No firm proof exists, but Lancaster's methods and experiences would resonate in Hudson's own conduct, particularly on his final, fateful voyage of 1610.

The circumstantial evidence suggests that Henry Hudson was connected to influential circles in trade, commerce, exploration, and politics for years before materializing as an explorer in 1607. But none of it confirms that he was working secretly for English interests on the 1609 *Half Moon* voyage. The Dutch would not know what to make of him or his performance when the voyage was over: some would suspect he had in fact hoodwinked them, deliberately avoiding making a discovery in the northwest that would benefit the Dutch rather than the English. But as we shall see, Hudson's behavior at the voyage's conclusion, as documented by Van Meteren and Holland, suggests that he may never have been working for anyone other than himself; that in making off with the *Half Moon* he seized an unparalleled and possibly unrepeatable chance to pursue his own agenda and salvage his career. There had never been a voyage of exploration like this before, and never would be again.

CHAPTER 6

HUDSON HAD BEEN ENTIRELY PREPARED to fail in carrying out his sailing instructions from the VOC for the *Half Moon* voyage. When the Northeast Passage thwarted him—or when Hudson grasped the earliest defensible opportunity to declare that nothing good was going to come from pressing the effort—he was ready to steer in new directions.

The details of Hudson's decision to reverse course with the *Half Moon* and sail for eastern North America rather than Amsterdam are murky. The *Half Moon*'s log is long vanished, and the most complete surviving account, the journal of Robert Juet, falls conspicuously silent for two weeks of crucial sailing, from the moment the *Half Moon* cleared Norway's North Cape on May 5, steering east across the Barents Sea toward Novaya Zemlya, to her reappearance off that same cape on May 19, now making west for the New World. Juet's journal (as published in 1625) offers only a fragmentary sentence as explanation for how and why Hudson had turned back: "after much trouble, with fog sometimes, and more dangerous of ice." And nothing in Juet's journal indicated when or why Hudson embarked on his rogue plan.

The Dutch consul in London, Emanuel Van Meteren, who saw Hudson's journal account on his return and paraphrased its contents, provided a few more details. After passing the North Cape on May 5, Van Meteren would write, Hudson "directed his course along the north coasts towards [Novaya Zemlya]; but there he found the sea as full of ice as he had found it in the preceding year, so that he lost the hope of effecting anything during the season. This circumstance, and the cold which some of his men who had been in the East Indies could not bear, caused quarrels among the crew, they being partly English, partly Dutch."

Ships and crews were so poorly equipped for arctic passage-making that it is a tribute to sheer fortitude that anyone made a living in the northern whale and walrus fishery. There was no central heating on board, nor was there coffee or tea to warm the gullet or the hands clasping a mug while on watch. The sails had to be worked with coarse hemp cordage that froze stiff with salt spray and jammed in wooden blocks. There was little or no shelter from the elements on the open deck (not to mention while perched at the bow in the beak, defecating into the sea), and the crew had to ward off the cold and the freezing ocean spray with the early seventeenth century's limited clothing technology. The list of apparel purchased for George Waymouth's 1602 expedition to the Northwest Passage is a rare survival among accounts of the era. It reveals the crew being outfitted with leather breeches and hooded cassocks lined with lamb's wool, and leather gowns lined with frieze (a looped pile fabric), as well as fur-lined leather mittens, cotton waistcoats, linen shirts, woolen socks, and leather boots and shoes.

These garments doubtless were the best any northern mariner could expect, but the notoriously skinflint VOC would not necessarily have agreed to spend so generously. For one thing, Waymouth had been expected to overwinter in the Arctic, where Hudson's *Half Moon* voyage was meant to be a summer reconnaissance. With Petrus Plancius still advocating the existence of a temperate region above the arctic circle (and with Hudson readily agreeing with him), funds may not have been supplied to dress the crew properly for the frigid experience actually awaiting them. Hudson would have known better, based on his experiences with the *Hopewell* in 1607 and 1608. But as he had other plans for this voyage assuredly from the beginning, he was probably little concerned that Dutch sailors accustomed to tropical torpor in the East Indies trade might soon be close to freezing to death and demanding that he turn around.

IF HUDSON WAS now going to alter course and sail west, across the North Atlantic, he would have to make his move no later than returning to North Cape, so that he could set a southwesterly course to the Faeroe Islands, some one thousand nautical miles away. There, he could take on freshwater and replenish the ship's larder by harvesting wild birds in preparation for an extended voyage.

On the 1608 voyage, he was still at anchor off Novaya Zemlya when he made his pitch to the crew of trying for the Northwest Passage. Although rebuffed on that occasion, he seemed to have learned at least from his 1607 voyage. The strange circumstances of that first voyage's conclusion indicate that he had tried to surreptitiously bend that enterprise toward the Northwest Passage, and delayed for as long as possible in owning up to the crew what he had in mind.

On the return leg from Spitsbergen in 1607, he took the *Hopewell* about five hundred miles off course to the west, before correcting back toward London. He was so far off course that he discovered a new landfall, a volcanic speck north of Iceland, which he named Hudson's Touches. But Hudson gutted his journal account of the details of the return leg, thus costing himself the credit for finding it. When a Muscovy Company captain named Thomas Edge inspected the *Hopewell*'s log in 1610 he noticed Hudson's discovery, and it only become public knowledge when Edge's observation of that fact was published in 1625. In the meantime, whalers out of Hull called it Trinity Island in 1611; the Dutch who found it in 1614 gave it the name that would endure, Jan Mayen Island.

The best explanation for Hudson's peculiar decision to ignore the discovery in the 1607 voyage journal was that he was loath to address a crew insurrection that might well have erupted around that time, when the men realized where he was trying to take them. For his course, in delivering him to Jan Mayen Island, had been pointed at southern Greenland and the approaches to the Northwest Passage.

While the crew's opposition to Hudson's apparent 1607 subterfuge could have been ugly, neither that revolt nor the demand to sail directly home in 1608 rather than try for the Northwest Passage deserved to be called a mutiny in a strict legal sense. The concept did not exist in English maritime law at the time for commercial voyages. Ships' crews might have been assemblages of rabble, but they were rabble whose rights were protected by laws of maritime commerce.* Hudson could no more make a radical

---

* For example, article 24 of a 1597 set of laws for merchant vessels from the towns of the powerful Hanseatic League in the northern Netherlands and Germany prescribed: "If the master changes his voyage, and steers another course than was intended, he ought to have the

change in his exploration plans than the master of a collier shunting coal from Newcastle to Harwich could summarily announce midpassage that the vessel was instead bound for Java.

A ship's master's success or failure in convincing mariners to go along with alternate plans, either at the wages they had agreed to on departure or with some top-up arrangement, was a labor relations issue, nothing more. In Hudson's English law, if the crew of a commercial vessel forcibly took control of the ship in the course of sailing where they'd agreed to go, then it was a case of spoliation, or piracy, not mutiny, which was exclusively a naval offense. If lives were lost in the process, then there was murder besides. But a dispute over where to sail next, and for how much money, was a workaday grievance. For vessels out of London, that dispute could be addressed, once home, by taking the case to the elder brothers of Trinity House on Deptford Strand, which licensed masters and pilots like Hudson and held legal sway over employment issues in commercial shipping out of the City.

Subterfuge hadn't persuaded fellow Englishmen to go along with Hudson's plan B on the 1607 voyage, and a direct appeal on the 1608 voyage had been so soundly rejected that Hudson was compelled to provide the crew with a signed certificate protecting them from any charges of insubordination, and to set down that fact in his journal. Which makes it all the more curious that he was able to get the *Half Moon*'s crew to go along with his plans in 1609.

Not only did the Dutch outnumber the English aboard three to one: the master's mate, the second in command, was a Dutchman, and he must have known the essentials of Hudson's instructions from the VOC. And a Dutch majority seems unlikely to have been predisposed to defy the orders of so powerful a domestic employer. Then there was the sheer scale of the insubordination. Hudson wasn't talking about making an unauthorized side trip to La Rochelle to score a few guilders in the French wine trade. He was asking them to sail clear to the other side of the Atlantic, and presumably to keep on going to China if his hunch about an alternate passage proved correct.

---

consent of his mariners, or pay them what the major party of them shall adjudge to be due to them for his changing of the voyage; and if then any one of them will not obey him, he shall be punished as a mutineer."

Hudson may not have been able to promise additional wages out of his own pocket. One might imagine an unknown source of funds, provided perhaps by a wealthy and surreptitious English backer. But it is much simpler to conclude that Hudson succeeded in getting his Dutch charges to go along with his insubordinate scheme by offering them another means of recompense. And the very nature of the *Half Moon* is the most important clue.

EMANUEL VAN METEREN would write that Hudson was equipped with a *vlieboat*, a design the English called a flyboat. Broad-beamed with a shallow hull and a high stern, it was well suited to negotiating rivers and streams and shoaling waters. (The Vlie was the estuary of the river IJssel, which gave its name to the island of Vlieland.) The flyboat proved suitable to the exploration game because it could sail in unknown coastal tidewaters with minimal risk of damage in the event of a grounding. George Waymouth had used a flyboat, the *Discovery*, in his 1602 voyage to the Northwest Passage, and the design had also been employed by recent English voyagers to North America: the *Susan Constant*, commanded by Bartholomew Gosnold for the Virginia Company, was such a design.

Van Meteren might well have understood that a flyboat was what Hudson thought he would receive. But VOC records indicate that he was instead provided with a *jaght*, a variation on the vlieboat. *Jaght* means "hunter" or "chaser." It had less cargo capacity than a vlieboat, and while it might not have been more ferociously armed, being relatively swift and nimble made it useful for chasing down pirates, and capable of conducting piracy of its own. The evolving jaght became a favored design of Dutch burghers wishing a private pleasure vessel, and it gave us the modern term "yacht."

Hudson's ship's name clearly was inspired by the half-moon medallion worn by Dutch privateers. Called "sea beggars" (*watergeuzen*), they were often financed by leading Dutch merchants. They had played a leading role in the Dutch revolt against the Spanish since the first squadron was organized in 1568, and enjoyed folklore status for the damage they inflicted on Spanish property, at sea and on land. They also laid the foundation for the Dutch navy; Admiral Heemskerck had started out as one. While state control of maritime affairs was formalized in 1597, sea beggars continued to operate, with or without proper letters of reprisal authorizing attacks on enemy property. They could be ruthless in their conduct and unscrupulous in their choice of targets.

Not even stalwart Dutch allies were spared. On the 1602 voyage to Norumbega by Bartholomew Gosnold, the English were waylaid west of the Azores by sea beggars who at first feigned camaraderie. But once they had Raleigh Gilbert, commander of the *Mary and John,* aboard with several gentleman companions, they treated them badly (and, as historian David B. Quinn has suggested, probably with drunken amusement). Recalled the *Mary and John*'s pilot, Robert Davis (or Davies), the sea beggars alleged that Gilbert "was a pirate and [were] still threatening himself and his gentlemen with him to throw them all overboard and to take our ship from us." Gilbert and his companions were held against their will from ten in the morning until eight at night, with the Dutch "using some of his gentlemen in [the] most vile manner," delivering beatings and slapping leg irons on some, before deciding to let them go.

One of the most outrageous incidents involved an assault on the French trading post of Tadoussac in the lower St. Lawrence River in 1606. The *White Lion,* a heavily armed Dutch vessel about four times the size of the *Half Moon,* used the guidance of a French turncoat to strike a near-fatal blow to the local trade monopoly of the Sieur de Monts—carrying away the furs and armaments from two of de Monts's four vessels, devastating his proceeds for the year, causing a diplomatic incident, and igniting legal actions that lasted until 1621.

Such lawlessness (in which the English also were prone to indulging) was par for the course, and had been for many years. "Although the kings of Spain and Portugal are friends and allies of our own Sovereign Prince," the French royal geographer André Thevet had noted in *Cosmographie universelle* in 1575, "the sea pilots, sailors, and captains pay no attention to such alliances, or whether there is peace or war on land."

Almost no one on the high seas could be trusted to behave himself, regardless of the state of relations between nations and monarchs or what official commission a ship's commander might be carrying. Dutch and English merchant ships were routinely heavily armed, as able to give as good as they received, and trading voyages sometimes involved some side action in robbery. While the English were nominally constrained from attacking the

Spanish and Portuguese by the Treaty of London from 1605 onward, the Dutch continued to strike at them. And with the Twelve Year Truce not having been signed until three days after the *Half Moon* cleared Texel, her crew would have been able to claim a convenient ignorance of the new era of ostensible high-seas civility.

The VOC, in providing Hudson with a jaght, had ensured that this single-ship expedition would be able to thwart aggressors. Far from the oversight of the company directors, Hudson found that the vessel's character was of some advantage to his particular ambitions. The VOC would not have supplied such a potent vessel without including crewmembers that could fight at sea. Many of them could have had experience as sea beggars, although even crews of VOC merchant vessels had to know how to handle weapons.

There would be no hijacking of this voyage by Hudson without such a crew's consent. According to Van Meteren, some time after the Dutch and English crewmembers fell into quarreling about their circumstances in the ice and fog off Novaya Zemlya, Hudson presented them with two alternate plans. Neither involved returning to Amsterdam. Predictably, one was to investigate the Northwest Passage in the vicinity of Davis Strait, which would mean testing the Furious Overfall last overcome by Waymouth. The other was to look for a passage right through North America, around latitude 40. Van Meteren's account does not indicate that the crew chose one option over the other, only that they agreed to the general plan of not going right back to Amsterdam. But Van Meteren never explained why they acted this way.

Hudson could have proposed that if the Dutch majority went along with his alternate plans on the far side of the Atlantic, they could thieve their way to additional compensation. Already, these men were probably chafing at their wages, as the VOC paid mariners less than almost any other Dutch maritime employer, its stinginess surpassed only by the navy's. Privateers and independent traders paid better. The mortality rate of VOC crews was also appalling. About one in five ships in the Dutch service to the East Indies between 1598 and 1606 was lost, and disease further ensured that one sailor in three perished.

So it may not have been difficult after all for Hudson to convince these men to abandon the VOC's assignment and try something that promised far greater rewards. But as the voyage record would prove, the VOC had placed together in one well-armed vessel the inflammatory combination of an insubordinate commander and a ruthlessly opportunistic crew that was as capable of defying their master as their master was his employer.

BEYOND THE FACT that the *Half Moon* was a jaght, we have no firm knowledge of what she was like. Ships were not built from plans at the time, so no drawings survive. On December 29, 1608, two of the Amsterdam chamber's directors, along with the chamber's chief boatswain, Dirck Gerritsz, were instructed to look out for "a suitable vessel [*scheepgen*]" of twenty-five to thirty-five *lasten*, or "lasts," for Hudson's voyage. Something around the size of Willem Barentsz's ship thus was imagined, but later VOC documents indicate the *Half Moon* was forty lasten.

Two unnamed jaghts were built for the VOC in 1608, and they were probably seventy and eighty feet long, from stem to sternpost. While neither of them necessarily was the *Half Moon*, she could have been the larger of the two, which would have been in keeping with a capacity of forty lasten. But recordings of lasten are not especially helpful, because the definition of this measurement was extremely inconsistent at the time. Thomas Holland's observation that the *Half Moon* looked to be about seventy tons' burden is a little more informative, as we have a better grip on what this volume measurement meant, and it would suggest a smaller vessel. But the calculation of tonnage was also so flexible in Hudson's time that it is still a challenge to come up with absolute dimensions. We can imagine her hull to have been anywhere from sixty-five to as many as eighty feet long, and around fifteen to twenty feet wide. Her draft, or depth below the water, was around eight or nine feet.

Juet's journal confirms she had a mainmast, a foremast, and a bowsprit, and while he never mentions a mizenmast, we can be confident her sailplan conformed to the standard rig of Dutch ships in contemporary drawings. She thus had three masts, as well as the bowsprit, with a total of six sails. It was a simple arrangement of canvas, and all but one sail was cut square and supported by horizontal yards. The exception was the triangular lateen on the smallest mast, the mizen, which emerged from the highest, sternmost deck, the poop. An aid to steering, it seldom seems to have been set. Contemporary illustrations of ships at sea usually show the mizen furled, and Juet never refers to it in the entirety of his journal.

The bowsprit extended forward from the blunt profile of the bow like the tusk of a narwhal, supported by the beak. We're accustomed to thinking of a figurehead being mounted on the beak of historic sailing ships, but the *Half Moon* probably didn't have one. The bowsprit had a single square sail, the spritsail. The mainmast, which was stepped on the keel about halfway along the ship's length, featured the mainsail, and above it, on the topmast, the main topsail. At the very bow, and raking slightly forward, was the foremast, shorter than the mainmast and with two sails of its own, the fore course at the bottom and the fore topsail above it. Sails could be expanded in lighter winds by attaching an additional strip of canvas, called a bonnet (which Juet notes), to their lower edges. Alternately, rows of rope sewn into the sails allowed them to be reefed, or reduced in area. This multipart spread of canvas was harnessed by a cat's cradle of rope and wooden turning blocks: halyards to raise and lower sails, tacks and sheets to trim them, standing rigging to keep the masts upright, ratlines to allow sailors to ascend the rig and keep a lookout (although her masts would not have had crow's nests), and more. She would have flown at least the flag of the VOC, an orange-white-blue horizontal tricolor with the VOC logo on the white field.

As to armaments, Juet refers to a falconet, which was a small cannon about four feet long that typically fired an iron ball two inches in diameter. Weighing more than four hundred pounds, it would have been mounted in a carriage at a gun port, and the *Half Moon* probably had at least four of them. Juet also refers to stone-shot "murderers," which were small rail-mounted cannon that could be swiveled and aimed along the ship's length to repel boarders and otherwise inflict damage in close-quarters combat. Muskets are also mentioned.

We're fairly at sea in deciding what the hull was like. Because no hard evidence survives for interior layouts of most ships of this time, the *Half Moon* included, the issue of how many decks to include has preoccupied efforts to build replicas (or more precisely, informed-guesswork imaginings). Deck nomenclature can be confusing. By "single deck" we mean that there was one main deck, with no "walk-through" interior decks directly below it, above the hold. Choosing multiple decks creates a more complex interior, and also a taller hull. The larger of the two jaghts built for the VOC in 1608 had some kind of two-deck arrangement. A plan with both a main deck and a lower one called the orlop (with three interior deck levels in the stern) was

The Australian replica Duyfken *displays the high, narrow transom of a VOC jaght. (Photo courtesy Nick Burningham.)*

chosen for the *Half Moon* replica built in 1989, although in size (sixty-five feet from stem to sternpost) she might be more like the smaller vessel built for the VOC in 1608, which was single-decked.*

To help understand the seagoing world of Henry Hudson and his men, we can look to the *Duyfken* (Little Dove), a jaght built in 1595 that was in VOC service in the East Indies from 1601 to 1608. Variously described as having been twenty-five to thirty lasten, she might have been slightly smaller than the *Half Moon*, but we really cannot be sure. The design team responsible for the Australian replica launched in 1999 went to considerable lengths to create a faithful circa 1600 jaght and drew up a variety of configurations based on computer analysis of hull shape, archaeological evidence, shipbuilders' contracts, surviving ship models, descriptions in logs, and contemporary illustrations. Unusual for such research efforts was

*The 1989 replica appears fairly similar to the original *Half Moon* replica, built by the Netherlands for the 1909 Hudson-Fulton Celebration, although its published length from stem to stern was just fifty-eight feet six inches. It was destroyed by fire in 1931.

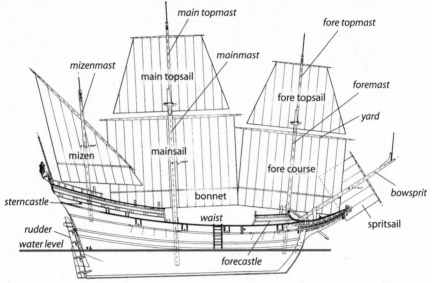

A typical three-masted configuration of a Dutch jaght of the early seventeenth century, shown here in the sail plan drawing of the 1999 replica Duyfken. *(Drawing by Nick Burningham, with labels by the author.)*

their emphasis on creating a ship that could live up to the performance criteria indicated by historical records, as so many "replicas" have left us with a jaundiced view of the capabilities of historic vessels. (The first replica of the *Half Moon*, launched in 1909, essentially could not sail toward the wind and was impossible to tack without the use of the mizen sail to swing the stern around.) They were also blessed by the fact that an eyewitness sketch of the *Duyfken* at anchor exists, something that cannot be said of other individual jaghts, the *Half Moon* included. The team concluded that a single-deck layout made the most sense in their case.*

Juet's mention of waistboards—temporary defensive screenings that increased the height of the bulwarks to protect the crew from hostile fire—confirms that, as in the case of the *Duyfken* replica, the *Half Moon*'s main

---

* While I am partial to the 1999 *Duyfken* replica's more rakish interpretation of the jaght, I must emphasize that this does not make the 1989 *Half Moon* "wrong." All attempts to create an example of a ship of this era require a considerable amount of educated guessing, and no one who has done so has ever expected to produce a definitive version of an unknowable original.

deck was broken into higher "castles" at either end, with a lower exposed area, or waist, between them. Forward was the forecastle; aft was the sterncastle. These were not substantial elevated areas, along the lines of sixteenth-century ships. The sterncastle, which supported the quarterdeck, probably was only a few steps higher than the main deck. A further slight rise in the quarterdeck toward the tall, narrow stern created the poop deck, which provided headroom in the master's cabin. The helmsman was sheltered beneath the forward end of the poop at the whipstaff and peered out of his hutch along the quarterdeck, where the officer conning the ship stood. Forward, the foredeck similarly was elevated slightly above the waist of the main deck, enough to provide headroom to the compartment below it, the forecastle.

The master's cabin featured shuttered windows on the high stern, which in the case of a jaght had a square transom, rather than the rounded one often found on vlieboats. Narrative evidence suggests Hudson shared the cabin with Juet, and possibly with his son John as well. The door from Hudson's cabin led directly to the helm station, with its whipstaff and compass binnacle. Ahead was the main cabin.

Below the master's cabin was a low-ceilinged space known as the aft peak, or tiller flat—so called because the tiller swept across its ceiling, which would have been a creaking distraction to anyone trying to sleep. While this cabin could have featured a cannon poking out of a gun port in the transom, it would have been home to senior crewmembers. While no crew manifest survives, a master's mate, a carpenter, and a cook appear in Juet's journal. A boatswain (who was responsible for the physical state of the ship) also would have been on hand. The crews of Hudson's earlier *Hopewell* voyages were too small to include a barber-surgeon, and there may not have been one aboard the *Half Moon*, either.

The *Half Moon* likely followed long-standing convention in granting little consideration to the privacy or comfort of the general crew. The hammock had not yet been invented. If hard wooden berths were not available, the crew would have slept off-watch wherever they could make themselves comfortable.

Crews routinely dozed out-of-doors in fair weather, rather than breathe belowdecks air fouled by rotten food, bilgewater, and rat piss, which braided aromatically with the general odor of a ship's company with no opportunities (or inclinations) to bathe. Sailors literally pitched camp on the upper

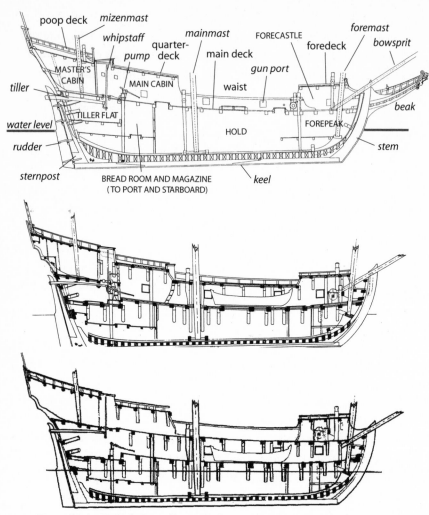

Top: a basic single-deck configuration for a jaght about the size of the Half Moon, *as chosen for the* Duyfken *replica of 1999. Two- and three-deck configurations (middle and bottom) were also investigated, but judged to be too top-heavy and not in keeping with the performance attributed to the original ship. (Drawings by Nick Burningham, with labels by the author.)*

decks, sleeping in tents or leather-covered "kennels" of their own making, which likely was the practice aboard the *Half Moon*.

In higher latitudes, the forecastle would have been an attractive gathering place, as it usually housed the ship's stove, the only source of heat. English ships often had a stove down in the hold, but as nautical archaeologist and *Duyfken* replica designer Nick Burningham has noted, Sir Walter Raleigh for one disapproved. Apart from the fact that such stoves rather incredibly were not properly vented, thus filling the hull with smoke, he complained that spilled food spoiled in the bilge and caused the ship's timbers to rot. Dutch vessels like the *Half Moon* instead employed a portable iron cooking stove (*combuis*) that was located (with a proper chimney) in the forecastle.

This stove, however, could be moved about. After Willem Barentsz's ship was trapped in ice in the winter of 1596–97 at the northern tip of Novaya Zemlya, the stove was shifted one deck lower, into the forepeak, to afford the crew warmer accommodations. The stove as a result wasn't vented, with nearly fatal consequences for the crew—not from asphyxiation but from consumption by polar bear. When a bear boarded the vessel, the crew "came above hatches to look on her and to shoot at her, but we could not see her by means of the exceeding great smoke that had so sore tormented us while we lay under hatches in the foul weather," according to the bestselling account by ship's carpenter Gerrit de Veer.

While a single-deck *Half Moon* still would have had elevated castles, she was probably more rakish and predatory looking than usually has been depicted. The distance from the main deck to the water might have been only about six feet midway along her length, and her cannons would have been placed on this deck, to be fired through ports in the protective bulwarks. The stone-shot murderers would have been positioned on the castles. But the fierce look probably was compromised by a strange village of tents and kennels, in the words of Nick Burningham, "cluttering all the decks like the most desperate kind of refugee camp."

CHAPTER 7

H
UDSON PAUSED IN THE FAEROE ISLANDS for a few days to provision, killing a fresh supply of meat in the seabird colonies. Such
breeding colonies of murres, auks, and other birds were well-known
supply depots for northern seafarers. Whenever possible they restocked the
larder with them, and set seines for fish: anything to avoid having to rely
exclusively on the typical stores of wormy biscuits, dried peas, cheese, meal
that could be cooked into a sort of porridge, and pickled or salted pork
and beef. Water was stored in casks, which Hudson replenished ashore in
the Faeroes, but sailors generally drank beer, wine, and spirits, which
kept better.

Hudson then turned to the literature of exploration on June 2 for the
next item on his revised voyage agenda. As Juet recounted: "At noon we
steered away west south-west to find Busse Island, discovered in the year
1578 by one of the ships of Sir Martin Frobisher, to see if it lay in her true
latitude in the chart or no."

Busse Island had been sighted by the crew of the *Busse of Bridgewater* on
their return to England on Frobisher's final voyage. The island reportedly
was fully twenty-five leagues long—seventy-five miles, hardly a speck of
rock. Such a major landfall should not have been difficult to find again, yet
somehow it was. Nevertheless, the island became fixed on the most authoritative charts.

At noon on June 3, a position of latitude 58 degrees, 48 minutes was determined for the *Half Moon*. They were about one and one-third degrees

70

north of the latitude at which the *Busse of Bridgewater* had established the island's southernmost point. "We accounted ourselves near Busse Island,"
Juet wrote. They gave themselves another twelve hours of sailing before actively searching for it. "By midnight we looked out for it, but could not see it."
The sun did not set until after ten P.M. and rose just after four A.M.: it
should not have been difficult to spot an island seventy-five miles long on
an empty ocean, and it would have been obvious against the horizon in the
slanting light of dusk or daybreak.

Hudson's inability to find Busse Island was understandable, since it
didn't exist.* But the fruitless searching could not have inspired much confidence in Hudson's charts, already made suspect by the Faeroes landfall,
which Juet said showed the islands to be placed too far west by fourteen
leagues, or forty-two miles. Any thought among the crew of agreeing to
steer west toward the Furious Overfall may have evaporated when Busse Island failed to materialize. Besides, according to Van Meteren, the Dutchmen already had their fill of arctic weather in the attempt to overcome
Novaya Zemlya.

From that point, the *Half Moon* steered progressively to the southwest,
shedding latitude, making for North America's eastern seaboard and the
lure of a midcontinental passage to the Orient. As strange as it might seem
to us today, the idea of reaching China by cutting through the heart of
North America was a powerfully persuasive idea in Hudson's time, which
owed its currency to arguments made in a little book that had recently been
a bestseller. It was a publishing phenomenon that Henry Hudson could
not have avoided reading and owning.

APPROACHING LONDON FROM the west, a traveler on the north side of the
Thames, in crossing the conveyor of offal that butchers had made of the
river Fleet, was immediately greeted by the spectacle of Ludgate. It was a
city entrance as well as a hulking prison, and the name also applied to a

---

* Like other false landfalls, Busse Island would enjoy extraordinary longevity, proving that
once dry land was fixed on a chart, it displayed barnacle-like resistance to removal. A Captain
Shepard would even claim to have charted it in 1671, encouraging the Hudson's Bay Company to secure a patent in 1675 from Charles II for its fishing rights. By the early nineteenth
century, Busse Island had been not so much erased as sunk, reclassified as a seamount,
which it also wasn't. In all likelihood, the 1578 observation had been of a great ice field.

conveniently located hill with fine sight lines for public executions. Arrive along Fleet Street on the right day, and one could be entertained by a condemned man being hanged until not quite dead, then watch as his entrails were cut out before his still blinking eyes. Like other gates around the ancient walls (as well as London Bridge), Ludgate was an opportune place to display the drawn and quartered remains, the heads, limbs, torsos, and bowels of the condemned that were denied a Christian burial. Ducking beneath the crow's feast of rotting body parts, a traveler would brace himself for the bouquet of a riverside metropolis without sewers and descend the slope of Fleet Street from Ludgate Hill. Ahead was St. Paul's, and the curious commercial bustle of its churchyard.

Publishers, printers, and booksellers rented space from the bishop for their stalls. Like London buildings in general, the stalls were known not by a street address but by their signage—in the case of the churchyard spaces, by such names as the Ball, the Bull Head, and the White Greyhound. The retailing arrangements made the churchyard the heart of the thriving English publishing trade. The stationers' company, which held the publishing monopoly, had its hall—which doubled as a book warehouse—immediately west of St. Paul's, and the premises of the publishers and printers ranged along Fleet Street, beyond Ludgate's visceral welcome.

The book business's offerings (properly licensed by the stationers and otherwise) ran from the high-minded to the low, from plays and poetry and Latin texts to shocking Italian illustrated pornography. Illicit pamphlets also circulated, along with bootleg editions of Shakespeare's plays and sonnets, but the publisher of a particular new offering in the autumn of 1602 did things by the book.

George Bishop was a leading member of his trade, who had served as Queen Elizabeth's printer and helped to produce some of the most important books in the realm. He co-published Richard Hakluyt's first edition of *Principal Navigations* in 1589; Bishop and two other partners then produced the three-volume second edition of 1598–1600, an influential and weighty bestseller. He had already participated in the publication of the *Chronicles of England, Scotland and Ireland* of 1587, which Shakespeare mined in creating his "history" plays. But this new work, with a main essay of about four thousand words, was far less of a financial burden to print than Hakluyt's recent opus, and Bishop handled it on his own.

The book was *A Briefe and True Relation of the Discoverie of the North Part of Virginia*, the official account of the voyage of Bartholomew Gosnold to Norumbega in the summer of 1602. The author was John Brereton, a Cambridge graduate (M.A., 1598), ordained deacon and priest from Norwich, who seems to have gone along as the chaplain of the expedition's small bark, the *Concord*.

According to the book's title page, the voyage had been made "by the permission of the honourable knight, Sir Walter Ralegh." But that was a lie. Gosnold had made the voyage without Raleigh's knowledge. The first that Sir Walter knew anything about it was when he discovered (as he complained in a letter to Sir Robert Cecil, on August 21) that someone had returned from the New World with a cargo of sassafras, a plant used to brew medicinal tea. In 1584 Queen Elizabeth had granted Raleigh the exclusive right to exploit "remote, heathen and barbarous lands, countries, and territories, not actually possessed of any Christian Prince, nor inhabited by Christian People." Raleigh insisted that his right as applied to eastern North America still existed, and the Gosnold voyage's backers had to come to a swift rapprochement with the knight. They concocted the fiction, set down in Brereton's title page, that Raleigh had approved of their initiative all along.

In the vernacular of the modern publishing trade, Brereton's was an "instant" book. Speed to market was paramount. Bishop had published enough travelogue material with Hakluyt to know marketable novelty when he read it. *A Briefe and True Relation* was the first published account of a voyage to Norumbega of any significant length, in any language. Released in late 1602, the book was an immediate success and quickly led to a second edition, which also carried the date 1602 but may have waited until early 1603 of the modern Gregorian calendar to reach Bishop's stall at St. Paul's. The second edition was in fact an entirely new book, the type reset and the page count expanded, as it was crammed with additional material. It sold twice as many copies as the first edition, veritably flying out of the stationers' hall warehouse.

For the second edition, Brereton's account of the Gosnold voyage became almost secondary, as the volume was inflated with content meant to lure investors to the cause of exploration and colonization. Some older items were gathered for George Bishop to typeset, probably with the help of Richard Hakluyt, an old hand at trade-and-exploration propaganda. But a key component of both editions was a treatise by a dear associate of Sir Humphrey Gilbert, Edward Hayes, on colonization and exploration. The treatise was included anonymously in the first edition, but Hayes received full credit in the second. The Hayes treatise was a culminating statement of some two decades of scheming, theorizing, and intelligence gathering. And it proved massively influential, within England and without.

As HISTORIAN DAVID B. Quinn documented, Edward Hayes was an idea man who pestered the English court with schemes of impressive if bewildering intellectual breadth. When he wasn't advocating coinage schemes for Ireland or the creation of an English militia, he was pressing his vision for overseas colonization and exploration. His persistence may have been exhausting, even exasperating, to those who dealt with him, but his coinage proposals were put into action, and on overseas matters he held the respect of influential men. Among the Elizabethans who dreamed of New World opportunities, Hayes's name would never have the same cachet as that of his associate Sir Humphrey Gilbert or of Sir Walter Raleigh. Yet his influence was considerable, if now largely unappreciated. He was a principal architect of the basic scheme for exploring and exploiting eastern North America in the first decade of the seventeenth century.

Hayes's thesis had been evolving for almost twenty years—or, rather, was repeatedly adapted by him to the cause at hand. If an overseas venture needed a theoretical framework to convince royalty to provide a monopoly and induce men of means to provide capital, Hayes was the one to write it. The son of a successful merchant from Liverpool, he had been an investor and a participant in Sir Humphrey Gilbert's ill-fated 1583 colonization venture, whose flotilla had claimed Newfoundland for England. The flotilla was sailing on for Norumbega when its supply ship, the *Delight*, foundered on Sable Island. On the voyage home, Hayes, commanding his own ship, the *Golden Hind*, witnessed Gilbert's loss in his little *Squirrel*. Hayes memorably recounted how Gilbert had shouted across to him, "We are as near to Heaven by sea as by land!" shortly before the *Squirrel*'s light vanished as a tempest swallowed him.

Hayes never again saw North America, but its possibilities remained vivid for him as his theorizing produced an increasingly persuasive counterpoint to the opportunities of polar passage-making. Hayes teased into shape the landscape of opportunity that ultimately drew in Henry Hudson.

Hayes argued that a route to the Orient could be found through the continent of North America, instead of above it, and advocated a search not for a pure ocean passage but rather for a transcontinental course employing rivers, lakes, and portages. He also believed that colonization was a precursor to making a passage search, expanding on an idea expressed by Richard Hakluyt in his *Discourse of Western Planting*, the brief he composed and presented to Elizabeth on Raleigh's behalf in 1584, which argued successfully for Raleigh's charter. Hakluyt had proposed how "by these Colonies the Northwest passage to Cathay and China may easily, quickly and perfectly be searched out as well by river and overland, as by sea."

Hayes initially, in the late 1580s, advocated a fresh attempt at establishing a settlement in Newfoundland, but he began promoting the colonization of the St. Lawrence in the early 1590s, in a treatise he co-wrote with Christopher Carleill—the same Carleill who had mounted a colonization expedition for eastern North America with Muscovy Company funds approved by Christopher Hoddesdon, which detoured to Ireland in 1584. The treatise probably inspired the failed English attempt in 1597 to drive independent French and Basque hunters from the rich walrus hunting grounds of the Magdalen Islands and install a Brownist colony there. That misadventure likely involved Peter Hilles, who owned a fleet of merchant ships and was active in the St. Lawrence walrus fishery. He may have been a relative of one Thomas Hilles, who was aboard the *Hopewell* with Henry Hudson in 1608, which would help explain why Hudson returned that year from Novaya Zemlya with a severed walrus head.

Hayes then shifted his theoretical focus yet again, to the Norumbega coast, around 1601. The latest iteration was written to drum up support for the Gosnold voyage of 1602. The trading post Gosnold established in the Elizabeth Islands, near Martha's Vineyard (conceived with almost paranoiac concerns for security, on an island in a pond in the middle of an island), was abandoned in late July rather than risk an overwintering with an insufficient food supply. Within months of the expedition's return, Brereton's account, to which Hayes's treatise was anonymously appended, was published.

While Gosnold's attempt to establish a permanent English presence in Norumbega was a failure, the underlying treatise by Hayes proved to be enduring and influential. Hayes had no time for the notion of a balmy polar region long ago proposed by Robert Thorne, which shortly was to be seized upon by Henry Hudson as he began his own passage-seeking career. Hayes argued: "I will show how trade may be disposed more commodiously into the South sea through these temperate and habitable regions, than by the frozen Zones in the supposed passages of Northwest or Northeast," where, he warned, "are we like to be frozen into the seas, or forced to Winter in extreme cold and darkness like unto hell: or in the midst of Summer, we shall be in peril to have our ships overwhelmed or crushed in pieces by hideous and fearful mountains of ice floating upon those seas."

Inspired by the river systems of Europe and western Asia, Hayes proposed that there must be also great rivers in North America draining not only eastward, into the Atlantic, but also westward, into the Pacific, within the temperate zone. The midcontinental gap between the headwaters of these as yet undiscovered rivers he imagined to be perhaps one hundred leagues, or three hundred miles. Goods could be transported overland between them by horses, mules, or "beasts of that country apt to labour" such as elk or buffalo, or "by the aid of many Savages accustomed to burdens; who shall stead us greatly in these affairs."

Bundles of Chinese silk crossing between the headwaters of two great North American rivers on the backs of buffalo and indentured or enslaved natives: it seemed almost too far-fetched to take seriously. But Hayes had produced a compelling framework for moving forward in exploration and colonization, and his passage-making premise was at the core of English designs on eastern North America. Both the Jamestown and Kennebec colonies of the original Virginia Company were sited with the idea of exploiting a river course that met Hayes's transcontinental criteria, and much of the initial energy at Jamestown was devoted to investigating such a route, initially on the river James.

"When it shall please God to send you on the coast of Virginia," the first flotilla of the London wing of the Virginia Company was instructed by its backers in 1606, "you shall do your best endeavour to find out a safe port in the entrance of some navigable river, making choice of such a one as runneth farthest into the land." And if they discovered several suitable rivers, among which one had two main branches, "if the difference be not great, make choice of that which bendeth most toward the North-west for that way you shall soonest find the other sea."

This "other sea" was the South Sea, the East India Sea, the "Back" Sea: the Pacific Ocean. The quest to establish a colony in the Chesapeake adhered to Edward Hayes's theory of the riverine nature of the transcontinental passage, adapting it to an idea, which endured from the voyage of

Giovanni da Verrazzano in 1524, that the New World at this latitude was pinched into a narrow isthmus.

The 1606 flotilla instructions for the Virginia Colony on the Chesapeake also echoed the precedent Hayes had cited in the different river systems that Muscovy Company adventurers had used to reach Persia from Arkhangel'sk: "You must observe if you can," read the instructions, "whether the river on which you plant doth spring out of mountains or out of lakes. If it be out of any lake, the passage to the other sea will be more easy, and [it] is like[ly] enough, that out of the same lake you shall find some spring which run[s] the contrary way towards the East India Sea; for the great and famous rivers of Volga, Tan[a]is and Dwina have three heads near joined; and yet the one falleth into the Caspian Sea, the other into the Euxine [Black] Sea, and the third into the Paelonian [White] Sea."

Some thirty years after a ship captain named Thomas Hudson made this journey for the Muscovy Company from the White Sea to the Caspian Sea, a ship captain named Henry Hudson had sailed to the New World, to see if North America could be crossed the same way.

CHAPTER 8

O<small>N JUNE 15, THE *HALF MOON* WAS</small> tossed about by a "great storm," hammered by wind and pelted by rain. The foremast snapped and went over the side; for the next three days the crew did little more than endure. Canvas was reduced to only the mainsail, and the seventeenth brought "a stiff gale of wind, and so great a swelling sea out of the west-southwest, that we could do nothing." On the eighteenth, the conditions eased, and the next morning, a piece of the broken foremast was jury-rigged so that at least the fore course could be set again. But the punishing weather quickly returned, with the fore course splitting on the twenty-first in "much wind and a great sea." Hudson carried on under reduced sail, working his way southwest and easing down below latitude 45 by June 22.

With light winds and flat water, the *Half Moon* was probably capable of being steered within seventy degrees of the wind's direction, or twenty degrees above a right-angle reaching course. But sideslipping could erase much of the gain in course made good toward the wind. The difference between course steered and course made good is an angle called leeway, and mariners were advised to trail a rope over the stern so they could know at a glance how badly they were skidding away from their intended course. For the most part Hudson needed the wind behind him in order to make good progress. The *Half Moon*'s top speed, under a full spread of canvas in a strong breeze, was likely about eight knots; a good day's continuous running would amount to about a hundred nautical miles, with an average speed of four knots. And if there was little or no wind, Hudson had to drift, or anchor and wait for the breeze he needed, as the *Half Moon* was too large to row. Ships often fell to pirates not in running battles of cannon fire but in simple boardings as they sat becalmed near a disreputable shore and their attackers rowed out to claim them.

A cooperative wind blew out of the southeast on the evening of June 22, and so "we steered away west for Newfound Land," according to Juet. Hudson now kept the *Half Moon*'s course around latitude 44. He was using the most basic strategy for an ocean crossing: bring the ship to the latitude of the destination, then use fixes from the sun and stars to stay on this track. And the latitude he chose to follow indicated he was making for the Georges River, where Waymouth had proposed a midcontinental passage could be found.

But it was plain that the *Half Moon*'s crewmembers had ambitions of their own. It was around noon on the twenty-fifth that they spied a sail "and gave her chase, but could not speak with her."

Calling upon another ship at sea to exchange greetings and information was common practice, but Robert Juet was being altogether too coy: as he admitted, this chase lasted six full hours and was in an easterly direction, taking *the Half Moon* terrifically off course. So determinedly did they press the pursuit that they must have had more in mind than a courtesy call on an unknown vessel. A Spanish or Portuguese fishing vessel would have provided the Dutch crew with the bounty they were seeking. But they were unable to close with her. The broken mast and its reduced canvas could not have helped. Making proper repairs would be a priority once land was reached.

ON TUESDAY, JULY 1, Hudson began feeling for the eastern edge of the Grand Banks. Because of the near impossibility of accurately measuring longitude and the multifold errors to which latitude fixes were prone, navigators of Hudson's time routinely groped their way forward along the bottom as they approached landfalls. The tool of choice was the lead line. In shallower coastal waters, a ship would use a shorter sounding line and a weight that could be heaved and retrieved while under way. But when seeking the edge of the continental shelf, a deep-sea ("dipsie") line was employed, which required a special shipboard ritual of deployment.

As marine historian D. W. Waters intricately documented, a light line between 150 and 200 fathoms long was attached to a heavier plumb weight of about fourteen pounds. The line was laid out on deck in a series of coils from bow to stern, with a crewmember assigned to each coil. The ship would be halted as a crewmember heaved the lead at the bow and noted how his coil ran out. For a deep-sea line, only the twenty-fathom intervals were initially marked, by pieces of string with knots in them; further along the line, the marks were increased to every ten fathoms. As each successive coil ran out, the crewmember minding it would call out "watch, there, watch" to the man in charge of the next coil. When the line stopped running out and the bottom was reached, whoever was overseeing the coil in question would note the fathom mark. If all the line ran out without the bottom being sounded, the call "no bottom" was made; Juet preferred the term "no ground."

The plumb weight was then retrieved and inspected. It was hollowed out like a bell, with tallow smeared into the recess so that the weight could retrieve a sample of the ocean bottom. (If the bottom was expected to be muddy, a wad of cotton cloth, secured with tallow, was instead used for sampling.) The snaggings of the tallow could be compared with information in the private notebooks pilots maintained called rutters or *routiers*. Coastal regions had unique compositions of gravel, sand, mud or ooze, shells, and even worms. Reading the bottom, in both depth and composition, was one of the few measurements a pilot in Hudson's time could make with any certainty. To this day, bottom composition is included on nautical charts, if only to aid in anchoring.

The *Half Moon* paused at eight in the evening on July 1 in "close, misty and thick weather" and heaved the deep-sea line. From the raised deck of the forecastle, along the waist and up onto the quarterdeck, the coils snaked into the sea. "No ground," went out the call. Thousands of feet of ocean depth were still beneath the keel.

At eight the following morning, Hudson was met with a light westerly. As the little ship paused, facing into the wind "in stays" as she laboriously changed course to the south, the lead line was cast again. Hudson promptly discovered he was over the bank, in thirty fathoms, as the lead returned with its tallow sprinkled with white sand and shells. It was hardly *terra firma*, but Hudson had made contact with the New World.

THE MASTER'S MATE was a nameless Dutchman, but Hudson obviously had wanted a few fellow countrymen serving at his side, and so had insisted on bringing three along. In addition to one unknown Englishman who we can be fairly certain was his own son John, Hudson had included Robert Juet and John Colman.

Colman had served as mate for part of the 1607 *Hopewell* voyage after Hudson shuffled the ranks midvoyage, but he had not been in the 1608 crew. We can only guess at why Hudson chose him for this voyage. As Colman—and not Juet—would be given command of the ship's boat in an important reconnoiter that was otherwise manned by Dutchmen, it's possible that Colman could speak Dutch, and so could serve as a shipboard liaison between the English and Dutch factions, particularly in directing or conning the ship. Steering the *Half Moon* was complicated and required a high degree of coordination between the senior command on the quarterdeck, the helmsman at the whipstaff, and the crew trimming the sails. Unless Hudson was making do with a simple creole of nautical terms, he would have benefited from having at least one capable Englishman who could converse intelligently in Dutch. If Colman was that man, he probably also bunked with the senior Dutch officers in the tiller flat.

In Colman's absence on the second *Hopewell* voyage, Hudson had Robert Juet aboard, who in the opening roll call of that expedition's journal was called the mate.* Samuel Purchas had possessed Juet's journal for the 1608 voyage, but for "brevity's sake" (as a margin note explained) omitted it from *Purchas His Pilgrimes* of 1625; the original, like so many other priceless papers in Purchas's possession, has never been seen. But the select references to Juet's journal that Purchas included in the margins of Hudson's 1608 voyage account nevertheless underscored Juet's wayfinding skills. Although Hudson was formally listed as the voyage's pilot, Juet was clearly his equal as a navigator, if not his superior. There was a telling moment early in the voyage when Hudson was puzzled by an error in his dead reckoning: he couldn't get his estimated position to agree with a noon sun sight. Purchas noted that Juet had detected the problem: Juet's journal identified a change in magnetic variation that Hudson had not.

While the journals of the 1607 and 1608 *Hopewell* voyages were chockfull of keenly observed navigational detail, Hudson's skills sometimes

---

*The mate's role switched so illogically back and forth between Juet and Arnold Ludlow in the 1608 journal as published by Purchas in 1625 that the seemingly capricious changes may have been a simple editing error, in which Ludlow should have been identified as the boatswain's mate and Juet should have remained the mate all along.

seemed rudimentary, even archaic. Writers have almost reflexively saluted Hudson's alleged skills by noting how he determined the *Hopewell*'s latitude on the 1607 voyage with a high-latitude observation of the summer sun at midnight rather than noon—in other words, at its lowest point in the arctic sky, rather than at its highest. But this was no great feat. The calculation involved simple arithmetic and was explained (with a diagram) in William Bourne's *Regiment for the Sea* of 1587. The journal description makes it sound like Hudson was navigating by "cookbook," directly consulting Bourne in order to know what to do, as he even used an instrument called the cross-staff (as recommended in Bourne's explanation) to make the sighting. The journal's confused description of applying a correction for observation error indicates Hudson was using the old single-vane cross-staff design. Cross-staffs had since come into use with three vanes in order to minimize observer error; what is more, John Davis had invented a far more accurate device, the back staff, whose use Davis had described and illustrated in his *Seaman's Secrets* of 1595.

By the time the *Half Moon* was upon the Grand Banks, Robert Juet's journal was making clear his leading role in the *Half Moon* voyage, even if he had no apparent formal rank. With the 1608 *Hopewell* voyage, Juet had come to form a seagoing partnership with Henry Hudson. How he entered Hudson's career is no clearer than how Hudson himself had started that career. Juet's *Half Moon* journal would provide further evidence of his navigational skills. A journal can also provide subtle clues to a writer's origins. John Smith signaled his Lincolnshire roots in *A Map of Virginia*, his 1612 history of the Jamestown colony, when he called crumbling ore "moskered." A brief extract by Purchas from Juet's 1608 journal provides a similar dialectic clue, as Juet reported detecting a "slake" on the sun. This reference to a "smear" (which was probably an observation of a high-latitude distortion in the sun's appearance, rather than a historic observation of sunspots, as has often been proposed) indicated that Juet most likely was a "borderer" from the Anglo-Scots frontier. His name is a further clue. At one point in Hudson's 1608 journal Juet was called Everet. As we would use *w* where Hudson used *v*, Juet's "real" name was probably something like Ewart, a surname from the borderer region.

Juet would be described by a fellow participant in Hudson's 1610 voyage as "an ancient man." As most men were fortunate to reach the age of forty at this time, he might have been in his fifties or sixties. But he was far from frail. The journals of the 1608 *Hopewell* and 1609 *Half Moon* voyages capture him leading shore parties (including a walrus hunt), climbing the rigging to sight land, taking to the ship's boat to make soundings, and handling weapons.

They were an unusual partnership. Hudson must have been about ten or twenty years younger than Juet, but his knowledge and skills belonged to an older man. Where Hudson's navigational efforts were outmoded or imperfect, and his writings reflected the pseudo-scientific and quasi-mystical ideas of the sixteenth century that underpinned northern passage-making schemes, it was Juet, the older man, who appeared most familiar with concepts of the increasingly scientific art of navigation.

Given his evident borderer roots and the academic streak that emerged in his navigational knowledge, Juet might have arrived in London as part of the sprawling entourage of court figures introduced by James VI of Scotland when he succeeded Elizabeth as James I of England in 1603. Navigation had become a fashionable subject among gentlemen, who bought up the new works on mathematics and navigational methods published in London and attended lectures by the leading theorists sponsored by Sir Thomas Smythe. We might imagine that Juet came to Hudson's attention through Sir Thomas Challener, who encouraged an interest in scientific inquiry in Prince Henry and an enthusiasm for proving a northern passage to the Orient. But Juet's Limehouse address, the familiarity he demonstrated with ship's weapons aboard the *Half Moon*, and his other duties tell us he was no armchair theorist or dabbler from the gentry.

Juet could have been placed aboard the *Hopewell* in 1608 at the insistence of one of the voyage investors, in part to serve as a personal observer. But for the VOC's *Half Moon* voyage in 1609, Juet was along solely at the discretion and insistence of Hudson. His precise role is impossible to label. Calling him the pilot reflects his navigational duties but is probably not technically correct. He was more of an adjutant, a right-hand man for Hudson, even something of a co-conspirator in carrying out Hudson's real intentions for the voyage while the Dutch master's mate was marginalized, left to worry about the day-to-day workings of the ship in consultation with Colman. The fact that Juet composed a journal is in itself noteworthy. As the VOC would not have expected Juet to keep and submit one along with the rest of the ship's papers, his motivations for doing so consequently warrant consideration.

Companies like the VOC and the Muscovy Company expected senior crewmembers—the master, master's mate, and pilot—to maintain their own records and to compare navigational findings with each other. On a voyage of discovery especially, a longer journal narrative was also expected to be composed for the investors, and Sir Thomas Smythe made a practice of providing these to Richard Hakluyt. The duty of producing one fell to the master, although the job was often handed over to someone on board who had a way with words, and this person would consult the logs of the senior crewmembers in composing it. The 1607 *Hopewell* voyage journal as published by Purchas, for example, is attributed to a participant named John Playse, although it is generally felt that Playse's account is based substantially on one already prepared by Hudson. Gentleman participants in voyages routinely produced journal accounts that drew on the logs of the senior crew.*

There should be little doubt that, given his sheer volume of navigational duties, Juet kept his own log or table of course, which he consulted to compose his fuller narrative journal. That log is gone, but the narrative journal survives, having come into the possession of Richard Hakluyt and then been passed along to Purchas for eventual publication, long after Juet—and Hudson—had died.

Juet would never have produced a full narrative account for the benefit of the VOC. His journal—and likely his log as well—was written for English eyes, and as such was attuned to English interests. It would not have been intended for publication: nothing Hakluyt gathered from English voyages after the third volume of *Principal Navigations* in 1600 made it into

---

*The nomenclature of ship's papers can be confusing. "Journal" and "log" are sometimes used interchangeably, but by the time of the *Half Moon* voyage, evolving standards in record-keeping by the leading trade companies were creating a more consistent approach. What we call a "log" today was what the English generally called the "table of course." It was divided into a series of columns, and each day's entry typically would provide information on course, wind direction, the noon sun sight, compass variation, and the estimated distance covered over the past twenty-four hours. The column farthest to the right was reserved for brief comments, and it was called the journal. William Baffin on his 1615 arctic voyage referred to the table of course, including the right-hand margin journal, as the "brief journal." But "journal" also referred to a fuller narrative account of a voyage, and it would draw on the contents of the entire table of course, including items in the journal column.

print until after Hakluyt died in 1616, when Purchas, his presumptive liter-
ary successor, bought his papers and finally used them for *Purchas His Pilgrimes* in 1625. Juet's journal may have been the only account of the *Half
Moon* voyage that the English were able to read, as it appears that Hudson's
narrative journal went to the VOC without a copy being made that Hakluyt
could preserve.

Juet's account as published by Purchas overlooked (or was loath to admit) certain facts, but it also revealed indirectly on more than one occasion
that Hudson was relying on privileged unpublished information, charts
even, for which Hakluyt was a likely source. Juet surely intended to produce a journal that would reach important and influential English figures
in the overseas exploration and colonization business, Hakluyt among them.
Such a journal would add to the chronicler's store of exploration lore that
Hudson and Juet had been able to tap into in directing the *Half Moon* to
North America.

WITHOUT THE SUN or stars, an ocean navigator was blind, save what his
dicey compass could tell him and what he could learn from feeling his way
along the bottom when closer to shore. Arctic exploration was especially
trying because the perpetual daylight of summer defeated the glimmer of
stars, while atmospheric distortions played havoc with sun sights. On the
Grand Banks, Hudson and Juet had another problem: fog. When a sailor
was not socked in altogether, scarcely able to see the ship's bow from the
quarterdeck, an overcast sky could obscure the view of the heavens. Hudson and Juet knew more or less where they were—on the Grand Banks—
but not necessarily where they were going. Juet had no latitude fix on July 1,
2, and 4 and so was unable to offer a distance run or a compass direction
for the net daily progress from one noon position to the next.

It also turned out that they had only clipped the southeastern edge of the
banks on July 2, as they could not find it again that day. The next morning,
Thursday, July 3, brought "fair sun-shining weather, with a fair gale of wind
at east north-east." The *Half Moon* turned west, and Hudson found himself
among a great fleet of French fishing boats working on the open ocean,
some 250 nautical miles southeast of Newfoundland. The deep-sea line
went over the side again at ten that morning: the weight struck at thirty
fathoms and returned with its tallow flecked with gray sand. They were able

to secure a noon sight and arrive at a latitude position of 43 degrees, 41 minutes.

The next day, Hudson sailed off the bank and was in deep water again, still pursuing his westerly quest around latitude 44. Ahead on that very latitude was the sobering hazard of Sable Island, a shape-shifting crescent of sand surrounded by extensive banks about ninety nautical miles southeast of Nova Scotia. Poorly charted and constantly on the move, Sable's shoals extended tens of miles east and west from the island's low profile of dunes and marram grass, shallowing so rapidly that an unwary ship in fog could quickly be aground.

Hudson was stumbling his way forward, aided by intermittent clues as to where he might be. On July 5, Juet secured a latitude fix from the noon sun of 44 degrees, 10 minutes, then confirmed it with fixes that night from both the pole star, Polaris, and the "scorpion's heart," the red star Antares in the constellation Scorpio. On July 7, after crossing back over deep water, Hudson came to another bank, where he found the bottom at fifty-nine fathoms, with white sand. He had reached the eastern edge of the Banquereau, a productive fishing grounds south of Cape Breton.

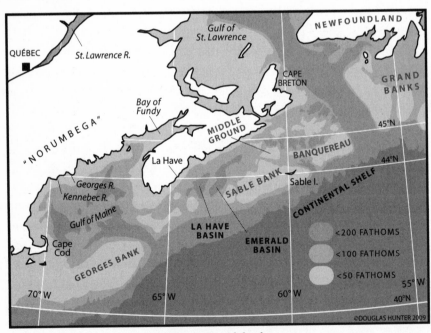

East Coast with banks.

Hudson stopped here on the eighth to top up the ship's larder, landing and salting 118 cod. After landing a few more cod on the ninth and depleting his supply of salt, Hudson was on the move again, but having to sail south because of contrary winds. The breeze was driving him right into Sable's clutches, and the fickle Labrador current, sweeping him westward at probably a knot or more, was only further confusing his location and direction.

"The irregular currents are said to be one of the principal causes of the frequent wrecks on Sable Island," the British Admiralty's *Sailing Directions for the South-East Coast of Nova Scotia and Bay of Fundy* of 1885 would warn. Indeed, the Labrador's flow (joined by the Belle Isle current when it has reached Sable) is unpredictable in direction and strength, but it was known by the nineteenth century to hurry vessels along generally westward on the north side of Sable. To the south of Sable, the Gulf Stream follows the nearby edge of the continental shelf, conveying warm water in the opposite direction to the cold water of the Labrador. The convergence of these two great currents is considered to be at least partly responsible for Sable's very existence. The tide meanwhile flows north and south, across the extensive and dangerous bars at either end of the island, while wind strength and direction influence the day-to-day character of near-shore currents. And when the warm water of the Gulf Stream meets the air chilled by the Labrador current, a persistent veil of fog descends over this calamitous maelstrom of currents and tides.

Hudson sailed westward, perhaps a half-dozen miles to the north of Sable, without seeing its low-lying hummocks of sand. The region was essentially uncharted in any practical way, and it is by no means certain that Hudson even knew Sable was close by. Edward Wright's 1599 world chart placed Sable far to the east of its true location—and showed it as a pair of islands labeled *I. Sables*—and included instead around its proper position a much larger island, St. John, which had been appearing in sixteenth-century charts in various guises. It was depicted as *S. Juan Estevanez* in a 1529 world map by Diogo Ribeiro. The Atlantic in this region had been peppered with such phantom landfalls, which according to Sable Island historian Lyall Campbell may have been part of a scheme by the Portuguese to lay claim to Sable as a supply depot for the fishery. For Sable to be Portuguese rather than Spanish, it would have to lie east of the meridian that lay roughly at today's longitude 60, which divided the New World's possessions according to the Treaty of Tordesillas. Longitude 60 also happens to divide Sable Island clean in two. (Ribeiro's pseudo-Sable, S. Juan Estevanez, was placed east of this critical meridian, in Portuguese territory. Ribeiro was Portuguese by birth; his world map of 1529 was drawn for the Spanish crown.) The theory goes that false landfalls were deliberately placed on charts by the Portuguese in support of their claim to an island they knew in practice was further west than plotted.

Where Hudson went next remains as confusing to us as it evidently was to him. These waters south of Nova Scotia feature an array of glacial sand and gravel banks that formed a chain of barrier islands when the ocean's level was about fifty fathoms lower at the end of the last ice age. Sable remains the only feature to break the surface. While the island continues to be constantly reshaped (and the degree to which it has migrated along its larger surrounding bank is debated), the soundings of the region's banks are also subject to rapid changes, as ocean currents and storms resculpt tremendous volumes of these vast glacial deposits. Although it is impossible to match any single sounding by Juet to a specific location in latitude and longitude, the general trends of the soundings do help indicate Hudson's course—and especially how close he came to having the *Half Moon* meet the same fate as the *Delight*, a supply ship in Sir Humphrey Gilbert's 1583 flotilla.

Sailing west* after fishing on the Banquereau, Juet reported the soundings to retreat to fifteen fathoms on "a fishing bank" on July 9. He had also secured a noon fix of 44 degrees, 27 minutes. The *Half Moon* had either just crossed the north-south ridge of the Middle Bank, immediately west of the Banquereau, or had cruised right over the North Spur (assuming it existed four hundred years ago), the submarine extension of the dangerous bars of Sable Island's west end that lies directly south of the Middle Bank. The latter course was more likely, as Hudson then began sailing westward across an extensive bank where his soundings returned depths of around thirty fathoms. When he spotted a French fishing vessel that evening, he

---

*I have given Hudson's course in general terms. Juet's journal entries record courses according to the thirty-two points of the compass, with which even experienced sailors today are not fully familiar. His courses are further complicated by the fact that they are usually stated before a correction for local magnetic variation (which Juet gives as seventeen degrees westward; today it is about nineteen degrees) is applied. While I have paid attention to corrected compass bearings in working out Hudson's most likely course, the intricate details need not burden the reader.

could not help himself and broke the operating silence he had observed while surrounded by French fishermen on the Grand Banks. After the *Half Moon* hailed the vessel for a chat, one of the first things Hudson surely asked was "Where am I?"

There was no shame in admitting uncertainty, and it would have been on this fisherman's word that Juet had the confidence to assert that they were now on the "bank of Sablen"—the Sable Bank, which sprawls about a hundred miles to the east and west and fifty miles to the north and south, with Sable Island occupying its northeastern extreme. Although Juet never mentioned Sable Island by any name in his journal, the *Half Moon* could not have been unaware of it, or its hazards. Richard Hakluyt had published Edward Hayes's harrowing account of the loss of the *Delight* (and the near loss of the entire 1583 flotilla) at Sable in *Principal Navigations*.

The flotilla had set out from Newfoundland for "the Island of Sablon," as they understood the Portuguese had left cattle and swine to breed there. Hayes recounted how, on the morning of August 29, accosted by rain and a strong southerly breeze, they were "altogether run and folded in amongst flats and sands, amongst which we found shoal and deep in every three or four ship's length, after we began to sound: but first we were upon them unaware, until master Cox [of Hayes's *Golden Hind*] looking out, discerned (in his judgment) white cliffs, crying (land) withal, though we could not afterward decry any land, it being very likely the breaking of the sea white, which seemed to be white cliffs, through the haze and thick weather." The soundings shrank to as few as three fathoms as the *Golden Hind* desperately clawed clear of the shallows. Almost a hundred lives were lost as the *Delight* "struck aground, and had soon after her stern and hinder parts beaten in pieces."

The *Delight* was the first of more than 350 wrecks to have been documented in Sable's waters. Beyond any wrecks, the island's recent history was a gruesome one. In 1598 the Marquis de la Roche had established a colony populated by French convicts. The wrongheaded experiment failed in 1603, when starving colonists who had been all but marooned on this hopelessly impractical oasis murdered their guards.

Yet the location of Sable remained poorly understood. Hayes wrote that it lay on the route from Newfoundland's Cape Race to Cape Breton and "lieth to the sea-ward of Cape Briton about 25 leagues," which was grossly incorrect, although in agreement with the location assigned to it, to the east of Cape Breton, in Edward Wright's 1599 chart. The French fishing vessel Hudson spoke with could have attempted to set him to rights, but if Hudson thought he would find any island in this area, it was probably the St. John of Wright's map, which was depicted by Wright as a fairly large island south of Cape Breton. When the 1602 Gosnold expedition came over the Georges Bank en route to Norumbega, "some thought it to be the sounding of the Westernmost end of Saint John Island," according to the account of Gabriel Archer.

None of this cartographic confusion would have mattered, had the wind not then turned against Hudson, compelling him to retreat almost due east.* Having safely cleared Sable Island and its shoals on the north side, he was now sent scurrying along its south side by the weather. And he still had not seen it, nor did Juet give any indication they were aware of or concerned about it.

They sounded regularly, with Juet noting the parade of measurements: forty-eight fathoms at noon, fifty at two o'clock, then forty-eight at six o'clock. When they could find no ground at eighty fathoms at eight o'clock, they knew they were over the edge of the Sable Bank, as the seafloor plunged steeply to more than a mile of depth over the lip of the continental shelf.

Juet wrote that after the soundings turned up no ground, they "stood along," which indicates they followed eastward the edge of the shelf, paralleling the unseen coast of Sable, which was about twenty nautical miles to the north. Hudson held this course for four hours, then turned west again at midnight, as the wind shifted and the calendar turned to July 11. He may have been confident that Sable (if he was even conscious of it) was well clear to the north and steadily falling astern. But it appears that the Gulf Stream, coursing along the continental shelf, was hurrying along his easterly progress and then defying his westerly intentions. And we cannot be sure precisely how the tide, flowing at right angles to his course, at the same time would have transported him to the north with the flood. Captain Joseph Darby, superintendent of the island, did caution the editors of Edmund Blunt's *American Coast Pilot* in a letter reproduced in the 1847 edition: "The flood tide sets across the bar to the northward and eastward very

---

* Juet gave the course as "south-east and by east," which is a bearing of 123 degrees. With his correction for magnetic variation applied of 17 degrees, we arrive at 106 degrees: 16 degrees southward of east, hence my description "almost due east."

strong." Darby also described a confusion of currents running in different directions and strengths, depending in part on the wind. Hudson, in short, was trying to make his way in one of the most dangerous and confusing corners of the eastern seaboard, without personal experience, adequate navigation tools, or charts of any use, and likely without any idea that the very hazard of Sable was so close at hand.

The weather on July 11 was "very thick and misty." Hudson was sealed in a fog bank, unable to secure a noon sight, assuredly unaware of how far east he had actually sailed (and been carried by current and tide) the previous day, how far north the flood tide might have pushed him, and how little progress he was actually making back to the west. At noon he sounded without result and kept steering westward, continuing to search fruitlessly all the while for the bottom at fifty to sixty fathoms. Then at midnight, wrote Juet, "I sounded and had ground at 15 fathoms, white sand."

Neither Hudson nor Juet knew it, but they had gone past Sable on the tenth, turned around, and spent the eleventh sailing right back at the island. The twelfth was "very foggy," and Hudson paid the fifteen-fathom sounding (which was trying to tell him he was coming into the shoal waters near the island) no special mind as he continued to hold his westerly course. Suddenly, at eleven in the morning, they saw land: "low white sandy ground, right on head of us; and had ten fathoms."

Hudson turned away from the startling sight, running south for four glasses, or two hours, before heading back toward the land again, "thinking to have rode [anchored] under it." Perhaps Hudson thought he had found the St. John Island of Wright's chart, and hoped to have a better look. But as he came closer "the fog was so thick that we could not see; so we stood off again." The decision may well have saved them all, as they retreated until the soundings reached sixty-five fathoms that midnight.

Hudson would not give up his probing. At eight o'clock on the morning of July 13, he ignored the fog and turned back for another glimpse of the strange shore but could see nothing ahead. He changed course toward the west, and the fog lifted enough for him to secure his first noon sun sight in four days: 43 degrees, 25 minutes, which placed him somewhere to the south of Sable. He carried on roughly westward the rest of the day, over the Sable Bank, until at six that evening the island reappeared. It would have been the western end, and Juet was able to record: "the land by the water's side is low land, and white sandy banks rising, full of little hills."

Hudson's unwitting jousting with one of the most dangerous landfalls in all of eastern North America mercifully ended as he continued westward on July 14. The soundings increased, from the twenties to the thirties and forties, then "50, 70, 90, 70, 64, 86, 100 fathoms, and no ground." Sable Bank fell astern as they steered over the Emerald and La Have basins and on toward the mainland as Hudson reacquired his desired course of around latitude 44. The following morning, July 15, was "very misty," and as the soundings retreated to twenty fathoms, "we made account we were near the islands that lie off the shore. So we came to anchor, the sea being very smooth and little wind, at nine of the clock at night." The following morning, the weather cleared, "and we had sight of five islands lying north, and north by west from us, two leagues."

Henry Hudson had safely reached the mainland of North America. But was Hudson actually where he thought he was?

CHAPTER 9

ENRY HUDSON'S DETERMINATION since June 26 to keep on a
westerly course around latitude 44 suggests he was aiming at the
Georges River area, and his arrival on July 15 at a group of "five islands" near the coast at that latitude certainly fit the bill. Hudson would
have known even from Rosier's published account of the 1605 Waymouth
voyage that he would first encounter a group of islands—the Georges—a
few miles offshore, where Waymouth had initially paused in a roadstead he
named Pentecost Harbour before proceeding north, into the river.

But Hudson was not at the Georges Islands. He was on the right latitude, but entirely the wrong coast. The *Half Moon* had fetched up in the island group at the mouth of the La Have River on the shore of Nova Scotia.

Hudson had rather strikingly committed the same essential error made
two summers earlier by the ships carrying one hundred colonists for the
Kennebec colony of the Plymouth wing of the Virginia Company. Which
makes one wonder if Hudson's arrival was indeed an error at all. Did Hudson know, based on information from the Kennebec flotilla, where he was
headed—and have every intention of pausing at La Have before proceeding
on to the Georges River? Alternately, did the mistake only occur to him after he arrived there? Or did the mistake not sink in until after he left La
Have, when the geography that then unfolded indicated he had been in the
wrong place for the past few days?

The Kennebec flotilla had made a suspiciously similar final approach to
La Have. The two vessels, the *Mary and John* and *Gift of God*, had employed

the typical transatlantic crossing stratagem of the English bound for eastern North America, sailing first for the Azores before turning westward with the trade winds. On July 27 their persistent sounding in search of the continental shelf finally paid off with an abrupt result of just eighteen fathoms. Pilot Robert Davis reckoned they were at latitude 43⅔ degrees. Although he made no mention of sighting Sable Island, the two ships knew they had come upon the Sable Bank, where they "fished three hours and took near two hundred Cod very great & large fish." Three plodding days were then required to cover what Davis estimated to be only thirty-six leagues before they reached the mainland. But the shore that they expected to be modern Maine turned out to be modern Nova Scotia. They had arrived early, longitudinally speaking, as the Nova Scotia peninsula got in their way. After pausing for several days at La Have, the two ships worked their way southwest, around the peninsula, and then northwest across the Gulf of Maine. They called at the Georges Islands, taking note of a cross Waymouth had erected, before moving on to the Kennebec, where the short-lived Sagadahoc colony was established.

However accidentally the feat was achieved, the 1607 flotilla was the only contemporary English voyage known to have approached Norumbega from the Sable Bank and Nova Scotia before Hudson fell into almost exactly the same approach after he made his own acquaintance with the Sable Bank. And he ended up calling at La Have, just as Davis's flotilla had.

So much of what Hudson relied on in the way of navigational intelligence is unknowable because so much of the material that would have been available to him has vanished. No original charts survive from Hudson's 1609 voyage, or from any of the English ones to Norumbega dating back to 1602. The 1607 journal of Robert Davis, however, is a rare survival. Copies circulated after his return, and one was used by William Strachey (who according to David B. Quinn may have secured it as early as 1610 from Virginia Company officials in London) in preparing his account of the Virginia initiative's history. Hudson thus could have had his own copy of the Davis narrative, which included crude but valuable sketches of how landfalls appeared from the deck of a ship.

If so, a copy of the Davis narrative was but one item in Hudson's personal trove of geographic intelligence. Robert Juet's journal would shortly indicate that Hudson was equipped with at least one confidential source from the 1602 Gosnold voyage to Norumbega: the unpublished journal account of senior member Gabriel Archer. When the *Half Moon* reached Cape Cod on August 9, Juet would write: "and this is that headland which Captain Bartholomew Gosnold discovered in the year 1602, and called Cape Cod, because of the store of cod-fish he found thereabout." An innocent enough observation, except for the fact that the official voyage account did not name Cape Cod and was so vague about its location that it would have been impossible to divine from a simple reading. Nor had any chart been published that showed it so named. In fact, Captain John Smith's famous map of New England of 1616 would call it Cape James, a name that didn't stick. But Archer's unpublished account (which Hakluyt possessed) did say: "near this Cape we came to anchor in fifteen fathom, where we took great store of Codfish, for which we altered the name, and called it Cape Cod."*

Juet's phrasing was so close to Archer's that the Archer narrative was the most likely source. If Hudson had the Archer narrative from Hakluyt, he could also have been carrying copies of the journals lost to us from the earlier Norumbega voyages by the English. And Gosnold could have been known personally to Hudson. He became a key figure in the Jamestown venture of the Virginia Company's London wing (as did Archer), and his wife, Mary Golding, was a first cousin of Sir Thomas Smythe. A chart based on the findings of the 1602 Gosnold voyage or the 1607 Kennebec flotilla also would have been invaluable, and within the realm of possibility for Hudson to have possessed.

One clue that Hudson in fact possessed such confidential cartography is the so-called Velasco Map of 1611–12, which is thought to be based on a lost master chart belonging to the Virginia Company. (See chapter 27.) It shows La Have with five islands. There are actually more, but that also happens to be precisely how many Juet said there were, and Hudson didn't stay long enough to discover otherwise. Rather than Hudson having been the original source for what is shown in the Velasco Map, it's more likely that he had a copy of the source chart that was incorporated into the company's master chart. That source chart would have originated with the 1607 Kennebec flotilla.

And so perhaps Hudson's arrival at La Have was premeditated, and assisted by documents from earlier English voyages which he had so

---

*Archer never mentioned the original name that Gosnold altered. See chapter 13 for a discussion of early place names on this coast.

carefully gathered, waiting for the day when a subverted assignment like the *Half Moon* voyage would provide him with the opportunity to employ them.

As HENRY HUDSON was about to discover (or reconfirm), La Have was an important center for the Mi'kmaw* people who traded with Europeans. The explorer Samuel de Champlain had called there in 1604, on his first visit to Acadia and Norumbega in the company of the French trade monopoly holder, the Sieur de Monts. Coincidentally or not, Champlain had nearly piled up on Sable Island on his own approach, after his ship's pilot underestimated their westerly progress on the Atlantic crossing by forty leagues, causing them to come up over the Sable Bank before they had a chance to start sounding for the continental shelf.

La Have (which the French knew as Port de la Hève) was something of a magnet for landfalls because of its prominent headland, Cap de la Hève, which rises more than one hundred feet above sea level and provides a ready target for a mariner offshore seeking solid ground. Neither Hudson nor Juet gave the name of their landfall, and an arrival in Maine, in the general area of Penobscot Bay and the Georges River, traditionally has been proposed. But Juet's journal, despite the problems of its fragmentary navigational information, most firmly supports La Have.

Henry Hudson was still at anchor on July 17, waiting for the fog to lift so that he could approach the anchorage beyond the island group off La Have, when the Mi'kmaq turned out to welcome him. "At ten of the clock two boats came off to us, with six of the savages of the country, seeming glad of our coming," Juet wrote of the visitors. "We gave them trifles, and they ate and drank with us."

The next day, the *Half Moon* moved north, anchoring near a Mi'kmaw village. "We went into a very good harbor," Juet reported, "and rode hard by the shore in four fathom water . . . We went on shore and cut us a foremast; then at noon we came aboard again, and found the height of the place to be

---

*At the time of Hudson's visit, the English knew the ancestors of modern Mi'kmaq as the Tarrantine. Champlain called them the Souriquois. Note that the adjectival version of Mi'kmaq is Mi'kmaw.

in 44 degrees, 1 minute."* Hudson and his crew set themselves to repairing
sails, cutting and shaping the new foremast, gathering water, and fishing for
cod and lobster. Some of the Mi'kmaq came aboard the *Half Moon*; they
"showed us great friendship," Juet reported, "but we could not trust them."

Relations with the coastal people could be unpredictable and violent, but
the Mi'kmaq were well acclimatized to the French (and French-speaking
Basques) and demonstrated nothing but goodwill. On July 20, Hudson
spotted two "French shallops full of the country people" entering the harbor: Mi'kmaw traders were returning from one of their wide-ranging
coastal cruises. The English who preceded Hudson to eastern North America had been unprepared for the acculturation and commercial sophistication of such Mi'kmaq. Bartholomew Gosnold for one was plainly shocked
to discover natives who may have had several generations of casual familiarity with Europeans and were actively trading with them, to the point of
having become fully integrated as active middlemen in a mature commercial network. The Mi'kmaq were far more sophisticated than prevailing notions of "savages" could accommodate.

On arriving on the Maine coast around Cape Elizabeth in 1602, Gosnold
had been greeted by a shallop powered by sails and oars, crewed entirely by
natives. Their commander (as Gabriel Archer related) was unforgettably at-
tired in "a waistcoat of black work, a pair of breeches, cloth stockings,
shoes, hat, and band. One or two more had also a few things made by
some Christians. These with a piece of chalk described the coast thereabouts, and could name Placentia of Newfoundland. They spoke diverse
Christian words, and seemed to understand much more than we, for want
of language could comprehend." These Mi'kmaq lived in Nova Scotia, but
as trade middlemen they ranged in shallops along the Atlantic seaboard
from Norumbega to Newfoundland. They exchanged goods for furs from

---

*This latitude figure may have been a typographical error by Purchas in publishing Juet's
journal, although it is still a very good result for La Have. Johanne de Laet would cite the
ship's papers that belonged to Hudson in asserting in *New World* (1625) that the landfall was
at latitude 44 degrees, 15 minutes, which is perfect for La Have. But in his description of the
land of Cadie (Acadia) in 1633, de Laet gave a position of 44 degrees, 5 minutes for La Have.
Of course, neither Juet nor Hudson ever identified the landfall by name. Cap de La Hève is
thought to have been named by the Sieur de Monts and Champlain in honor of the prominent cliffs in the suburb of St. Adresse, where they had departed France at Havre de Grace in
March 1604, although the name could have predated their visit.

local natives and delivered the furs to French and Basque fishermen. They had been making a local sales call when Gosnold appeared.

The 1607 Kennebec flotilla had been similarly greeted at La Have. Robert Davis noted how "here we had not been at anchor past two hours before we espied a Basque shallop coming towards us having in her eight Salvages & a little salvage boy." They spoke to the English "in their language," which actually might have been a trade creole. When the Mi'kmaq could not make themselves understood, they became reticent about further contact but were persuaded to board Davis's ship, and three even stayed the night. Davis presumed that "the French hath trade with them for they use many French words. The Chief Commander of these parts is called Messamott."

The chief, who was known to the French as Messamouet, may have been the commander of the shallop Gosnold had encountered in 1602, resplendent in European clothing. By then, he had actually visited France with an independent trader. He came to know Champlain and traveled with him in his coastal explorations.

Hudson evidently had a copy of Archer's unpublished journal of the 1602 Gosnold voyage (and also would have availed himself of Brereton's official account, which also mentioned the Mi'kmaw traders), and quite possibly had documents from the 1607 flotilla that had called at La Have. And so he would have been primed for the likelihood of a similar encounter with Mi'kmaw traders who spoke French (as Juet noted), were led by a chief dressed in European clothing, and roamed hither and yon in shallops.

Juet never mentioned if they too met Messamouet, but the Mi'kmaq pressed for the opportunity to trade. "They brought many beaver skins and other fine furs, which they would have [ex]changed for red gowns," Juet explained. "For the French trade with them for red cassocks, knives, hatchets, copper, kettles, trivets, beads and other trifles." The key words penned by Juet were that these Mi'kmaq *would have* exchanged furs for any number of items. But they obviously didn't.

While Hudson had managed to satisfy his initial visitors in the two canoes with some "trifles," these would have been odds and ends scavenged from the ship. He would not have sailed with a proper stock of barter goods and had no appointed "cape merchant," a crewmember assigned to oversee trade. Having been hired to search for the Northeast Passage, Hudson never would have been provided with goods to trade with natives in eastern North America. And while Hudson had been given funds to outfit the voyage, either the need to stock up on trade goods hadn't occurred to him or they were beyond his budget. (Laying them in, furthermore, would have indicated to the VOC that he had designs on a course other than the one specified in his sailing directions.) Hudson could have tried to address the trade-goods shortage in anticipation of such a meeting by bartering with the French ship he spoke with on the Sable Bank. But he obviously had nothing to offer experienced Mi'kmaw traders—no treasured red gowns, no iron kettles or trivets for cooking.

The lack of trade sophistication aboard the *Half Moon* must have perplexed the Mi'kmaq. So would the apprehension the *Half Moon*'s men radiated, as Juet attested that the Mi'kmaq "offered us no wrong, seeing we stood our guard." It would have been absurd for the Mi'kmaq to attempt to attack a potential trading partner (and one so heavily armed). Juet's words underscored the Hudson crew's basic mistrust and hostility. It would have struck the Mi'kmaq that these foreigners were nothing like the French or Basques with whom they regularly traded, and nothing like the English visitors—inept at trade but otherwise agreeable—who had called here two years earlier. Perhaps, after the Mi'kmaq were turned away empty-handed by Hudson, local sentiments began to turn against Hudson's persistent presence. *Why, they would have begun to ask themselves, is this ship here among us?*

SEBASTIAN CABOT, AS governor of the venture chartered in 1553 to prove the Northeast Passage that was the forerunner of the Muscovy Company, had provided specific guidance on how indigenous peoples should be plied for information. As Cabot advised in Ordinance 23, "For as much as our people, and ships may appear unto them strange and wondrous, and theirs also to ours: it is to be considered, how they may be used, learning much of their natures and dispositions, by some one such person." Cabot (who had visited eastern North America perhaps twice at the beginning of the sixteenth century and may have practiced his techniques himself) understood that "one such person," a conscripted ambassador, would have to be either charmed on board the ship or forcibly taken—or both. Once the ambassador was on board, the voyager could "learn as you may." But the intelligence was to be gathered "without violence or force, and no woman to be tempted, or entreated to incontinency, or dishonesty."

Cabot was firm about the captive's treatment. The "person so taken" was to be "well entertained, used, and appareled, to be set [back] on land, to the intent that he or she may allure other[s] to draw nigh to show the commodities: and if the person taken may be made drunk with your beer, or wine, you shall know the secrets of his heart."

Cabot's ordinances (or some direct variation) were standard issue for ships dispatched by merchant adventurers well into Hudson's time and were published by Hakluyt in *Principal Navigations*. Almost from the moment of his arrival at La Have, Hudson had plied the Mi'kmaq for information about local resources, although we don't know what inducements he offered. The Mi'kmaq, according to Juet, "told us that there were gold, silver, and copper mines hard by us."

Hudson—for now—drew the line at abduction. Fellow English explorers who were probing eastern North America and the Northwest Passage were less restrained in adopting Cabot's intelligence-gathering methods. It would have become clear very quickly that meaningful language skills could not be developed over beer and wine during a shipboard visit. The guests of English mariners needed to come back home with them, whether they liked it or not, so that the fact-finding and cross-cultural indoctrination could proceed at greater leisure. Martin Frobisher and John Davis had snatched Inuit in the Arctic. At the Georges River in 1605, Waymouth had done his utmost to cultivate the trust and friendship of the local people, the Pemaquid, and had then kidnapped five of them.

There is no denying the traumatic nature of the abduction experience for the natives, however strange and wondrous they might have found England. But the kidnappings were usually carried out with the idea of eventually returning their captives (four of Waymouth's abductees managed to see home again), so that they could serve as friendly liaisons between the English and their home communities. And the English, somewhat to their credit, were occasionally willing to leave their own people behind, to learn the native languages and customs. The Jamestown colonists made a gift of an English boy to the powerful chief Powhatan. Waymouth had carried two men in 1605 that he was "to leave in the Country, if we had thought it needful or convenient." They were Welshmen: Waymouth (or his backers) were laboring under a long-standing delusion that Norumbega had been colonized in the fourteenth century by a Welsh prince, Madoc, and so someone who could speak Welsh would be able to understand the natives. Waymouth's would-be interpreters obviously found the Algonquian language of the Pemaquid incomprehensible.

Hudson neither grabbed an unwary Mi'kmaq nor proposed leaving anyone behind, as he was not at La Have to pursue colonization. For another three days, through July 23, the *Half Moon* remained at anchor as some of her men completed the work on the new foremast while others fished for cod, halibut, and lobster. Juet had already noted that the river "runneth up a great way," but he provided no evidence that it was actually explored by Hudson.

Juet's comment suggests that Hudson might in fact have thought that he was at the Georges River, whose penetration of the continent had been greatly exaggerated in Rosier's account of the 1605 Waymouth voyage. Rosier had claimed that the river was greater than the Severn and a rival to the Thames, and that Waymouth explored forty miles of it, when there were only twenty miles to see. Rosier also had Waymouth's men pressing twenty miles up a tributary on which a falls would have stopped them cold after six. Rosier (presumably with Waymouth's connivance) had contrived to make the Georges River appear to reach far deeper into the continent than it actually did, in order to meet the requirement of the Hayes treatise that a settlement placed on a river would provide the eastern portion of a midcontinental passage.

With the *Half Moon* finally repaired and replenished, the opportunity was now at hand for Hudson to get on with exploring. If he was under the mistaken impression that he was actually at the Georges River, he could see for himself if it provided the promised route into the continent. Or he could get on with looking for a midcontinental passage elsewhere. But Hudson was sitting on a powder keg of insubordination. It didn't take long to blow, with appalling violence.

JUET WROTE LITTLE about the nature of the Mi'kmaq, beyond the fact that they treated the *Half Moon*'s crew well, albeit while raising unelaborated suspicions. By the time Hudson had sailed for North America in the *Half Moon*, there was ample evidence available of the violent and unpredictable relations the English were experiencing with natives at the Virginia Company's colony of Jamestown, in both published and unpublished accounts.

The recent record was riddled with violence and treachery. Gabriel Archer had been wounded in the hand when the first boatload of colonists to row ashore at the Chesapeake in 1607 was welcomed with a shower of arrows. The general perception emanating from Jamestown was that natives would use deceit and surprise to achieve their ends, feigning friendship where necessary. Juet especially took this to heart and adopted the same monotonously distrustful attitude that Rosier attributed to George Waymouth in his account of the 1605 voyage to the Georges River, even though the Pemaquid gave Waymouth no specific cause to doubt their friendship. In the end it was Waymouth who turned savage by abducting five of them. And it was an entirely agreeable people whom the crew of the *Half Moon* brutally assaulted on the morning of July 25, 1609, charging into their settlement with weapons blazing.

Robert Juet's explanation for the atrocity at La Have was brief and feeble. The *Half Moon*'s men "took the spoil of them, as they would have done of us." But Juet could not offer up a single incident that would have justified their concerns or warranted the ferocious assault by the European visitors.

The work on the mast had been completed on July 23, and Juet reported the weather to be "very hot." Sails were repaired the next morning; more fishing followed in the afternoon. Anticipation must have been building in both camps as to what the *Half Moon* would do next. Trade was minimal or nonexistent. Perhaps some of Hudson's men (if not Hudson himself) were coiled with apprehensive tension, their mistrust fueled by accounts of native attacks on the Chesapeake. The strangers were now simply encroaching on Mi'kmaw territory, helping themselves to local resources. The natives could have sensed the peculiarity of this group of visitors: the language barrier between the *Half Moon*'s English and Dutch factions could have been as high as the one between the natives and everyone on board.

The Dutch, doubtless growing surly in the heat, without a single prize to show for almost three months of sailing, developed their own ideas about how to proceed. If the *Half Moon* had nothing to offer in trade with these natives, then they should just take the furs of the Mi'kmaq and gather whatever European goods were in the village at the same time, to use as trade items in future encounters along the coast. Juet's detailed list of the items the French offered in trade might well have been an inventory of the things stolen from the Mi'kmaq by the *Half Moon*'s men. Notwithstanding Juet's feeble excuse, the Mi'kmaq most likely were assaulted because the majority of the crew sensed weakness and opportunity.

For some Dutch, there was little moral restraint where dealings with natives were concerned. Sea beggars already had a casual disregard for human life, wherever it was found, and the VOC wasn't much better. In establishing itself in the Far East, the company had used its military force to smash the Portuguese presence, subjugate and intimidate the local peoples, destroy indigenous trade networks, and deny ships from England's East India Company access to Southeast Asian ports, forcing the English eventually to focus their trading on India. The concept of predestination in the strictest tradition of the Dutch Reformed Church (which was advocated by Petrus Plancius, who was one of its theologians and ministers) also rendered indigenous peoples subhuman. The church (as with some other Protestant strains) was not concerned with saving souls, with converting pagans to Christianity. Natives were born inferior and, like Africans who made Protestant merchants in England and Holland (and eventually America) rich in the slave trade, were destined to remain that way.

Still, the Dutch were pragmatically flexible when it came to relations with indigenous peoples. In Surinam, where the Dutch used African slave labor on plantations, they entered into alliances with tribes being enslaved by the Portuguese, as it suited their strategic purposes. And once the colony of New Netherland was established, with Manhattan as its locus, there would be conversions of natives to Christianity under the Dutch, even while African slaves were imported, indicating that not every Protestant in the New World thought natives had souls incapable of redemption.

But there would also be incidents of grotesque violence. When traders realized that wampum, made of shell beads, served as native currency, some resorted to vicious extortion to gather it in order to gain furs essentially for free. In 1622, Hans Jorisz Hontom testified in a court case to having captured a Mohawk chief and held him for ransom. After it was paid, Hontom castrated the chief anyway, and the man bled to death. In 1626, a native approached Fort Amsterdam in lower Manhattan with his nephew to trade furs. Three farmhands of the colony's director-general, Peter Minuit, robbed him, then killed him in cold blood in front of the child. The failure of Minuit and his council to take action against the thieves and killers, either according to the demands of their own legal system or by making amends through gifts to the victim's family as native custom expected, underscored the fact that natives were not considered to be people with any individual rights. As would be the case with Minuit's unrepentant and unpunished servants, killing a native American would not have been much different than killing a dog for a sea beggar loose in the New World.

While Hudson's English contemporaries ultimately were better behaved than some Dutch traders who proved to be absolutely ruthless in their quest for material advantage, the English who visited Norumbega in the first decade of the seventeenth century were often clumsy in their interactions with natives, generally arrogant in their behavior, and not averse to inflicting terror. On a 1603 voyage to this coast, Martin Pring brought from Bristol "two excellent mastiffs, of whom the Indians were more afraid than of twenty of our men." Mastiffs were bred for bear-baiting rings, and these particular slobbering brutes were named Fool and Gallant; one of them ran around with a half pike (a weapon eight feet long) clamped in its jaws. Whenever Pring tired of the presence of natives, "we would let loose the mastiffs, and suddenly with outcries they would flee away." Rosier, in his account of the Waymouth voyage, mentioned how the natives "much feared our dogs," which suggests that Waymouth followed Pring's example. It was the smallest of mercies that the only domestic animal known to have been aboard the *Half Moon* was a cat.

The best explanation (which essentially was Hudson's own explanation) for what happened at La Have would come in the published account by Emanuel Van Meteren. Hudson found the area to be "a good place for cod fishing, as also for traffic in skins and furs, which were to be got there at a very low price. But the crew behaved badly towards the people of the country, taking their property by force; out of which there arose quarrels among them. The English fearing that they would be outnumbered and worsted [by the natives], were therefore afraid to make any further attempt [at trade]."

The plotting had begun in the heat of the twenty-fourth, according to Juet, when members of the *Half Moon*'s crew "kept good watch for fear of being betrayed by the people, and perceived where they laid their shallops." On the morning of the twenty-fifth, six men, armed with four muskets, went aboard the *Half Moon*'s scute (a flat-bottomed fishing boat not unlike a Grand Banks dory), and stole a Mi'kmaw shallop. It was placed alongside the *Half Moon*; now a dozen men (which coincidentally was the sum total of Dutch on board) took to the scute and the ship's boat, armed with muskets and two stone-shot murderers unmounted from the ship's rail.

And so a dozen heavily armed men went ashore and "drove the savages from their houses," as Juet put it. He said no more. Not about the prizes taken, how much blood was spilled, the casualties among men, women, and children. The two murderers would have produced a devastating cross-fire as the muskets poured directly into the wigwams, with the weapons then being leveled at the backs of natives who, having been roused from sleep with terrifying discharges of powder and shot, were fleeing for the safety of the woods.

When the assault was over, Hudson had the *Half Moon* moved down to the harbor's mouth and rode there at anchor all night, without any fear of immediate reprisal being expressed by Juet. The destructive sweep of the village must have been absolute, and they could have counted on a counterattack not occurring until at least the next day. Since the Mi'kmaq only had bows and arrows, and the *Half Moon*'s men had just demonstrated the horrendous effect of musket balls and stone shot, the natives were unlikely to have been in any hurry to respond.

Hudson would demonstrate some sympathy for and tolerance toward the natives he encountered on this voyage, as much as any Englishmen of this time. Did he attempt to reproach the Dutch majority for their behavior? Did the differences of opinion over the action cited by Van Meteren erupt into bitter arguments, made more infuriating by the crew's lack of a common language? A wind blowing in from the sea, along with mist and rain, kept the *Half Moon* in the harbor for the night. The breeze would have carried the angry, incomprehensible words to the ears of whoever might have survived the attack.

There would be one clue in an otherwise silent historical record as to the scale of the *Half Moon*'s inexcusable assault at La Have—or at least as to its impact. Seven years later, a Jesuit missionary in Acadia, Pierre Biard, would write in his order's *Relation* of 1616 how "towards the end of the year 1611," a Dutch ship appeared at La Have, "the Hollanders merely wishing to land at Cap de la Hève to take in some fresh water." The ship was the *Vos*, under the supervision of the merchant Pieter Aertszoon de Jonge. It had been sent out by Dutch investors with another vessel, the *Craen*, in large part to investigate Hudson's findings.

When the Dutchmen came ashore, Biard wrote, "our Savages assailed them fiercely, and made away with six of them, among whom was the Captain of the ship." All six, including de Jonge, were lost, and Biard (who was in Port Royal at the time of the assault) seized the incident as evidence of the need for a Christian influence among these heathens. He had no idea that the Mi'kmaq had taken vengeance on the first boatload of Dutchmen to appear at La Have after the *Half Moon*'s rabble inflicted their horrors. What Hudson's men had sown, de Jonge and his men had reaped.

IN THE EARLY morning hours of July 26, the wind swung to the north-northwest; the weather cleared, and at five A.M. the *Half Moon* left behind La Have and its shameful carnage. Hudson guided the VOC ship around the southwestern extreme of the Nova Scotia peninsula and turned north-west, sailing by Juet's estimate twenty-seven leagues more or less north-west across the Gulf of Maine. Hudson's course seemed to be taking him toward the Georges River, but at five o'clock in the afternoon on July 28, the *Half Moon* suddenly turned south. At noon on the twenty-ninth Juet recorded a latitude fix of 42 degrees, 56 minutes, and Hudson began mak-ing his way westward again. Five days later, on August 3, he was anchored off Cape Cod.

Perhaps he had become completely disoriented about his location: per-haps he thought that La Have had in fact been the Georges River, and that his opportunity to explore Waymouth's discoveries had been squandered when his Dutch charges had turned to berserking. Regardless of where he thought he had just been, Hudson likely was rattled by the destruction wrought by his charges and the capacity they had demonstrated for having things their way, violently if necessary. He would have been fearful of mak-ing another landfall immediately after the La Have atrocity, of being unable to control his crew whenever another group of natives agreeably came call-ing to trade. And if Robert Juet had not actually joined the Dutch crewmem-bers in the assault, his account of it was approving, which may have given Hudson cause for worry about his loyalty.

Yet there seemed to be no turning back. After pausing briefly at Cape Cod, Hudson was bound for the Chesapeake. In his voyage through the literature of exploration, he was now taking up the intelligence of a midcontinental passage said to exist in the vicinity of the English colony at Jamestown.

CHAPTER 10

O N JUNE 2, 1608, FRANCIS NELSON was about to sail for England from Chesapeake Bay when a large open boat, called a barge, descended the river James, emerged from Hampton Roads, and struck out across the lower bay, hoping to reach Nelson's pinnace, the *Phoenix*, before she cleared Cape Henry and ventured irretrievably into the Atlantic. Aboard the barge were fourteen men, led by Captain John Smith, who were embarking on an exploration of the upper reaches of the Chesapeake. Smith was carrying at least one lengthy report, which was addressed to an unknown recipient—"Kind Sir, commendations remembered"—who could have been a senior member of the Virginia Company or a friend or both.

The barge reached the pinnace just in time. Smith's report on the convoluted, faction-riddled history of the first fourteen months of the Jamestown colony enjoyed a speedy ocean crossing, and Nelson had it in England by early July. Whoever Smith intended to read the report, it was quickly set upon by a commercial opportunist. John Tapp, a leading publisher of mathematical and navigational texts, registered it as a new book with the stationers' company that August, without Smith's knowledge, let alone permission. *A True Relation* was soon on sale at the Greyhound in St. Paul's Churchyard. Tapp initially misattributed the account to an anonymous "gentleman" of the colony, then to a man named Thomas Watson, before finally accrediting it to Smith in yet another printing before the end of 1608.

As Smith's report was addressed to an anonymous "worshipful friend," there is a gleam of possibility that Henry Hudson was the recipient. According to Emanuel Van Meteren, Hudson had proposed to the *Half Moon*'s crew that they sail to latitude 40 on the American coast because he had been "most moved by letters and maps which one Captain Smith had sent him from Virginia, by which he indicated a sea [suitable] for sailing around their Southern Colony on the north, and from there go into the Western Sea, which if it were so (although experience up to now shows the contrary) would have been a very profitable thing, and a short route for sailing to the Indies." While *A True Relation* lacked the passage-making insights that Hudson would have craved, the published account seems to have undergone a choppy editing, and as no original survives, it's impossible to know what was excised in order to protect important passage insights.

The mystery of the correspondence from Smith to Hudson involves not only how or when it got there but how the two men even knew each other—and why Smith would have entrusted Hudson with such confidential information.

BORN IN 1580 to Lincolnshire farmers, John Smith was at least ten years younger than Hudson and had been away from England on sundry exotic travel and military adventures from the age of fifteen before reappearing in England in 1604. He had endured more near-death experiences in a few short years than could be imagined in several lifetimes. He had fought the Spanish in the Low Countries, then signed on as a mercenary with Austrian forces battling Turks in Hungary. He would recount an incredible tale of having been wounded, taken captive, and enslaved by the Turks. By killing his captor, he made his escape through Russia and from there regained England.

In December 1606, with Hudson four months away from embarking on his first known voyage of exploration in the *Hopewell*, Smith sailed with Christopher Newport to Virginia, to found the Jamestown colony. Smith spent some time clapped in irons on the passage to Virginia, suspected of plotting against its leadership, only to be released before the Chesapeake was reached. Once in Virginia, the sealed instructions provided to Newport by the backers revealed that Smith was to be named to the governing council. Proving to be a man of considerable practical experience and daring,

Smith moved to the forefront of the colony's explorations, and into the midst of its many controversies.

If Smith was close enough to Hudson to entrust him with confidential information, particularly a chart and his ideas about where a midcontinental passage might be, they must have gotten to know each other well in the short span of time between Smith's return to England in 1604 and his departure in late 1606 for America, from which he had not yet returned. Perhaps it was in reaching England from Russia that Smith made critical connections with the merchant adventurers and mariners affiliated with the Muscovy Company. And there would have been a remarkable coincidence to share with Hudson. In escaping his Turkish captors through Russia, Smith had re-created something of the epic overland journey Captain Thomas Hudson had made for the Muscovy Company from the White Sea to the Caspian Sea (and back) in 1579–81—an expedition whose accomplishments were cited in the instructions to the Jamestown colonists for finding a way to the Pacific.

The colony's initial hopes that the river James would lead toward the Pacific had quickly proved false. But there were more rivers to investigate along the Chesapeake's western shore, and by the spring of 1608, Smith already knew enough about the possibility of one in particular that the details could have been conveyed to Hudson in a message carried home by Nelson aboard the *Phoenix* that June. The most promising river was called the Patawomeke—the Potomac. Although it had not yet been visited by the English, its passage-making potential was suspected by then, as it would also be discussed in a deposition to the Spanish in 1610 by an Irish defector, Francis Magnel, who had left the colony for England with Christopher Newport on May 21, 1608.

According to Magnel, natives had told the colonists of numerous passage options to the South Sea. "Twelve leagues from the entrance of that river where the English are, there are four other rivers, which one of those Captains [John Smith] reached in a pinnace, who says that one of those rivers is of very great importance, and the natives affirm that fourteen leagues beyond the four rivers to the north-west there is another big river which reaches far inland until it joins another big river which comes from the South Sea."

As for the chart (or charts) Van Meteren said Smith sent to Hudson, a map did return from Jamestown in that same June 1608 bundle of dispatches carried by Nelson, which was more than likely drawn by Smith. He might have created several copies of the crude cartographic sketch and sent it to various people, including Hudson. One of the copies was soon in the hands of the Spanish ambassador, Don Pedro de Zúñiga, and being sent back to Spain; its survival in the Spanish archives at Simanca is the only reason we know about it.

This critical 1608 map shows that Smith confused the Potomac, which he had not yet reached, with the very head of Chesapeake Bay, rather than realizing it was a river that branched away about halfway up the western shore. In Smith's view, if a ship navigated to the head of the bay, which seemed to be in the vicinity of latitude 40 (and is in fact at latitude 39 degrees, 30 minutes), the celebrated midcontinental passage might be waiting. Here was the passage around latitude 40, to the north of the Jamestown colony, that Van Meteren said Hudson proposed to seek.

Critical intelligence from Smith may well have reached Hudson in Nelson's care in the summer of 1608, regardless of whether it was part of the report seized upon by Tapp for publication or a separate communication. It would have been waiting for Hudson when he returned to London from the second *Hopewell* voyage, to Novaya Zemlya, on August 26, 1608, and before he headed to Amsterdam that autumn to discuss the *Half Moon* voyage.

But as Van Meteren wrote that Smith sent "letters and maps" to Hudson, we can presume that there was more than one package. And so additional intelligence could have come later, carried by Christopher Newport as he arrived in England from the colony in mid-January 1609. With this later delivery, Smith would have been able to tell Hudson what he had learned in the explorations on which he was just embarking when he rushed his report to the *Phoenix* on June 2, 1608. For Smith was bound for the Potomac after the rendezvous with the *Phoenix*, and he reached its mouth on June 16.

Two participants, Walter Russell and Anas Todkill, contributed an account of the investigation to Smith's *A Map of Virginia*. They reported enthusiastically on its passage-making potential after penetrating it thirty miles, writing of "the good news of our discovery, and the good hope we had (by the Savage's relation) our Bay had stretched to the South-sea." Had Hudson returned to London from Amsterdam in March 1609 and found a jewel of

a missive waiting for him from Smith, the information on the investigation
of the Potomac would have been a major factor in his decision to make off
with the *Half Moon* and try for a midcontinental passage somewhere north
of Jamestown.

Smith's willingness to share such valuable information with Hudson,
who was not a member of the Virginia Company, suggests Hudson was indeed close to the men around Sir Thomas Smythe who were overseeing
the colony on the Chesapeake. Smith surely never imagined that Hudson
would show up in a VOC ship in the summer of 1609 and attempt to exploit the passage before Smith could.

Even if Hudson could count John Smith (who secured the settlement's
presidency in August 1608) among his friends, no VOC vessel or shore party
would have been welcomed in probing a passage in the heart of the Virginia Company's territory. The Dutch at Bantam in 1604 had severely re-
pelled the English East India Company flotilla under Sir Henry Middleton,
thus beginning years of tense competition in the Indies trade. Hudson
might have argued that he was acting within the bounds of a newly articulated principle of trade composed in 1608 and published in 1609. *Mare
Liberum*, known by its English translation as *The Freedom of the Seas, or the
Right Which Belongs to the Dutch to Take Part in the East Indian Trade*, was
commissioned by the VOC during the negotiations that produced the Twelve
Year Truce from the Dutch jurist Hugo Grotius (Hugo de Groot). Grotius
argued that the seas belonged to no one, that all nations could take advantage of navigable waters for trade: "every nation is free to travel to every
other nation, and to trade with it."

Russell and Todkill would report that the Potomac was nine miles wide
(while the entrance is indeed about ten miles wide, the river's lower reaches
are about six miles wide). If this intelligence had been shared with Hudson, he might have been tempted to argue that a river of such breadth,
should it represent a passage that could be employed for trade, was equivalent to the high seas. In Hudson's general discussions of his passage-
seeking assignment with Petrus Plancius and others in and around the
VOC, the work commissioned from Grotius surely came up.

All that said, Hudson's use of a VOC ship to search for a passage that
Smith intended to find for himself and exploit for the Virginia Company
would seem to have been a serious breach of his friend's confidence. And
to reach it Hudson would first have to sail right into the company's claimed

territory on the Chesapeake and past the entrance to the James. Regardless of the learned opinion of Grotius, Hudson's plan was so reckless that he had to hope no Englishman would notice his arrival, or be able to do anything to stop him as he made for the broad reaches of the Potomac, seventy miles north of the James.

But as Hudson steered toward the Chesapeake, he was completely unaware that his reception could turn out to be far harsher than one the Virginia Company's colonists might offer a trespassing VOC vessel. For Francisco Fernández de Écija was on his way there as well in command of a Spanish warship, to destroy the colony, and then continue his cruise north to deal with any other Protestant heretic interlopers along a coast that the Spanish continued to insist was theirs alone.

TO FIND JAMESTOWN, one had to know where to look for it. And by the autumn of 1608, the Spanish knew. Their intelligence efforts in England had secured a copy of the map of the Chesapeake that had arrived in England with Francis Nelson that June, which Smith had likely drawn. It lacked such basic navigational information as latitude, depth soundings, distances, or compass bearings, but it did show Jamestown's location, as well as a simple plan of the triangular fort. Henry Hudson and Don Pedro de Zúñiga probably studied copies of the same map and formed distinct ambitions. For Hudson, who wanted to go nowhere near Jamestown, it promised a passage to the Orient in temperate latitudes. For the Spanish ambassador, it located Jamestown fairly precisely and provided an opportunity to destroy the hated Protestant outpost.

Zúñiga had arrived in London as ambassador in 1605 and had been indefatigably urging Philip III to strike decisively against the Virginia venture once he had learned of it. "It would be very advisable for Your Majesty to root out this noxious plant while it is so easy," he had counseled on September 22, 1607, alleging that the English "are mad about the location, and frightened to death that Your Majesty will throw them out." With this new map in hand, the Spanish had something concrete to follow in ridding themselves of the upstart English presence. It was only a matter of deciding to act.

Several years of discussions of moving against the English in Virginia had thus far come to nothing. Philip III, who had ascended to the throne on the death of his father in September 1598, had made conciliation with his European enemies a priority. A brittle peace had been secured with France in 1598, in the last months of his father's reign, and hostilities at last ended with England through the Treaty of London, negotiated in 1604 and ratified in 1605. But the Spanish still considered eastern North America to be their territory, and Zúñiga would not let the issue of the Virginia colony drop, constantly goading his king to do something about the Protestant infiltrators.

Zúñiga had also done well to keep track of the north Virginia effort, sending a plan of Fort St. George to his king. But with the failure of the Kennebec colony, Zúñiga's venom became focused on Jamestown. By early 1609, Zúñiga was practically howling for English colonists' blood, his personal outrage inflated by the anti-Catholic invective of the recently published *Nova Britannia*. Captain George Kendall, a gentleman member of the first company and the Jamestown council, had been executed there in late 1607 on suspicion of fomenting a Catholic overthrow of the enterprise. *Nova Britannia* advised not allowing any Catholics in the colony: "If they grow so bold and desperate in a mighty settled State, how much more dangerous in the birth and infancy of yours? Therefore if you will live and prosper, harbor not this viperous brood in your bosom, which will eat out and consume the womb of their mother."

Such prejudice would have been cause enough for Spain to eradicate the Protestant heretics, as the Spanish claim to the eastern seaboard was based on a papal decree. "Let Your Majesty command that they be crushed as quickly as possible . . ." Zúñiga urged on March 15, 1609. "It would be a service to God for Your Majesty to stop a villainy and a swindle like this." Zúñiga literally showed him how, marking for Philip on another map of unknown source (which does not survive, but which may have been a copy of a 1608 map by Robert Tindall)* "a line to the entrance of the river, which shows the depth there. And I show where the English are . . . Your Majesty should command that this be summarily stopped." On April 12, Zúñiga further urged, "I hope [you] will quickly command the extirpation of these insolents."

* Robert Tindall's simple map did not include soundings but did sketch in shallows in the river, which would satisfy the ambassador's description in his letter to Philip III that the map showed "depth."

And so, finally, the command went out to Pedro de Ibarra, governor of Florida, at his headquarters in San Agustín: eliminate Jamestown.

On Sunday, June 21, 1609—a day on which the *Half Moon* tore her fore-sail in heavy winds and high seas in the north Atlantic—Francisco Fernández de Écija left mass at the Franciscan mission church of Nombre de Dios in San Agustín for an audience with Pedro de Ibarra. He strolled across the plaza of the town, an imperial backwater of about 275 souls, to the gover-nor's residence, accompanied by everyone who would join him on the im-pending cruise, including twenty-five soldiers and their officers.

Ibarra addressed them on their assignment. They were to sail north and destroy the Jamestown settlement, then carry on as far as latitude 44 de-grees, 30 minutes, eliminating any Protestant interlopers they came across. No one preserved exactly what Ibarra said, but he surely urged them on in forceful language that would have delighted the perpetually incensed am-bassador Zúñiga.

After his speech, Ibarra embraced each man in turn, and he would have paused especially for Fernández. The ship's captain was the most experi-enced man for the job of ridding the Chesapeake of the English. Ibarra had promoted him to captain in 1605, when he was sixty years old, by which time he had some forty years of experience on the coast of what the Span-ish called Florida, which not only took in the peninsula of the modern state but reached north through Georgia and the Carolinas, to the region around the Chesapeake they knew as Ajacàn.

Fernández had particularly distinguished himself by making short work of the last English interlopers to show their faces in Ibarra's jurisdiction. A joint Anglo-French trade venture had raised alarms when one of its ships was spotted at the entrance to San Agustín, in February 1605. Ibarra gave Fernández the task of hunting them down. He sailed north, discovering the two ships of the expedition trading with natives in St. Helena Sound. He demanded the surrender of the larger vessel, the *Castor and Pollux*, and then closed in, pounding the ship with cannon fire and setting her alight. With the flames doused and the crew captured, Fernández took possession of the ship, and her smaller companion as well, and delivered them back to Ibarra in San Agustín.

Later that same summer, a ship from Le Havre paused on the Carolina coast. It had been trading illicitly in the Spanish territories, and five men were sent ashore to gather freshwater. A storm brewed up, forcing the ship out to sea and marooning the Frenchmen. Natives killed two; two more were captured and turned over to Fernández when he arrived soon afterward, on a cruise in his small brigantine, *La Asunción de Cristo,* in search of Sir Walter Raleigh's "lost" colony on the Carolina Banks. The remaining marooned Frenchman from the Le Havre ship eluded Fernández, spirited away into the interior by native captors.

Some of Fernández's prisoners from 1605 ended up enslaved in galleys. Others were turned over by Ibarra to native allies in Florida, to use as they pleased, and were never heard from again.

The fate of the Anglo-French expedition was cause for considerable diplomatic activity. Spain made no apologies. This is what happens to trespassers, the actions of Fernández and Ibarra effectively allowed the Spanish diplomats to say. And in 1606, Ibarra sent Fernández cruising north again, to follow up rumors that there were as yet survivors from Raleigh's lost colony. But when Fernández could not find his way past Cape Fear, he returned to San Agustín.

Now he had a choice undertaking that would draw on all his experience on the coast north of San Agustín, while asking him to negotiate latitudes he had never visited. For all of Spain's insistence that the eastern seaboard was its exclusive territory, no Spanish ship had seen Chesapeake Bay since Vicente Gonzalez was sent north in 1588 to search for Raleigh's colony. Mistakenly believing that the colony was in the Chesapeake, Gonzalez explored it fairly thoroughly, all the way north to the Susquehanna River.

It wasn't at all certain that Fernández could even find the bay, which the Spanish alternately called the Bay of Santa Maria and the Bay of the Mother of God of Jacán. Fortunately, among the men who gathered with him in the governor's residence was an ensign, Juan de Santiago, who had seen the bay with Gonzalez, and could help Fernández identify the landmark at its entrance the English called Cape Henry.

After the audience with the governor, Fernández proceeded to his ship. *La Asunción de Cristo* had been specially prepared for the assignment. Two cannons, one bronze, one cast iron, had been brought aboard, and enough munitions for the artillery and the soldier's muskets to eradicate the noxious English weed.

Sails were hoisted. Cries of *buen viaje* hurried them down the channel, toward the narrow gap in the sandbar that shielded the port from the Atlantic. The voyage's chronicler noted how "we left in high spirits."

Fernández worked his way methodically up the coast of what is now Georgia and the Carolinas. He called upon native groups, gathering from them what intelligence they could offer of the location and state of the English settlement, the strength of its fortifications, the shipping activity, and the alliances the colonists had struck with local tribes. Along the way, he gathered the missing Frenchman who had been marooned in 1605. At last, they gained Cape Henry. Jamestown was within easy striking distance.

But at five o'clock in the afternoon, as Fernández prepared to bring *La Asunción* into the Chesapeake, a sentinel in the crow's nest shouted that a ship was anchored in the bay.

To THIS DAY, no one knows the identity of the ship that *La Asunción de Cristo* found anchored in the Chesapeake, with Francisco Fernández de Écija on the verge of attacking Jamestown. It may have been the *Mary and John*: Samuel Argall reportedly arrived at Jamestown on July 23, one day before *La Asunción* spotted the strange ship.

Whatever her identity, she was larger than *La Asunción*. The two vessels waited out the night of the twenty-fourth before beginning to maneuver for an advantage. In the sober light of a new day, the Spanish found themselves up against "a ship incomparably greater in burden than ourselves, because we saw that it carried two topsails and a great flag at the masthead, and because the ship was very long and flush-decked." At one point, when the strange ship turned, it "revealed a stern which was like a castle." The ship aggressively pursued Fernández out of the bay before returning to station. On balance, Fernández felt that she was in fact an English guard ship.

It is not at all certain this was the case, however. The *Mary and John* could have been large enough to intimidate *La Asunción*, as she had been able to transport a hundred colonists to the Kennebec settlement in 1607. But a vessel tasked to carrying human cargo in 1607 and to fishing for sturgeon in 1609 seems unlikely to have been the daunting craft that so rattled the professional Spanish soldiers and sailors. As well, Argall was reported to have had the *Mary and John* upriver at Jamestown on July 23, and he was still there more than a month later when Gabriel Archer arrived. In which case, why would Argall's vessel have been at anchor in Chesapeake Bay at five in the afternoon on July 24? Further, in their close-quarters maneuvering, Argall would have recognized that his quarry was a Spanish warship. While Jamestown records and reports are admittedly fragmentary (and nothing from Argall himself survives for his 1609 voyage), it is strange that such a momentous event—the appearance of a hostile Spanish naval vessel, loaded with a company of soldiers and their artillery—never factored in any private letter or contemporary published account, in particular John Smith's *A Map of Virginia*.

Fernández and his fellow officers could have greatly exaggerated the size and capability of the ship they encountered to excuse their retreat. But a hunch Fernández held may have been right: that the ship was actually a pirate vessel—it would have been an English, French, or Dutch one—calling on the Chesapeake while sailing to or from a raid on Spanish shipping in the Caribbean.

Three or four leagues out at sea, Fernández called together his pilot, the ship's master, the ensign, and the master gunner. He recounted how his orders required him to continue sailing north, to latitude 44 degrees, 30 minutes, but he wished to have their opinions. And all of them were of the opinion that this was not a good idea, as it was now so late in the season. Hurricanes would have been on their minds, but so too would have been the prospect of having their way home later blocked by the aggressive guard ship if they now chose to sail on north.

The senior officers of *La Asunción* decided not only to abandon their attack on Jamestown without having fired a shot but also not to sail any farther north, into the path of the shipload of heretics under Henry Hudson's command, who were making their own way to the Chesapeake. On July 24, the very day that Fernández reached the Chesapeake in preparation for an attack on Jamestown, the *Half Moon*'s men were preparing to launch their own assault on the Mi'kmaw village at La Have.

"The six and twentieth, fair and clear sun-shining weather," Robert Juet had then recorded, with the *Half Moon* back at sea. He took a noon fix and arrived at latitude 43 degrees, 56 minutes. The *Half Moon* was within the northernmost limits of Fernández's sailing orders and should have been closing with the Spanish patrol. But with Fernández abandoning the cruise north and steering for home, the way to the Chesapeake was clear for Hudson.

CHAPTER 11

O N August 4, the *Half Moon* was in the general vicinity of Cape
Cod, probably just north of Nauset Harbor, when Hudson came to
anchor off a headland. They heard voices and sent a boat ashore to
investigate, "thinking they had been some Christians left on the land; but
we found them to be savages, which seemed very glad of our coming," according to Juet. One was brought back to the ship. They "gave him meat,
and he did eat and drink with us. Our master gave him three or four glass
buttons, and sent him on land with our shallop again."

"Our" shallop was the one they had stolen from the Mi'kmaq. As much
as Hudson may have lamented the brutality of the attack at La Have, the
shallop would have been a treasured prize. Powered by oars and sails, a
shallop was anywhere from twenty to thirty feet long and was well suited to
coastal surveying. Explorers in Hudson's time often brought one along
knocked down, to be assembled when they reached their destination. Hudson had been without one on his 1607 voyage, which almost spelled the
end of him, when off Spitsbergen a becalmed *Hopewell* was thrown toward
a sea of grinding ice floes by waves left over from an earlier blow. The ship's
boat had been too small to offer an effective tow. Only the sudden appearance of a beneficial wind allowed Hudson to escape. He made sure he had
a shallop on the 1608 voyage to Novaya Zemlya.

Not being issued one for the *Half Moon* voyage could have been a bone
of contention between Hudson and the Amsterdam chamber's chief
boatswain, Dirck Gerritsz. But Hudson didn't have the stolen shallop for

long. After leaving Cape Cod, the shallop smashed into the stern of the *Half Moon* while under tow in rough weather and sank.

It would also become clear that, after the La Have raid, Hudson was properly equipped with all sorts of trade goods, and the glass buttons he provided the man at Cape Cod could have been the first of those goods to be dispensed. At least, in his treatment of the stranger at Cape Cod, Hudson had made personal amends for the behavior of his crew at La Have.

They sailed on for the Chesapeake. The gap along the Atlantic shore at the mouth of the bay is only about ten nautical miles wide, which was no simple thing for an early seventeenth-century mariner to locate. Bartholomew Gilbert failed altogether to find the entrance on a 1603 voyage. Hudson's geographic intelligence likely extended beyond having a crude map from John Smith along the lines of the Zúñiga map of 1608. Further information, based on Smith's June 1608 visit to the islands off Cape Henry, would have been useful.

Hudson also may have been able to debrief Jonas Poole, who had been part of the first Virginia Company flotilla to the Chesapeake in 1606–7 and had explored the James with John Smith. Once back from Virginia, Poole was recruited by Sir Thomas Smythe to exploit the train oil resources Hudson had uncovered at Spitsbergen in 1607 and was promised annual commissions in the trade. Poole sailed north from Blackpool in the *Amity* on March 1, 1609, about one month before Hudson left Amsterdam in the *Half Moon*. Poole's men were soon risking life and limb on the ice, slaughtering members of a herd of one hundred walrus and battling polar bears for their valuable pelts. Poole would be knifed to death for his cut of the proceeds on a London dock shortly after his return from a 1612 voyage.

Poole would have inspected the 1607 log of the *Hopewell* before making his first voyage to Spitsbergen, but he also would have welcomed discussing Hudson's 1607 voyage with the explorer himself. Smythe could have called the two men together, after Hudson returned from Novaya Zemlya in 1608 and Poole from Virginia, each man seeking his next opportunity, to ensure that Poole was properly prepared for his assignment.

Hudson would have elaborated for Poole on the challenges and opportunities of Spitsbergen and discussed his views of the temperate arctic theory, which Poole echoed in his journal for the 1609 voyage north. Such a meeting would have been another opportunity for Hudson to expand his personal hoard of intelligence. As a skilled mariner, Poole would have been an ideal source for the finer points of approaching the entrance to Chesapeake Bay.

Juet's journal indicated that *someone* had given Hudson specific coastal features to watch out for. He was confident enough to weigh anchor offshore and begin their approach to the entrance at four o'clock in the morning on August 18. They "stood into the shore to see the deepening or shoaling of it, and finding it too deep we stood in to get a rode: for we saw, as it were, three islands." In other words, they steered toward shore to see how the depths changed. When the water was deeper than their liking, they moved closer to shore. An ebb tide must have been flowing out of the bay, which would be faster in the deeper main channel, and moving into shallower waters would reduce the current opposing them. By "to get a rode," Juet likely meant to get a wind-rode, rather than to actually anchor. A windrode was a way of using the wind's force on the sails to hold a ship's position against the tide, until it was slack or turned to flood in their favor. And so they moved toward the three islands, which evidently they had been looking for and were using as a guide for their specific approach.

Once they saw the islands, "we turned to windward to get into a bay, as it shewed to us to the westward of an island. For the three islands did bear north of us." These three islands at the mouth of the bay were part of the Smyths Isles (so named for Sir Thomas Smythe) off Cape Charles that John Smith would include in his published 1612 map.* The 1608 map acquired by Zúñiga provided no information about these islands or the mouth of the bay. Smith did not visit the islands until June 1608, after delivering his package to the *Phoenix;* he made a quick reconnoiter of them before heading to the Potomac. It again suggests that at least some of the information Hudson possessed had come to him from Smith later than the *Phoenix* packet.

Hudson also knew there was a bar at the entrance to the bay, which Juet described in more detail than he could have gleaned from his own observations: "For in coming over the bar we had five and four fathoms and a half,

---

* In an area of ever shifting sands, it's impossible to identify for certain these three islands. They may have been some combination of dry land formed by what became known as Fisherman's Island and the Isaacs immediately south of Cape Charles, as charted in the nineteenth century. Today the Isaacs are all but subsumed by one crescent-shaped mass formed by Fisherman's and Adams Island, which serves as the foundation for the north end of the modern bridge-tunnel crossing from Cape Charles to Cape Henry.

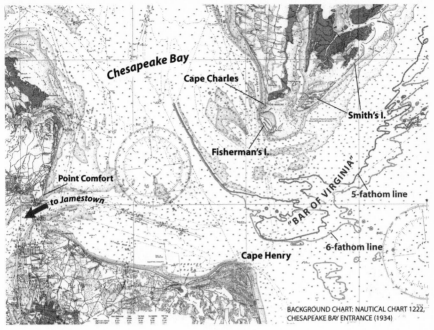

Chesapeake Bay.

and it lyeth five leagues from the shore, and it is the bar of Virginia. At the north end of it, it is ten leagues [30 miles] broad, and south and north, but deep water from ninety fathoms to five and four and a half. The land lyeth south and north."

Juet's continued description in fact sounded as much like instructions copied out of someone's rutter as his own observations. "This is the entrance into the King's [James] River in Virginia, where our English-men are. The north side of it [the entrance to Chesapeake Bay] lyeth in 37 degrees, 26 minutes: you shall know when you come to shoal water or sounding, for the water will look green or thick, you shall have ninety and eighty fathoms, and shoaling apace till to you come to ten, eleven, nine, eight, seven, ten, and nine fathoms, and so to five, and four fathoms and a half."

As Zúñiga was able to send to Philip III an additional unknown map in March 1609 that showed depths for the approach to the James, it's possible that whatever charts Hudson acquired from Smith (or even Poole) included far more detailed information than was in the 1608 map that survives in the

Spanish archives. But Hudson may have had still another source of geographic intelligence for the Chesapeake visit: the Dutchmen in his own crew.

THERE IS SOME indication that the Dutch had firsthand experience of the
Chesapeake before the Jamestown colony was established. The first flotilla
of the Virginia Company's London wing had serious difficulty reaching
America, as they overshot their anticipated sighting of land by three days
and considered turning back. Once the coast appeared, however, they entered the bay with such nonchalant confidence that historians have suspected someone in that fleet had been there before. The bay must have
been an established privateering base for striking against Spanish shipping
in the Caribbean and the Strait of Florida.

Pedro de Zúñiga found it odd that none of the initial settlers were
women and children and suspected that Jamestown was a colonizing cha-
rade that was actually a haven from which to attack the Spanish. Zúñiga
still clung to this interpretation in a letter to his king about Virginia Company rumors on December 10, 1609: "I believe they will again send people
out, because, no doubt, the reason they want that place is its apparent suitability for piracy."

A participant with privateering experience against the Spanish, such as
Christopher Newport or Bartholomew Gosnold, could already have known
the bay as such a safe haven. But Dutch sea beggars equally could have employed it as a refuge. Smith in *A True Relation* mentioned news he heard in
1607 of a ship that had been in the Pamunkey River the previous year—in
other words, well before the colonists had even arrived. Its captain was received warmly by the native people, "yet he slew the king, and took of his
people, and they supposed I were he." The incident sounded suspiciously
like the atrocity at La Have committed by Hudson's crew.

One clue that Hudson may have been relying on Dutch information
would come from Johanne de Laet, a director of the Dutch West India Company who had Hudson's ship's papers from the 1609 voyage. Writing in
1625, de Laet reported that Hudson gave the headland on the north side of
the entrance to the bay the name Dry Cape. It was peculiar that Hudson
would name a prominent feature that his friend John Smith already knew
as Cape Charles—both capes at the bay's mouth were named for the sons
of James I. As on his previous voyages, in which he was largely faithful to

place names assigned to charts by the explorers Willem Barentsz and Olivier Brunel, Hudson could have been using a Dutch precedent. *Drie* in Dutch means "three." And Cape Charles, as Juet's journal recorded, featured three islands that would indicate they had found the entrance to the bay that had eluded Bartholomew Gilbert.

Wherever he got the information that allowed him to enter Chesapeake Bay so confidently, Henry Hudson had scarcely gained its sheltered waters before turning around and leaving.

CHAPTER 12

I n describing the *Half Moon* arriving at "the entrance into the King's River in Virginia, where our English-men are," Robert Juet meant that they had at this point passed through the entrance to the bay. The James (or, as it was better known then, the King's River) was the first major tributary a ship encountered on arrival, fifteen miles west, and Hudson could not have intended to actually sail up it to Jamestown.

And after no more than a few hours in the bay, Hudson departed. Juet blamed a stiff northerly "with gusts of wind and rain" around noon for their abrupt exit, as they would have feared the *Half Moon* being blown ashore if she dragged her anchor. They moved back out to sea, where there was more room to maneuver, to wait for another opportunity to explore the bay. Lee shores were a particular terror to mariners in the age of sail, as they could not sail effectively to windward, but there may have been more to Hudson's retreat. With the wind out of the north, the *Half Moon* also could not sail northward up the bay to reach the Potomac. Instead, Hudson would have had to remain anchored and risk being discovered by the Jamestown colony.

Anchoring off present-day Norfolk would have put Hudson within five to ten miles of the colony's sentinel at Point Comfort, where the James empties into the Chesapeake through Hampton Roads. That was a comfortable distance, and he might have been assured of not having his sails spotted as he approached his stopping point. But the longer he remained in plain view, the more he risked being detected. Jamestown was desperate for relief and would have been keen to know of any arrival. The sight of the *Half Moon* at anchor would have invited immediate investigation. The colony was also in a perpetual state of tension, threatened from within as well as from without. A strange sail would not have soothed anyone's nerves. Indeed, an anonymous contributor to Smith's *A Map of Virginia*, in recounting the appearance of the relief flotilla of Sir Thomas Gates that summer, stated that Smith, "understanding by his scouts, the arrival of such a fleet (little dreaming of such supply) supposing them Spaniards, he determined and ordered his affairs."

The many machinations and traumas of the colony's first years are beyond the scope of our story, but suffice it to say that Jamestown was even more riven by factionalism than Hudson's crew. In little more than two years, the original president, Edward Maria Wingfield, had been deposed (with John Smith a ringleader in his overthrow), the fort had burned down and been rebuilt, Captain George Kendall had been executed on suspicions of fomenting a Catholic overthrow, Smith had narrowly avoided execution himself over allegations of gross insubordination, the settlement had come under attack by natives, and a famine had devastated the ranks, its victims including Bartholomew Gosnold. The settlement also had become caught up in intertribal warfare as one powerful chief, Powhatan (who took Smith prisoner for a time), strove to expand his territory, crush his enemies, and limit (if not eradicate) the English presence.

The *Mary and John* was still on hand, moored at Jamestown. Had Hudson lingered, Argall might well have headed downriver to size her up. Even if the *Mary and John* was not the ship that chased away the *Asunción de Cristo* one month earlier, Argall was a future admiral and fearlessly aggressive, capable of extending to the *Half Moon* and her peculiar complement of Dutch and English crewmembers a stern greeting.

It seems likely, then, that Hudson withdrew from the Chesapeake in no small part to await a wind that would allow him to steer immediately north, without having to linger anywhere near the James. Once back out at sea, though, Hudson had another problem: the colony's nine-vessel relief flotilla was arriving.

The fleet, which had departed England on June 18, using the traditional southerly transatlantic route to take advantage of the trade winds, had been ravaged by a fierce storm. The first four battered survivors "fell into the King's River happily the eleventh of August," according to Gabriel Archer, writing home to a friend after his return to the colony with the flotilla. But as Archer was using the old Julian calendar that remained in effect in England until 1751, the arrival in the river was actually August 21, according to the modern Gregorian calendar. The date shift is crucial, as Juet was using the Gregorian in his *Half Moon* journal because pilots employed celestial almanacs composed according to it. And so these first vessels of the flotilla would have been approaching the entrance to the Chesapeake on the twentieth, and a lookout in the rigging of the *Half Moon* could have spotted them out at sea on the nineteenth.

While Juet's journal had nothing to say about this arrival in force of ships, Hudson would have feared (as Smith apparently initially did) that these strange sails, appearing over the horizon from the southeast, might be Spanish and that he was about to end up slain or imprisoned—unaware of how closely he had in fact come to falling into Fernández's hands. Hudson also may have recognized these vessels as English, and he well understood that Virginia Company ships would not welcome a VOC interloper.

The *Half Moon* remained at sea for several days, enduring rough weather. "This night," Juet wrote of the twenty-first, "our cat ran crying from one side of the ship to the other, looking overboard, which made us wonder; but we saw nothing." They eased south to the latitude of the Carolina Banks before returning to the Chesapeake for another try.

At noon on August 26, they fixed their latitude at 37 degrees, 15 minutes, "and we found that we were returned to the same place from whence we were put off at our first seeing land." They anchored offshore; in the morning they sailed closer and, able to see land clearly, assured themselves that they were back where they had started, at the entrance to the Chesapeake.

When the *Half Moon* concluded this voyage at Dartmouth, Thomas Holland would be left with the impression that Hudson had seen a fair bit of the Chesapeake. Holland would relate that Hudson had "sailed to the southward of the London colony [Jamestown] in Virginia, and trended that coast till he came to Cape Henry, and so sailed up into the bay of Chicepeiake, and there having viewed the coast and the fashion and trending of the land, he came forth out of that bay to the northward." But Holland did not appear to know that Hudson made two attempts to examine the bay, and his account was a blend of both: the approach from the south was from the second attempt, while any observation of the bay's coast and "trending of the land" was made on the first, when Hudson had gained the bay and anchored for a few hours at most—long enough to have a quick look around, even if Hudson never "viewed" the bay and its coast in a way that would satisfy a pilot or cartographer.

Juet's journal leaves no time for any inspection of the Chesapeake on this second visit. They made no effort to do so. There was a good reason, even if Juet never offered any explanation as to why the Chesapeake again was left untouched.

Since their moving offshore to mark time, another ship in the storm-wracked supply fleet—the *Diamond*, the flagship of the flotilla's vice admiral—had limped into the Chesapeake without a mainmast "a few days" after the arrival of the first four, according to Archer; the *Swallow* followed "three or four days" later.

The arrival of flotilla stragglers would have further interrupted Hudson's plans. Now that so many Virginia Company ships were on hand, Hudson's chance of exploring the Potomac unchallenged had vanished. After months of anticipating his arrival in Chesapeake Bay, Hudson was forced to abandon his investigation before it had even begun.

WHATEVER TO DO next.

Only a few days after Henry Hudson abandoned his plan to enter the Chesapeake and seek out the midcontinental passage at latitude 40, the directors of the VOC would gather and ask the Amsterdam contingent to distribute copies of Hudson's contract and sailing directions. He had been gone for almost five months and had spent most of that time defying his orders, using a company ship and crew to further his own agenda. He was 3,600 nautical miles from Amsterdam, on the wrong side of the Atlantic Ocean. And he had accomplished virtually nothing in all that time, over all those sea miles.

Yet the voyage was not over. Hudson was determined to keep the *Half Moon* in motion and nowhere near Amsterdam, so long as the Dutch majority still abided his wanderlust. He had one last chance to accomplish something useful on this quixotic passage, before summer turned to autumn and he had no choice but to recross the Atlantic and confront the wrath of his employers. And he may have had one more voyage from the recent annals of exploration to revisit. It would take him north, along the Atlantic seaboard, above latitude 40.

OF ALL THE English voyages to eastern North America in the first decade of the seventeenth century, none was more shrouded in mystery than that of Bartholomew Gilbert in 1603. The London goldsmith (who was no relation to the famous Gilberts of Devon) had participated in the Gosnold expedition of 1602 with his bark, the *Concord*. When that enterprise evoked the wrath of Sir Walter Raleigh—who had the *Concord* and its cargo of sassafras seized at Southampton—Gilbert came to a rapprochement with the celebrated sea dog. Gilbert would make a voyage for Raleigh, to help reassert his claim to Virginia under his 1584 charter from Elizabeth I. With that in mind, Gilbert was to attempt to locate the so-called lost colonists of the settlement on the Carolina Banks established by Raleigh in 1587. No relief vessel reached it until 1591, when it was found abandoned. Rumors persisted that the colonists yet survived, somewhere on the mainland. If colonists indeed were alive, then Raleigh's claim would be so much easier to defend.

Precious little would be preserved about the Gilbert voyage, and all of it secondhand. When the *Concord* returned to England, the crew discovered that in their absence, much had happened. Elizabeth I had died on March 24, and their employer's loyalty to the new monarch, James I, was immediately deemed suspect. Raleigh was incarcerated in the Tower of London on July 19, and that November he was found guilty of treason on trumped-up charges, although his life was spared as he remained a prisoner of the tower. Needless to say, he was also stripped of his patent rights in America. Any report, journal, or chart from the *Concord*'s voyage that would have been presented to Raleigh was lost like so many others of this era.

A few glimmerings of knowledge about the voyage would circulate. The *Concord* failed to find the entrance to the Chesapeake, and somewhere in the area, Bartholomew Gilbert was killed by natives when he went ashore. But it was also understood that the *Concord* had coasted the American shore north of the Chesapeake and had gone somewhere above latitude 40, perhaps as high as latitude 41. While what the *Concord*'s crew saw, charted, or experienced has been lost to us, we don't know how lost that intelligence actually was in Hudson's time. Only six years had passed, and there would have been eyewitnesses among surviving crewmembers. And then there was the unknowable fate of the *Concord*'s papers after her crew returned to London to find their employer clapped up in the Tower.

The *Concord*, to be sure, had seen some part of a length of coast that had gone surprisingly and persistently unexplored by any other known expedition for the better part of a century. It was a no-man's-land, as far as exploration, colonization, and exploitation were concerned. Hudson now pointed the *Half Moon* into this yawning gap of European knowledge.

DEPARTING THE GENERAL vicinity of Cape Charles, on August 27 the *Half Moon* coasted "a white sandy shore . . . full of bays and points." Hudson was working his way north, a half-dozen miles offshore, minding the barrier islands, tidal marshes, and embayments to the west. Around six that night they found themselves off "an harbour or river," according to Juet, "but we saw a bar lying before it; and all within the land to the northward, the water ran with many islands in it." This may have been Chincoteague Bay, behind Assateague Island, or perhaps Isle of Wight Bay, behind Fenwick Island at present-day Ocean City. Hudson paused here and sent the ship's boat to sound. He could not have been at ease anchoring exposed in the Atlantic, along a coast that would claim thousands of ships in the coming centuries, but he was unable to move the *Half Moon* inside the barrier islands.

The next morning, August 28, they sailed a dozen leagues, or thirty-six nautical miles, and by noon had reached a point of land where their soundings dropped rapidly from five to three fathoms to just ten feet, the threshold of panic for the *Half Moon*, before the soundings mercifully receded again. They had unwittingly tempted the dangerous Hen and Chickens Shoal off Cape Henlopen, a ship's graveyard waiting for its first ship. Beyond the cape, to the northwest, was "a great bay and rivers."

On his third voyage of exploration, Henry Hudson had finally come upon a significant corner of the world no European is known to have visited before him. He had discovered Delaware Bay.

Lying at latitude 39, the bay must have struck Hudson as a potential passage entrance. The entrance between Cape Henlopen and Cape May, about twelve miles, is slightly wider than that of the Chesapeake, and Delaware Bay is initially broader. According to de Laet, Hudson thought the north shore was an island, then realized it was part of the mainland: "standing in upon a course northwest by east, they soon found themselves embayed, and encountering many breakers." Delaware Bay is riddled with shoals, with long, sinuous channels reaching to the northwest, where its upper reaches are within about two dozen miles of the top of Chesapeake Bay. If Bartholomew Gilbert's *Concord* ever saw this bay, her crew plainly left nothing behind of practical navigational use to Hudson. The *Half Moon* could not have made it much past Brandywine Shoal, about twelve miles from Cape Henlopen, before the soundings and the sight of "breaches and dry sand," as Juet described them, persuaded Hudson to sail back nine miles and anchor for the night.

"Hudson suspected that a large river discharged into the bay, from the strength of the current that set out and caused the accumulation of sand and shoals," wrote de Laet. Hudson was right in that at its headwaters was a river, the Delaware, but he would never find that out for himself. He gave up his probing prudently, being poorly equipped to take risks. As Juet observed, "He that will thoroughly discover this great bay must have a small pinnace, that must draw but four or five foot water, to sound before him."

Also, though, Hudson gave up easily. While he had lost the shallop stolen from the Mi'kmaq, he still had a ship's boat, so methodically sounding ahead of the *Half Moon* was entirely feasible. But Hudson dedicated only about six hours to the bay, from his clearing Cape Henlopen to his turning back and anchoring for the night. Juet did not mention Hudson naming any feature: not the bay itself or the prominent points of Cape Henlopen or Cape May at its mouth. Hudson must have been determined to make better use of what little time he had left before winter arrived. And already he may have had his mind set on reaching another place, not much farther north, that he had reason to believe held much greater promise. Delaware Bay had been a brief diversion that someone else, someday, could investigate for himself.

At five o'clock the next morning, Hudson embarked on a meandering course in an effort to extricate himself from the bay's many shoals. He grounded once but cleared safely, and gradually the soundings increased as he regained the ocean proper. To port was Cape May, and beyond, stretching northeast, was more of the same sort of coastline that had greeted him north of Cape Charles: barrier islands, tidewater marshes and sheltered waters, and long white stretches of pristine, surf-pounded beach, but now with shoaling waters extending many miles offshore.

They anchored well clear, becalmed, on the twenty-ninth, amazed at the

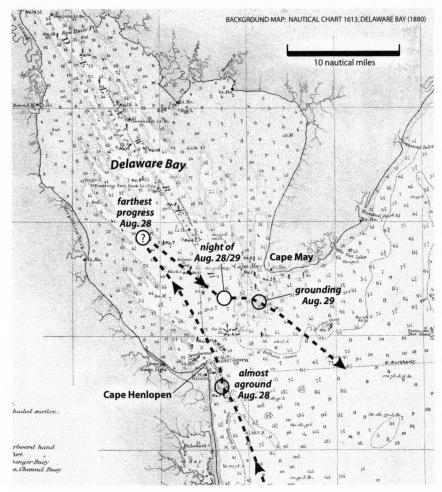

Delaware Bay.

fact there were only seven fathoms of water so far into the Atlantic. The next day they headed still farther out to sea. Twice Juet climbed to the main topmast head to see what he could make out, but he never glimpsed anything more noteworthy than the barrier islands. ("This shore makes broken land, when you are within two leagues of it," the *American Coast Pilot* would advise in 1796, "and at mast-head, you may see the water between these islands and the main land.")

They anchored and waited for the fickle wind to return. When it resumed out of the north-northwest just after midnight on the morning of the thirtieth, they accepted it, even though it meant sailing east-southeast, away from land as well as their intended course north. Hudson carried on until the persistent casting of the lead line returned twenty-six fathoms. They were beginning to tickle the edge of the continental shelf, some one hundred miles off present-day Atlantic City.

On the final day of August, a coastal current carried them backward, even as they thought they were again making northerly progress. Juet's noon sight indicated they had actually retreated south of the latitude of Delaware Bay, and it took another day and the push of a strong southerly breeze for them to recover the distance lost since the thirtieth. It was now September 1, and the VOC's directors were gathering.

The next day, Hudson anchored somewhere east of Sandy Hook. Juet took note of the "great stream" coming from Lower New York Bay and Raritan Bay. The outflow of the Hudson River estuary in fact was so great that it had produced the mysterious coastal current that had pushed the *Half Moon* southward off New Jersey.

Only a week earlier, the voyage had appeared to be all but over, as Hudson failed on his second attempt to enter and reconnoiter Chesapeake Bay. An entirely new voyage was now effectively beginning. Where Delaware Bay had scarcely held Hudson's interest for more than a few hours, this place would occupy him for a month, as he pressed for a success that he would never define.

CHAPTER 13

I N LATE 1523, A MERCHANT AND NAVIGATOR from an esteemed family near Florence departed Dieppe on a four-ship voyage of discovery. Giovanni da Verrazzano had persuaded the French king, Francis I, to sanction his country's first official expedition to the New World. Backing was provided by various merchants keen to profit from Verrazzano's main objective: to find a route to the Orient somewhere in the vicinity of the Gulf of St. Lawrence. The flotilla was quickly defeated by adverse weather, and in January 1524 Verrazzano continued alone in his flagship, a small caravel called the *Dauphine (Dolphin)*, from the Madeiras.

Verrazzano's discoveries would be recorded in influential maps later that decade, one by his brother, Gerolamo, who accompanied him on the *Dauphine*. The voyage's events otherwise were preserved by the explorer in a breezy letter to Francis I that survives in four different versions, the most authoritative being the one called the Cellere Codex, discovered in 1909, which includes annotations thought to have been made by Verrazzano himself.

The letter mentions only a few specific landfalls and is otherwise frustratingly devoid of practical geographic detail. Verrazzano seems to have arrived in North America around Cape Fear. After briefly coasting southward, he turned north, clear of any risk of running into the Spanish. Safe harbors persistently eluded him. Unable to find his way through the barrier islands, he anchored offshore repeatedly and allowed his imagination free rein when it came to deducing the nature of North America.

While anchored off the Carolina Banks, Verrazzano declared, he "found there an isthmus one mile wide and about two hundred miles long, in which we could see the eastern sea from the ship, halfway between west and north. This is doubtless the one which goes around the tip of India, China, and Cathay. We sailed along this isthmus, hoping all the time to find some strait or real promontory where the land might end to the north, and we could reach those blessed shores of Cathay."

Verrazzano had looked upon what was probably Pamlico or Albemarle Sound, across the barrier islands of the Outer Banks, and creatively surmised that these sheltered waters were the Pacific Ocean. For that to be true, the continent had to be squeezed at this point to a mere ribbon of sand. Verrazzano's idea of a narrow-waisted continent persisted into Hudson's time— its breadth expanding, to be sure, but nevertheless remaining sufficiently girdled to support the hope of men like Hayes, Hudson, and Smith that North America could be crossed by some river-based passage.

Verrazzano briskly coasted north and east as far as Nova Scotia and was back in Dieppe by July 8. In this whirlwind tour of the Atlantic seaboard, he naturally missed much. He never noticed Chesapeake Bay, for example, or Delaware Bay, or even the Bay of Fundy. But he did report finding "a very agreeable place between two small but prominent hills; between them a very wide river, deep at its mouth, flows out into the sea; and with the help of the tide, which rises eight feet, any laden ship could have passed from the sea into the river estuary."

At first he anchored off the coast, satisfied that the *Dauphine* was "well sheltered," explaining: "We did not want to run any risks without knowing anything about the river mouth. So we took the small boat up this river to land which we found densely populated."

Verrazzano had already encountered native Americans on this voyage, and he had been well treated, although his own behavior left much to be desired. Somewhere north of the Carolinas he went ashore with a party of twenty men from his Norman crew, and they marched two leagues inland, terrifying the people with their arrival: "Searching everywhere, we met with a very old woman and a young girl of 18 to 20 years, who had hidden in the grass in fear. The old woman had two little girls whom she carried on her shoulders, and clinging to her neck a boy—they were all about eight years old. The young woman also had three children, but all girls. When we met them, they began to shout. The old woman made signs to us that the men had fled to the woods. We gave her some of our food to eat, which she accepted with great pleasure; the young woman refused everything and threw it angrily to the ground."

Verrazzano's men snatched the boy from the old woman, to take back to France. They wanted the young woman as well, "who was very beautiful and tall, but it was impossible to take her to the sea because of the loud cries she uttered. And as we were a long way from the ship and had to pass through several woods, we decided to leave her behind, and took only the boy." Whatever became of the poor child is unknown.

The people they now met where the very wide river flowed to the sea "were almost the same as the others, dressed in birds' feathers of various color and they came toward us joyfully, uttering loud cries of wonderment, and showing us the safest place to beach the boat. We went up this river for about half a league, where we saw that it formed a beautiful lake, about three leagues in circumference. About 30 small boats ran to and fro across the lake with innumerable people aboard who were crossing from one side to the other to see us."

There was so much more for Verrazzano to see and do here, but he was soon leaving. "Suddenly, as often happens in sailing, a violent unfavorable wind blew in from the sea, and we were forced to return to the ship," he explained. A strong southerly had arrived, which would have threatened the exposed *Dauphine* with a catastrophic grounding if she dragged her anchor. Verrazzano was "leaving the land with much regret on account of its favorable conditions and beauty; we think it was not without some properties of value, since all the hills showed signs of minerals. We weighed anchor, and sailed eastward since the land veered in that direction, and covered 80 leagues, always keeping in sight of land."

There is little doubt that Verrazzano's landfall, which was fixed on charts as Angoulême (in honor of a dukedom of Francis I), was present-day New York. He had initially anchored offshore and sent ahead a boat to explore the narrows that immortalize Verrazzano's name. They likely beached the boat on Coney Island or at Gravesend Bay. After half a league of further investigation, the men found the "beautiful lake," Upper New York Bay, which teemed with canoes that seem to a modern reader of the Cellere Codex to be whizzing here and there like so many Yellow Cabs. Any glimpse Verrazzano might have caught of the entrances to the Hudson or East rivers went unmentioned. He then sailed eastward along the shore of Long Island and toward further discoveries no one had yet visited in Hudson's time: a "triangle shaped island" that was probably Block Island, and an "excellent harbor" that cartographers labeled *Port de Refugio* and was most likely Newport Harbor in Narragansett Bay.

Port de Refugio tantalized Europeans with its potential as a colony site in the first decade of the seventeenth century. Gosnold in 1602 was specifically looking for it and came up achingly short, by about thirty miles, when he decided instead to establish the quickly abandoned fort in the Elizabeth Islands. In 1606, the French explorer Samuel de Champlain came as close to finding it as sighting Martha's Vineyard after rounding Cape Cod, but the lateness of the season and an uncooperative headwind forced him back to Port Royal, on the Bay of Fundy.

Verrazzano's much praised Angoulême, however, remained unsought, falling into the farthest corner of that apparent dead zone of European activity between the Chesapeake to the south and the French and English efforts in Norumbega and Acadia to the northeast. If anyone else had seen it before Hudson came along, it may have been Bartholomew Gilbert or Estevão Gomes.

Gomes had been part of the Spanish circumnavigation voyage of 1519 commanded by a fellow Portuguese navigator, Ferdinand Magellan. But Gomes had refused to follow Magellan into the shrieking contrary winds of the strait named for the expedition leader near the tip of South America, returning instead to Spain with his ship. Gomes ultimately avoided serious punishment when the voyage's sheer scale of disaster was realized. Magellan was killed in the Philippines, and only 18 of 237 original participants completed the historic circumnavigation in 1522.

Gomes then convinced the forgiving Charles V to send him westward to find a passage to the Orient that was shorter and far less hazardous than the one through the Strait of Magellan. No original voyage chronicle survives, but recent evidence indicates he left La Coruña, Spain, on September 24, 1524, in a purpose-built caravel, *La Anunciada*, and sailed first to Cuba before coasting northward, all the way to Newfoundland's Cape Race, in 1525. Cartographic evidence supports his careful exploration of the Norumbega coast, where he made the horrific decision to abduct more than fifty natives and take them back to Spain as evidence of a potentially lucrative slave trade. Charles V was said to be so offended that he ordered them released, although no one knows what became of them.

What Gomes saw south of Cape Cod is a matter of conjecture. The sixteenth-century Spanish chronicler Oviedo inspected a report by Gomes for his *General and Natural History of the Indies* and asserted that Gomes made detailed explorations between latitudes 40 and 41, and a Spanish tradition developed that Gomes gave the Hudson River the name Río de San Antonio. James Grant Wilson, in his *Memorial History of the City of New York* (1892), would argue that the 1529 world map of Diogo Ribeiro, which is based in part on Gomes's lost cartography, showed that Gomes visited New York. Wilson identified Cabo de las Arenas (Cape of Sands), plotted at latitude 40, as Sandy Hook and associated a variety of other named features with the New York area—especially Río de las Gamas (River of Deer), which some still equate with the Hudson River.

Others have argued that Cabo de las Arenas was Cape Cod, and that the entire region labeled *Tiera de Estevan Gomez* by Ribeiro running north from there is New England, with Río de las Gamas being the Penobscot. But two maps by the Portuguese brothers Lopo and Diogo Homem in the 1550s may support the possibility that Portuguese or Spanish sailors were familiar with the New York area by the middle of the sixteenth century. Lopo Homem's 1554 world map, created for Cosimo I of the Florence Medicis, appears to show a prominent Bay of Fundy—the first time it appears in any cartography. About four years later Diogo created a one-of-a-kind atlas for England's Queen Mary and her husband, Philip II of Spain, which replicated the coast of Lopo's 1554 map and much of the labeling. While the great bay may actually be a gross misrepresentation of Penobscot Bay, the trend of the Atlantic coast in both Homem maps does make an interesting turn from westward to southward right where a Hudson-like river is.

Any prior visit by Gomes to the New York area would have been purely academic to Henry Hudson, as the Portuguese navigator left behind nothing of use to the *Half Moon* voyage in the historical record. Hudson would have known Verrazzano's account, which was such a fundamental part of the annals of North American exploration, especially where passage-seeking was concerned.*

---

* A version of the Verrazzano letter had first been published by Italian historiographer Giovanni Battista Ramusio in his multivolume *Navigationi et Viaggi* in 1556, and Hakluyt had included an English translation of the Ramusio account in his first compendium of exploration and travel literature, *Divers voyages touching the discovery of America and the Islands adjacent* of 1582. It was also necessarily included in Hakluyt's multivolume opus, the 1598–1600 second edition of *Principal Navigations* ("The relation of John de Verrazzano of the land by him discovered").

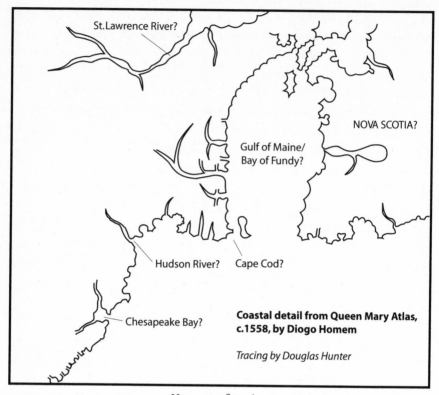

Coastal detail from Queen Mary Atlas, c.1558, by Diogo Homem

Tracing by Douglas Hunter

Homem 1558 tracing.

No surviving materials from Hudson's voyage indicate that the brain trust of the *Half Moon* was particularly conscious of Verrazzano's visit, as the Florentine navigator is never mentioned. There was little in the Verrazzano account to assist Hudson in his own arrival and exploration, and no crude and ancient chart derived from Verrazzano's sweeping survey of the Atlantic seaboard was of any use. Notwithstanding Hakluyt's dubious assertion that Verrazzano gave Henry VIII a chart of North America and even made a voyage for him, if Verrazzano (or specifically his brother) attempted a rough chart of the New York area, based on their brief visit, it had long since vanished.

Yet Verrazzano and Hudson were not so far apart in their experiences and goals as nearly a century of time would suggest. Hudson was still pursuing Verrazzano's dream of a passage to the Orient that could cross North America. And in his coasting northward from the Chesapeake, Hudson had been as frustrated as Verrazzano with the apparent lack of safe harbors, forced to anchor offshore as navigable gaps between barrier islands could not be found. Once in the vicinity of Sandy Hook, Hudson acted as Verrazzano had. He would have agreed wholeheartedly with Verrazzano's judgment that there was no sense running risks with the main vessel without first investigating with a ship's boat. Hudson could wait, and plan carefully. After his hurried reconnoiter of Delaware Bay, Hudson behaved now as if all the time in the world were at his disposal.

SOME THINGS HAD not changed in seamanship and navigation since Verrazzano's time. While efforts were being made to calculate longitude through lunar observation and global patterns of compass variation (the observed difference between true and magnetic north), arriving at a precise position along the north-south scheme of meridians remained out of reach. Nevertheless, there had been major advances in cartography, in navigational devices, and in the mathematics associated with both, within Hudson's lifetime. Commercial publishing had placed a huge amount of practical knowledge at the disposal of common mariners, in voyage accounts, celestial almanacs, and navigational treatises. The Copernican solar system remained controversial in Catholic Europe (Galileo would be compelled by the Vatican to recant the support he expressed for it in 1632), but it had been readily accepted in Protestant countries. Thomas Digges had published an illustration of the Copernican heavens in the family's *Prognostication* in 1576.

Also, as evidence in Robert Juet's journal indicated, theorists continued to work on one of the most fundamental puzzles of navigation: the nature of the magnetic pole.

As recently as 1595, Rumold Mercator had published the circumpolar map drawn by his late father, Gerhard, showing the North Pole to be a mountain of attractive lodestone, with a secondary magnetic pole placed above what we now call the Bering Strait to account for baffling patterns in compass variation. In Amsterdam, Petrus Plancius was collating compass observations recorded around the globe by VOC ships in an attempt to make sense of local differences. At the time of the *Half Moon* voyage, one of the most influential navigational works in England was Richard Polter's *The Pathway to Perfect Sayling*. Written by an official of Trinity House, it

Gerhard Mercator's 1595 circumpolar map Septentrionalium Terrarum de-scriptio *presented a fantastical view of the arctic realm. It proposed a polar land-mass called Septentrion segmented by four sea passages that flowed toward the North Pole. The pole was a mountain of magnetite, around which the sea plunged into the center of the earth. A second magnetic mountain above Septentrion was deployed in an attempt to account for magnetic variation. The map incorporated the recent discovery of Spitsbergen (t'Nieulant) in addition to Novaya Zemlya (Nova Zembla), as well as numerous nonexistent landfalls.*

perpetuated the notion that different lodestones (and the way they were ap-plied) magnetized compass needles to different headings, thus accounting at least in part for variation.

With the *Half Moon* anchored somewhere east of Sandy Hook on Sep-tember 2, Robert Juet's journal made a simple but telling observation that revealed his familiarity with a new theory of magnetism: "That night I found the land to haul the compass 8 degrees. For to the northward of us we saw high hills." Juet thus knew the work of William Gilbert, a physician to Elizabeth I who had published the six-volume *De Magnete* in 1600. It was composed in near-impenetrable Latin, and Juet most certainly never read it. Gilbert's findings, however, were promoted by the cartographer and navigational expert Edward Wright, and Juet would have readily grasped the gist of them.

Gilbert had conducted something like a scientific study, constructing a magnetized sphere that persuaded him the earth itself was a giant magnet. It was a great leap forward in insight, but Gilbert's ideas were also fundamentally wrong. He did not think there was an actual difference between the north magnetic pole and the geographic pole. Instead he argued that anomalies in the height of the earth's surface, such as ocean depths and mountains, caused local differences in compass direction. Juet as a result was convinced that nearby high ground was deflecting the *Half Moon*'s compass. Fortunately, the difference between true and magnetic north was not going to be a major issue for Hudson in his immediate explorations. A more proper understanding of magnetism was still more than two decades away, when it was established that in addition to the magnetic and geographic poles being two different places, the magnetic pole's location wanders over time.

Despite scientific advances, Hudson's countrymen had not fully extricated astronomy from astrology, or mathematics from numerology, or the earth from the center of the universe, or the hierarchies of angels in their particular celestial sphere from the observable cosmos. A Copernican universe cohabited the Diggeses' *Prognostication* with both astronomical data and astrological content. A leading Elizabethan figure of science like Dr. John Dee, who had done so much in the late sixteenth century to articulate the English concept of the polar region and how the Far East might be reached through it, could also serve as his queen's astrologer and converse through a lead crystal with archangels. (At the time of Hudson's 1607 *Hopewell* sailing, the old prognosticator was trying to summon the advice of one of the higher angels on treatment for his piles.)

Fate was literal: it was widely believed that the stars (which included planets, known as the "wandering stars") influenced and foretold the lives of men. Locked up in the Tower of London with plenty of spare time, Sir Walter Raleigh was working on his *History of the World*, the first volume of which would be published in 1614. He asked, "Why should we rob the beautiful stars of their working powers?" Raleigh pronounced the stars to be "open books, wherein are contained and set down all things whatsoever to come."

Hudson left no written clues to his own metaphysical leanings, beyond reflexively giving thanks to God whenever his vessel escaped from a tight spot. As an English ship's commander, he was expected to maintain ecclesiastical discipline, leading morning and evening prayers and holding common services. In 1553 Sebastian Cabot had set down ordinances for shipboard behavior for the forerunner of the Muscovy Company that became the template for such instructions in Hudson's time. In addition to the observance of religious services (which Rosier's account indicates Waymouth held on his 1605 voyage), Cabot had prescribed that "no blaspheming of God, or detestable swearing be used in any ship, nor communication of ribaldry, filthy tales, or ungodly talk to be suffered in the company of any ship, neither dicing, carding, tabling, nor other devilish games to be frequented, whereby ensueth not only poverty to the players, but also strife, variance, brawling, fighting, and oftentimes murder to the utter destruction of the parties." We don't know how well any effort by Hudson to impose such strictures went down with a shipload of raucous Dutchmen.

TIDAL ESTUARIES—COASTAL areas in which saltwater and freshwater converge through ocean tides and river outflow, and which feature mudflats, sandbanks and bars, often rapid currents, and large water level changes—were nothing new to a northern European mariner like Henry Hudson. In departing London in the fall of 1608 to discuss and ultimately accept employment with the VOC, he had passed through the Thames estuary's skein of treacherous shallows, where mariners trusted their vessels to known passages like the King's Channel and the Black Deep, contending with level changes of more than twenty feet while skirting such hazards as Shinering Sand, West Barrow, Knock John, Kentish Knock, and Girdler. And in departing Amsterdam aboard the *Half Moon* in April 1609, Hudson would have required a knowledgeable pilot to negotiate the many like traps of the Zuiderzee, the marshy, brackish inland sea in the northernmost provinces of the Dutch Republic.

New World locations like Delaware Bay and the Hudson River estuary have much smaller tidal ranges than the Thames estuary (which has the second highest in the world, after the Bay of Fundy) but nevertheless would have kept an Old World pilot fully alert. The most significant difference, of course, was that the difficult waters of the Old World had been charted and memorized by professional pilots, and by the late sixteenth century the English and Dutch were using fairly standardized navigation aids, with corresponding symbols on charts. In departing Amsterdam, the *Half Moon* had followed a shipping fairway marked by conical barrels blackened with pitch or tar, and the edges of sandbanks were picked out by beacons made of lamps hung in birdcage-like osier baskets atop poles. The same buoy and beacon system was used on the Thames.

Mariners who came to call on New York required unwavering attentiveness and wayfinding assistance. A mere fraction of the instructions for approaching the port from Sandy Hook in the 1822 edition of the *American Coast Pilot* reads: "steer up W. by N. until you bring the light-house to bear S.E. and Brown's hollow to bear S. ½ E. you must then steer up N. by E. ¼ E. for the bluff of Staten island, which will at that time bear exactly north from you; and that you may not be deceived with respect to Brown's hollow, it is the hollow which makes the termination of the high lands to the westward; by steering then as before directed, you will turn the S. W. spit— continue steering N. by E. ¼ E until you shoal your water, which you soon will do if it is young flood, as it sets from 2½ to 3 knots, to the westward."

No dauntingly detailed pilot's instructions (featuring illustrations of key landmarks such as Brown's Hollow as they appeared from sea), or carefully maintained buoys, beacons, and lighthouses, or a chart of any practical navigational use was available to Hudson as he weighed the task of safely probing the New York area. (Today, too, ships benefit from greatly simplified courses produced by massive dredging of channels.) Furthermore, he had no tide tables for a devilishly complicated region.

Tides would prove to be critical in Hudson's imminent explorations. He and Juet knew that the tides here, as at home, were semidiurnal, and so they could expect two high and two low tides each day. And they knew that the differences in the lunar and the earth calendars caused the daily tidal peaks to be twelve hours and twenty-four minutes apart, meaning that the tide cycle shifted forty-eight minutes later every day.

It would have been of great help to them to know the timing of the critical "spring" tides, when tidal ranges are the greatest in the monthly lunar cycle: high tide levels are their highest, and low tides their lowest. These peaks have nothing to do with the season of spring but coincide with the full and new moons, when through heavenly geometry the combined gravitational pull of sun and moon has the greatest effect on raising and lowering coastal sea levels. The timing of these peaks depends substantially on the global location of the tidewater.

A savvy mariner of Hudson's time could know the entire tide cycle of the lunar calendar for wherever he was by a method called "the establishment of a port." He would carefully observe the time of high tide during the first observable spring tide, which as noted would fall during a full or new moon. A new moon technically is invisible, but the mariner would look for its "change," when the first sliver of the quarter moon appeared. Since there were no reliable timekeeping devices, he used the position of the moon as his clock, by taking the full or new moon's compass bearing at the moment the associated spring tide was noted to be highest.

The mariner now knew, based on the bearing of the moon when in that particular phase, when to expect any future spring tide in this port. He could then determine the times of every other tide over the coming days, most easily by consulting a table. (It was also common for mariners beginning in the late sixteenth century to carry a pocket-watch-sized tide computer whose concentric dials could tell them when high water would occur on a particular day, by applying the establishment of the port.) The establishment of popular ports was already worked out. Dover's, for example, was said to be "North and South," which meant that during a full and a new moon, high water occurred when the moon's bearing was either north or south.

To "establish" New York, Hudson needed a full or a new moon, but he had arrived too late to take immediate advantage of either. The last full moon had occurred on August 15, when he was in the Atlantic, three days away from his initial attempt to explore the Chesapeake; the "change," or new moon, had come on August 29, when he was anchored miles out in the Atlantic, off the New Jersey shore. There wouldn't be another full moon for eleven days, on September 13. At the least, when the *Half Moon* anchored on September 2, Hudson would have known which days (if not the precise hour) would feature the greatest tidal ranges, according to the lunar cycle, and also which days would feature the lowest ones. These "neap" tides occur during quarter moons, and because the range—the height difference between low and high tide—is at its lowest then, high tides are

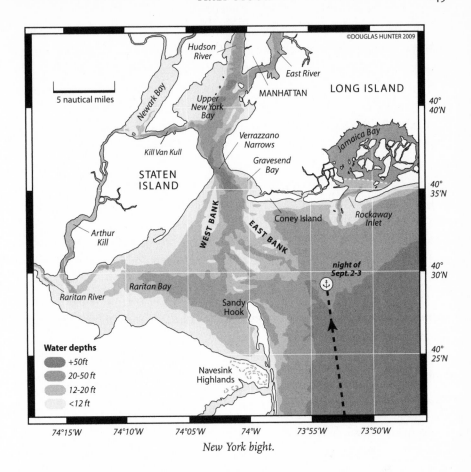

New York bight.

their lowest, and low tides are highest. The first quarter would fall on September 6, the last quarter on September 20.

What this all meant to Hudson was that, after arriving east of Sandy Hook on September 2, with the new moon having appeared on August 29, he could expect increasingly less water at high tide, should that prove critical to his explorations over the next few days. The peak level would continue to fall until the moon was in its first quarter and the neap tide visited on September 6. After that, tidal range would begin to increase again, building toward the spring tide of the next full moon, on September 13.

At an unknown landfall where Hudson had already seen dangerous shallows, the timing of these events was not trivial. If he began aggressively exploring when the tidal range was declining, he might be in trouble if he went aground on a high tide. With the high tide then becoming lower each day, he might not be able to float himself off again, until the tide cycle bottomed out at the neap and climbed back to the next spring. It might mean almost two weeks of waiting, if the grounding was serious and occurred at high tide around the new or full moon. And he might not ever get off again, if the ship in the meantime settled into shifting sand. If Hudson saw an opportunity for extensive exploration, it would be far better to wait until the neap was upon him, on September 6, so that he could count on increasingly higher high tides for about a week.

One seemingly useful fact Verrazzano left for Hudson was that the tidal range was eight feet. Verrazzano was probably using the old French foot, which was more than thirteen inches, and so his eight feet were closer to nine of our measure. As Verrazzano was only in the area for a day or two, and never said where he measured it, or when in the tidal cycle the measurement occurred, the figure wasn't of much use. And he greatly overstated the result: the mean tide range is around 4.5 to 4.8 feet at locations like the Battery on lower Manhattan, Coney Island, and the Narrows, with a spring tide adding about another foot to the range.

As Hudson soon would have recognized, he was contending with a location far more complex than a basic coastal port—so complex that the exercise of establishing the port would be useless if not conducted for an array of locations over a relatively small geographic area. The Hudson River estuary features convoluted tidal dynamics, as seawater floods and ebbs along its many miles and among its bays, straits, and feeder rivers, while opposing the outflow of freshwater, which itself follows a seasonal cycle in volume.

Tides in all river estuaries move as an enormous wave, changing speed and range according to the local geometry of the tidal course. (These waves are normally imperceptible but can build into a visible standing wave, or bore, in the higher reaches of an estuary.) Waters normally are "slack," neither flooding nor ebbing, around the times of high and low tides. But in an estuary like the Hudson, the tide typically continues to rise after the point of high tide, continuing for two hours into the ebb period.

Even in the general area of Upper New York Bay, the tide is highly idiosyncratic, complicated by the fact that tidewaters reach it from more than one direction. The flow in the East River (actually a tidal strait) is answerable to the tide on Long Island Sound, which is about 70 percent greater than that of the Hudson estuary and has a cycle that falls more than three hours later. While the mean tidal range at the Brooklyn Bridge is about four and a half feet, only eleven nautical miles away at Whitestone, near the entrance to Long Island Sound, it is more than seven feet.

Two hours after high water is marked at the Battery, the wavelike character of the tide means the ocean is still heading up the Hudson River at about one knot. But Upper New York Bay has already begun draining on the ebb through the Narrows at less than a knot—and moving seaward through the Ambrose Channel south of Coney Island at more than a knot and a half—while Long Island Sound is being replenished via Hell Gate at almost two knots. Three full hours after high water has been marked at the Battery, the nearby Hudson is finally slack, while the East River is ebbing at Hell Gate at four knots and the bay is exiting the Narrows at about a knot and a half and pushing through Ambrose at two and a half. And while all this is happening, the high water of the wavelike flood tide continues to ascend the Hudson River.

Hudson would never have time to comprehend all the tidal workings and seeming contradictions in the estuary in which he had just arrived. The best he could do was mind the lunar cycle, note the local indications of flood and ebb tides and the strength of their currents, make soundings in the ship's boat in advance of the *Half Moon* when prudent, and not do anything rash when the wind was opposing him.

CHAPTER 14

HENRY HUDSON'S PRECISE WHEREABOUTS in his first week in the vicinity of present-day New York have long caused debate and disagreement. A major challenge in deciphering the events of the *Half Moon* voyage is the fact that the geographic tableau has changed enormously in four centuries. Shorelines around metropolitan New York have been aggressively reengineered. While many of those changes have occurred over about the last hundred years, the process was quick to begin, as seventeenth-century Dutch settlers altered shorelines for shipping and began reclaiming tidal marshlands as they had in their native land. Below the water surface, mammoth dredging operations to benefit shipping more recently have obliterated bottom contours that seafarers negotiated well into the twentieth century. Greater New York circa 1609 is little more than a foundation of the modern cityscape: largely buried and invisible, an entirely different place belonging to an entirely different time.

But humans have not been the sole source of changes. With so many features of the lower bay and bight dependent on the state of shifting sands, particularly along the Long Island shore from Coney Island to Jamaica Bay, storms and coastal currents caused significant alterations in landforms, shoals, and harbors. The seventeenth, eighteenth, nineteenth, and twentieth centuries have each seen their own version of this mercurial shore. As well, sedimentary deposition from the Hudson River's outflow has changed some depth soundings. Less dramatic, but still noteworthy, is the incremental change in mean sea level. At the Battery, it is rising at a rate of 0.91 feet per century. The mean level thus was about 3.6 feet lower in 1609.

Another challenge in sorting out the voyage's events is the nature of observations from the *Half Moon*'s incomplete record, most of which come from the journal of Robert Juet. All of them are useful to some degree, but not many are absolutely reliable. Juet's reportage of a latitude fix of 40 degrees, 30 minutes on September 3, for example, does little more than confirm they were in the general area of present-day New York, as Juet would have done well to have an error margin in a sun sight made on a stationary ship of fifteen nautical miles, north-south. His distances are a general guide, as he had no reliable way of measuring them. When he says something is four leagues away, one cannot assume a literal distance of twelve nautical miles. It might actually have been eight, or fifteen. On the other hand, it would indicate he was most definitely not referring to something only a few miles away.

The measurements Juet made (or reported others having made) that can be considered reliable are soundings. Recording accurate soundings was one of the most important duties in coastal navigation. Even with some leniency accorded to sediment buildup and pre-dredging shifts in submerged hazards, the reported soundings are a highly useful tool in sleuthing where the *Half Moon* was from one day to the next—and where she could not have been.

It's impossible, as we have seen, for Hudson to have anchored the *Half Moon* to the west of Sandy Hook when he first arrived, as has sometimes been asserted, if Juet's soundings for the anchorage and distance from land are to be believed.* Once the *Half Moon* has been placed somewhere east

---

* The idea that Hudson anchored west of Sandy Hook on his arrival can be attributed in part to the terse account by Johanne de Laet, which states how after coasting the New Jersey shore, "they at length reached a lofty promontory or headland, behind which was situated a bay, which they entered and ran up into a roadstead near a low sandy point, in latitude 40°18'." This reference to a "low sandy point" has been interpreted in the past as Sandy Hook, and the bay they entered as Raritan Bay. But as noted, Juet's soundings don't agree, and Juet's detailed description of the arrival is a far better fit for entering Rockaway Inlet.

John Yates and Joseph Moulton, in their *History of the State of New-York* (1824) relate a local tradition that Hudson "first landed in Coney Island, opposite Gravesend (Long Island), and now a part of King's County, in this state." Given the shape-shifting nature of Coney Island, that's not far off an arrival at Rockaway Inlet, although the tradition could apply instead to Verrazzano, whose ship's boat seems to have come ashore in that very area.

of Sandy Hook on that first night, her course over the ensuing days, and the explorations by her men, become far more straightforward, provided one consults the earliest available (and reliable) nautical charts, made before so much of the coastline and the soundings in the heavily dredged main shipping channels were radically altered.

Because early charts show tremendous changes along the coast, from Coney Island to Jamaica Bay, it's not possible to remove all doubts in determining where Henry Hudson began his explorations on September 3. But we can propose with some confidence that it was Rockaway Inlet, on the south shore of Long Island.

MIST KEPT THE *Half Moon* at anchor off Sandy Hook until ten o'clock that morning. When a south-southeasterly wind brushed it aside, Henry Hudson sailed north. "The land is very pleasant and high," wrote Juet, "and bold to fall withal." (By "bold" he meant the water was deep enough for them to navigate close to this land; by "withal" he meant besides.)

By three in the afternoon they could see the entrances to "three great rivers." Farthest away, to the west, was a river (the Raritan, as well as Arthur Kill) they reasonably presumed to lie at the far end of Raritan Bay, helping to produce the "great stream out of the bay" they had noticed during the ebb tide the previous day. Closer at hand, to the northwest, were the Verrazzano Narrows. Closest of all, to the north, was Rockaway Inlet, the main entrance to the great saltwater marsh of Jamaica Bay.

The southern shore of Long Island, from Coney Island to Rockaway Beach, would be transformed beyond recognition in the twentieth century. Tourism and residential development carved an unruly shoreline into manageable waterfront real estate. No longer would currents, tidal streams, and Atlantic storms dictate the highly fluid nature of the sandy coast. Rockaway Inlet was particularly prone to natural resculpting: a cautionary note on the 1899 chart for this area warned, "The Point of Rockaway Beach is subject to great and frequent changes." The inlet nevertheless appears on Dutch charts in the seventeenth century and was a regular presence in eighteenth-century charts. When soundings were made and printed on charts in the nineteenth century, there was almost always some kind of bar guarding its mouth, featuring a shape-shifting sliver of sand called Duck Bar Island. The historic bar is an important clue to where Hudson made his landfall.

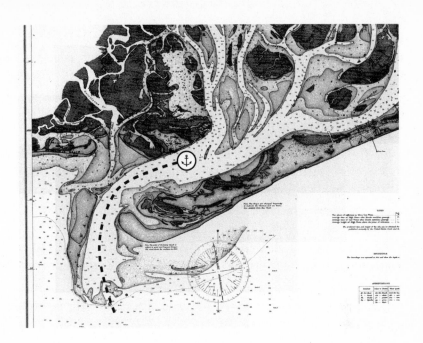

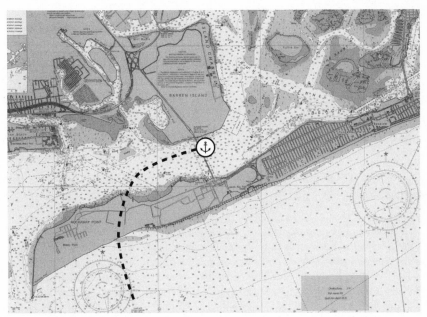

Henry Hudson's course into Rockaway Inlet is shown at the top on the 1899 Chart for Jamaica Bay and Rockaway Inlet. The same course today (as plotted above on chart 12350, 2001 edition) would require him to cut right across Rockaway Beach, due to the extensive terraforming of the twentieth century.

Approaching Rockaway Inlet on September 3, 1609, Hudson almost went aground in an instant. Sailing in some thirty comfortable feet of water, the *Half Moon* at once was upon "a very shoaled bar . . . ," according to Juet, "for we had but ten feet of water." The *Half Moon* immediately turned south, and once the soundings had recovered to six fathoms, Hudson anchored and launched the ship's boat to find a way into Jamaica Bay.

After ninety minutes, the boat returned with good news: soundings of no less than four to seven fathoms, which Hudson could follow in. The *Half Moon* was soon riding at anchor inside Rockaway Inlet in five fathoms. The waters teemed with edible life: they saw "many salmons, and mullets, and rays, very great."*

The next morning, they could see "good riding farther up," and the boat again went ahead to sound. Satisfied with the news of four to five fathoms only two cable lengths—about 1,200 feet—from shore, Hudson had the *Half Moon* moved farther into this "very good harbour." He seems to have stopped near what the Dutch would call Beeren (Bear) Eylant. The name was progressively corrupted in English, winding up as Barren Island, which the U.S. Army Air Corps would turn into Floyd Bennett airfield. Jasper Danckaerts (or Dankers) and Peter Sluyter, a pair of proselytizing Labadists from Friesland, traveled through the area in 1679–80 in search of a suitable settlement site for their Protestant sect. In a particularly informative journal (from which we'll be hearing much more) they described Beeren Eylant as being one of numerous islands "separated from Long Island by creeks and marshes overflown at high water." Of its one hundred acres, about thirty were upland. The rest was salt meadow, thick with cordgrass, a slender, haylike plant that typically forms whorls of wind-flattened growth and whose purple flowers still would have been in bloom when the *Half Moon* arrived.

---

*The presence of Atlantic salmon has been doubted, although according to Johanne de Laet, Hudson recounted catching them in the Hudson River. It has been proposed that Hudson's men probably caught weakfish, a sea trout common around New York in September and October. In Hudson's time, the distinction between salmon and weakfish would have been an esoteric issue. Animals were not organized into modern taxonomies, and names for creatures known in Europe were often applied to ones found in the New World, if they met the same general description and fit the same general purpose on the menu. However, it must be noted that Van der Donck (1655) also described salmon being in the Hudson River and was specific about their red flesh, and mentioned weakfish as well, suggesting he wasn't confusing the two species.

There was good depth for ships on the island's south shore in the nineteenth century, when it featured a hotel catering to sportsmen as well as two fertilizer factories (at least one of which relied on dead horses from New York City for its raw material); the 1899 chart indicated depths up to fifty-nine feet in the inlet, approaching and along the south shore of the island. The *Half Moon* was probably anchored in the shadow of Marine Parkway Bridge, where Flatbush Avenue crosses Rockaway Inlet to reach Rockaway Beach.

Some of the men went ashore and cast seines, replenishing the stores with "ten great mullets, of a foot and a half long apiece, and a ray as great as four men could haul into the ship. So we trimmed our boat and rode still all day."

On the night of the fourth, a strong wind arose out of the northwest, and the *Half Moon*'s anchor dragged. She was pushed ashore, likely on the north side of Rockaway Beach, "but took no hurt, thanked be God, for the ground is soft sand and ooze." For now, the *Half Moon* was stranded. The tide at least was near the bottom of its cycle: the neap would fall on September 6, and if they were not freed by then, they could count on increasingly higher floods to lift them off.

While waiting to float the *Half Moon* clear, Hudson found a more pressing issue to occupy him: the local people had found him.

CHAPTER 15

THE MEN WERE FISHING FROM THEIR dugout canoes beyond the river mouth, out where the sea widens, when they saw something that made no sense to them. It was still a great distance away, yet it was plainly very large, and was floating, or swimming. They could not tell.

They returned to shore immediately and told everyone what they had seen, which was not easy, because it defied description. Several others were convinced to return quickly to sea with them, to see this thing for themselves. It was still there—getting closer, and the sight of it was a great surprise to everyone who looked upon it.

They had no experience of any other people or technology, and it was a task almost beyond the capability of reason to make sense of the sight. The people debated what it must be. Some thought it was an unusually large fish or animal. Others, seeing a human touch in its angles and artifices, proposed that it was some kind of very great house that happened to be floating, and moving.

Those who had ventured out for that second look could not agree among themselves what it was, but they did agree that it was approaching land and that every tribe in the area should be notified and put on guard. And this was done. Runners and paddlers were dispatched in all sensible directions, to inform the chiefs that something extraordinary was approaching and that they should send every available warrior to prepare for the arrival.

The warriors poured in and assembled on a southern point of land. They could see the phenomenon approaching and came to their own conclusion on what it was. It was a large canoe or house, and it was carrying Mannito, the supreme being. Mannito was on his way to pay them all a visit.

The chiefs too now assembled here, and as it had been decided Mannito was approaching, they needed to agree without delay on how to receive him. The chiefs were unsure of the mood of the coming supreme being. Would he be pleased to see them, or had he made this unprecedented journey because he was angry for some reason? It would be best to prepare for every eventuality. A generous assemblage of animals was arranged for sacrifice. Women set to preparing the best possible foods. They brought together idols and sacred images, inspected their condition, and arranged them for display. They decided that a dance would be appropriate, because it would provide entertainment for Mannito and also segue neatly into a ritual sacrifice, should it turn out that Mannito in fact was in a bad mood and required appeasing.

As they waited for Mannito to arrive, the shamans were consulted. Never was their stature greater. All assembled, from chiefs to children, were in their thrall, hoping for a coherent explanation of what was about to happen and why.

"Between hope and fear and confusion," it would be recalled, "a dance commenced."

The dance was still going on when runners arrived with more detailed news of the approaching marvel. It was indeed a large floating house, and it had many colors and was crowded with creatures. Fresh runners arrived. Yes, it was a colorful house, but the creatures were people, albeit people of a different color than they were, and they were also dressed differently. One in particular was resplendent in red. This "person" must be Mannito.

Soon the floating house—or, as some were insisting, the great canoe— had approached closely enough for those borne by it to shout out a greeting, in a language they could not understand. This was a problem: if Mannito was about to visit, why were the people with him incomprehensible to them? The reaction was close to panic. Some were all for fleeing into the woods, but they were persuaded to stay. Those who were for staying were afraid that in fleeing, people would offend the visitors and prompt them to seek the offenders out and kill them.

The floating house that might actually be a canoe stopped moving. From it, a smaller canoe appeared. It carried a number of men, as well as the figure dressed in red, Mannito. When the canoe reached the shore, they all disembarked. Several men stayed with the canoe to guard it. The others accompanied the figure in red as he strode forward.

The chiefs and their advisers had formed a circle, and their visitors approached it. The figure in red greeted them with incomprehensible words, but his expression was friendly. They stared at the visitors, awestruck by their strangeness, the whiteness of their skin, the peculiarity of their clothing. The figure in red especially dazzled. His clothing had sparkling trimmings they could not explain. They were thoroughly convinced he must be Mannito, but they could not understand why Mannito would have such pale skin.

One of the men accompanying Mannito, whom they took to be a servant, approached with some kind of container, a supernatural version of their hockhack, or gourd. From it, a liquid poured into a small cup. The cup was handed to Mannito, and he drank from it, then returned it to be refilled.

Mannito turned to the chief next to him in the circle and handed him the brimming cup.

The chief sniffed at the cup cautiously but, rather than drink from it, passed it to the man next to him, who did the same. And so it went around the circle, each man sniffing at the cup but refusing to drink from it.

It was about to be returned untouched to Mannito when one of the assembled men, a great warrior, leapt up and delivered a scornful harangue. How dare they refuse to drink something offered to them by Mannito, after he had consumed the liquid? If they did not drink as Mannito did, they would greatly offend him, which could mean the death of everyone. He, the warrior, would drink from the cup. It was better that he alone would die, if that were to be the result.

So the great warrior drank, every last drop. His companions watched him carefully, to see what the effect would be. They saw him stagger, then fall, and as he slid into unconsciousness they feared that he had died. But then he returned to his feet, declaring that he had never felt happier than he did after drinking from the cup and that he wanted more of whatever had been in it.

Mannito granted the request. Everyone assembled now wanted some of this elixir, and it was provided. Soon, the chiefs and their advisers were quite drunk. Mannito and his attendants withdrew from the intoxicated gathering, waiting out the revelry in the security of their floating house.

So GOES THE main part of an oral tradition of the arrival of Europeans in New York. It is based on an account compiled by the Reverend John Heckewelder, a Moravian missionary who ministered in Pennsylvania among native peoples displaced by European colonization of the greater New York area. They were Lenape (Delaware), Mahican, and Munsee (actually a Lenape subgroup), and around 1760 Heckewelder had gathered their various recollections of their first encounter with the strangers who ultimately occupied their lands, condensing them into a single account. We have no idea if any of these people would have agreed with his compilation, although John Yates and Joseph Moulton, in their *History of the State of New-York, Including Its Aboriginal and Colonial Annals* (1824), would insist that this story "is told by all the Indians of the tribes of Delawares, the 'Monces,' and Mohiccans."

Adriaen Cornelissen Van der Donck had already told a similar (if terser) tale in *A Description of New Netherland* (1655) and related it explicitly to the arrival of Hudson in the *Half Moon*: "When some of them first saw our ship approaching from a distance, they did not know what to think about her, but stood in deep and solemn amazement, wondering whether it were a ghost or apparition coming down from heaven or hell. Others of them supposed her to be a strange fish or sea monster. When they discovered men on board, they looked upon them rather as devils than human beings. Thus they differed about the ship and men. A strange report was also spread about the country concerning our ship and visit, which created great astonishment and surprise amongst the Indians. These things we have frequently heard them declare, and we regard them as certain proofs that the Netherlanders were the first finders or discoverers and possessors of the New Netherland."

Van der Donck's account seemed fairly credible. He had arrived in 1641 as the first lawyer in New Netherland and learned at least something of the Iroquoian and Algonquian languages spoken by the native peoples. He was also recording recollections of the first encounter with Europeans within living memory of Hudson's visit.

Yet Van der Donck had an agenda in emphasizing that a Dutch expedition was the first to visit, and in dismissing notions that anyone other than the Dutch might have been there first. The Dutch claim to the colony of New Netherland was under siege from the English. He dismissed any idea of an original Spanish visit, in apparent reference to Gomes, but he failed to address the fact that the Dutch also knew the Hudson River by the suspiciously Hispanic name Rio de Montaignes. There was also the matter of Verrazzano's discovery, which he did not consider at all. And as we'll see, he rewrote many of the basic facts of Hudson's voyage to make his 1609 explorations as Dutch as possible.

About twenty-five years after Van der Donck's book was published, the Frisians Jasper Danckaerts and Peter Sluyter paused at Governors ("Noten") Island and questioned "Hans, our Indian, what Christians they, the Indians, had first seen in these parts." Their guide (who was likely Lenape) "answered the first were Spaniards or Portuguese, from whom they obtained the maize or Spanish or Turkish wheat, but they did not remain here long. Afterwards the Dutch came into the South River [Delaware River] and here, on Noten Island, a small island lying directly opposite the fort at New York, and to Fort Orange or Albany, and after them the English came for the first [time], who, nevertheless, always disputed the first possession." Even this memory was something of a compression: the first contingent of Dutch settlers did land on Governors Island in 1624, and the South River area was first settled in 1631, but there had been numerous Dutch trading visits before then, not to mention Hudson (who never touched Governors Island).*

The oral recollections of the first encounter, then, were as much a muddle as the rival European claims of discovery, not to mention the European efforts to give names to various peoples and subgroups and their territories. Heckewelder's specific mention of a ship captain in crimson garb with delicate trimmings of silk or silver thread does sound much more like the Ital-

---

* Native assurances that the Spanish were the first to visit the area were persistent. While in Albany, Danckaerts and Sluyter reported how "we took a walk to an island upon the end of which there is a fort built, they say, by the Spaniards. That a fort has been there is evident enough from the earth thrown up and strewn around, but it is not to be supposed that the Spaniards came so far inland to build forts, when there are no monuments of them to be seen elsewhere and down on the sea coasts, where, however, they have been according to the traditions of the Indians." They do seem to have been describing an old fortification on Castle Island, where the first Dutch trading post, Fort Nassau, was established in 1613 or 1614.

ian sailing for the king of France of 1524, or the Portuguese sailing for the king of Spain of 1525, than the Englishman sailing for the VOC of 1609. And as Heckewelder goes on to relate how agricultural tools were given to the natives, and how the strangers returned as promised the following year to settle and cultivate the land, it seems the Moravian missionary, gathering oral history more than a century after Van der Donck from different dislocated populations, produced an agglomeration of first-encounter experiences involving different visitors, even condensing different events within Hudson's own explorations.

In any case, none of the people who actually met Hudson when he made his initial landfall was from a tribe or confederacy named by these early ethnographers and travelers. The people who saw the *Half Moon* arrive in Jamaica Bay were Metoac, a confederacy of thirteen Algonquian-speaking peoples on Long Island. Specifically they were Canarsie (or Canarsee), the westernmost group of Metoac, whose territory encompassed the western and northern shores of Jamaica Bay and extended west to the Flatland of what would become the Dutch village of Breuckelen—the forerunner of today's Brooklyn. Their territory was acquired by the Dutch in 1636. The Canarsie would not survive war with both the Dutch and the Mohawk of the Iroquois confederacy to give their own version of the story.

ACCORDING TO JUET, the Canarsie appeared soon after the *Half Moon* was anchored in Rockaway Inlet, on Friday, September 4: "this day the people of the country came aboard of us, seeming very glad of our coming, and brought green tobacco, and gave us of it for knives and beads." The trade goods aboard the *Half Moon* were probably stolen from the Mi'kmaq in the raid at La Have.

There was none of the high drama and anxiety among the natives later related by Van der Donck and Heckewelder. If anything, the Canarsie got down to the business of trade with remarkable speed and apparent nonchalance. "They go in deerskins loose, well dressed," wrote Juet. Johanne de Laet recounted how the *Half Moon* was visited on its arrival "by two savages clothed in elk-skins [i.e., deerskin], who showed them every sign of friendship."

"They have yellow copper," Juet remarked. He probably meant brass, an alloy of copper and zinc, but he was mistaken, as no native American group could smelt metals. As Juet would note, they did have copper—"red copper" as he called it, which natives worked from nugget form into ceremonial and decorative items by hammering and annealing. "They desire clothes," Juet added, "and are very civil."

Few Canarsie archaeological sites would survive the coming colonization and aggressive development of the late nineteenth and twentieth centuries, and none of them would be excavated professionally. But the Canarsie are believed to have lived in permanent settlements, of which there were at least a half dozen close by the *Half Moon*'s anchorage, set on tidal streams and bays and occupying about an acre each.

The Metoac left behind enormous middens of shellfish, as well as bones from birds, mammals, and fish. While there has been some academic debate about how much agriculture they practiced (and if they did so before the Dutch came along), artifacts that include hoes, pestles, mortars, and even wooden grinding gears support the idea that corn was already a fixture when Hudson appeared. And as Juet reported, "They have great store of maize or Indian wheat, whereof they make good bread."

The following day, September 5, dawned without a breath of wind. Hudson was able to refloat the *Half Moon* on the flood tide and had the boat further sound the inlet. They found three fathoms "hard by the southern shore," by which Juet probably meant the south shore of Barren Island. They relocated the *Half Moon* accordingly, and the men then went on land.

At low tide, only a small stream divided Barren Island from the rest of western Long Island, and the *Half Moon*'s men may have walked a reasonable distance into the Flatland, for according to Juet they "saw great store of men, women, and children, who gave them tobacco at their coming on land. So they went up into the woods, and saw great store of very goodly oaks and some currants. For one of them came aboard and brought some dried, and gave me some, which were sweet and good."

De Laet described how on land Hudson's men "found an abundance of blue plums and magnificent oaks, of a height and thickness that one seldom beholds; together with poplars, linden trees, and various other kinds of wood useful in ship building."

"This day," Juet continued, "many of the people came aboard, some in mantles of feathers, and some in skins of diverse sorts of good furs. Some women also came to us with hemp. They had red copper tobacco pipes, and other things of copper they did wear about their necks."

Juet's careful notation of personal possessions of "yellow" and "red" copper was incidental ethnography. He was most interested in documenting the existence of valuable metals. They had already questioned the Mi'kmaq closely—almost immediately, even—about them on the *Half Moon*'s arrival at La Have. A mania about locating minerals and metals, gold especially, was preoccupying the first years of the Jamestown colony, to the point of nearly causing its failure. The contributors to Smith's *A Map of Virginia* railed against "our gilded refiners with their golden promises, [who] made all the men their slaves in hope of recompense[. T]here was no talk, no hope, no work, but dig gold, wash gold, refine gold, load gold, such a brute of gold, as one mad fellow desired to be buried in the sands, lest they should by their art make gold of his bones." Of course there was no actual gold, only a powerful distraction that detracted from the crucial labors of establishing a settlement in the summer of 1607. John Smith was dismayed by the scale and folly of the mania, which helped turn him against the original president, Edward Maria Wingfield, and principal figures like Christopher Newport and Gabriel Archer, and especially Captain John Martin, a gentleman adventurer who was the leading "refiner," or participant in the gold rush. Smith condemned the refiners in *A Map of Virginia* for "flattering themselves in their own vain conceits" that gold was at hand. He and Martin had differed bitterly over a return passage by the latter: Smith wanted to load the ship with cedar, but Martin insisted on burdening it with samples of "his fantastical gold."

The gold fever led directly to Richard Hakluyt and Sir Thomas Smythe and was most virulent when Hudson sailed in the *Half Moon.* In 1609 Hakluyt published *Virginia richly valued: By the description of the main land of Florida, her next neighbor,* an English translation of documents relating the explorations of Hernando de Soto. Hakluyt dedicated the work to his fellow participants in the new Virginia Company, stating that it "doth yield much light to our enterprise now on foot: whether you desire to know the present and future commodities of our country." Hakluyt considered the translated materials invaluable for their references to "gold and silver, and stones of great value" in the lands right next door to the colony.

Already, when Christopher Newport returned from the first expedition to establish Jamestown with news of valuable ores but no actual samples, Sir Thomas Smythe had written Sir Robert Cecil in exasperation: "And for as much as Captain Newport doth find his error, in not bringing of the same ore of which the first trial was made, he is now minded, to take upon him the present voyage again. And resolves never to see your Lordship before he brings that with him which he confidently believed he had brought before."

Indeed, it seems that Newport was soon being employed not by the Virginia Company but on a private venture that would have involved Smythe and perhaps Cecil and others like Sir Walter Cope. As related in *A Map of Virginia*, Newport reappeared in the colony in September 1608 in command of a relief vessel, having obtained "a private commission as not to return without a lump of gold, a certainty of the south-sea or one of the lost company of Sir Walter Rawley."

In his persistent inquiries about minerals and metals on the 1609 voyage, Henry Hudson seemed to be catering to the pet enthusiasms of these powerful men, if he was not actually employed by them in a covert private venture of his own. It was possible he made sure not to repeat Newport's error and brought home samples of the copper the natives possessed. As for the actual availability of copper, while mines would arise in the northeast during the colonial era, natives needed copper in nuggets that could be worked, rather than ore that could be extracted by smelting. Extensive native trade networks probably delivered those nuggets to the Canarsie from Lake Superior.

The visitors stayed aboard the *Half Moon* for a considerable time, not returning to land until darkness. Hudson and his men "rode very quiet" that night, by which Juet meant without incident, "but [we] durst not trust them."

It was Juet's nature to presume the worst of indigenous people, and given the unpredictable and sometimes violent encounters between natives and newcomers, he may have been entitled to this attitude. But he differed critically from his ship's master in this regard. Hudson, while prudent when it came to native peoples, also gave them an uncommonly large benefit of the doubt. He was much like John Davis, who on his three voyages in search of the Northwest Passage (leaving aside one lamentable if predictable kidnapping episode) was tolerant in the extreme of an Inuit tendency to steal iron at any opportunity, up to and including making off with a ship's anchor in broad daylight.

A rare surviving scrap of Hudson's own journal, quoted by de Laet, preserves his own impression of the Canarsie: "When I came on shore, the
swarthy natives all stood around and sung in their fashion; their clothing
consisted of the skin of foxes and other animals, which they dress and
make the skins into garments of various sorts. Their food is Turkish wheat
[corn], which they cook by baking, and it is excellent eating. They all came
on board, one after another, in their canoes, which are made of a single hollowed tree; their weapons are bows and arrows, pointed with sharp stones,
which they fasten with hard resin. They had no houses [a misunderstand-
ing by Hudson], but slept under the blue heavens, sometimes on mats of
bulrushes interwoven, and sometimes on leaves of trees. They always carry
with them all their goods, such as their food and green tobacco, which is
strong and good for use. They appear to be friendly people, but have a great
propensity to steal, and are exceedingly adroit in carrying away whatever
they take a fancy to." De Laet's account also paraphrased Hudson in stating
that the natives he encountered in the New World "are well disposed, if
only they are well treated." Presumably, then, they only behaved badly in
Hudson's judgment when they were treated badly.

It was the light-fingered behavior that must have set Juet's teeth on edge
when it came to the Canarsies' trustworthiness. After their visitors left the
ship that day, a large number of missing items would have come to light,
and no sailor enjoys being relieved of personal effects. But there was a difference between native visitors swiping the odd unguarded item and planning a massed assault. Hudson made no special defensive provisions after
that first full day in Rockaway Inlet. The *Half Moon* was secure, at last, in a
harbor that sheltered her from the Atlantic, with friendly, accommodating
natives and abundant natural resources. For now, this would do as a base of
operations.

CHAPTER 16

O N SUNDAY, SEPTEMBER 6, THE neap was upon them; the tide would now be higher with every successive day until September 13, the next full moon. Hudson decided to send out a survey party. He gave John Colman, the veteran of the 1607 *Hopewell* voyage to Spitsbergen, the command of the ship's boat and four Dutch crewmembers. Colman was to go "over to the north-side to sound the other river, being four leagues from us," according to Juet. And so Colman was to reconnoiter the nearer of the other two great rivers they had seen while anchored off Sandy Hook. It was around the corner, to their west, and more northward. Juet's distance was not terribly wrong for the Verrazzano Narrows, which are about eight nautical miles from Barren Island.

The departure would not have been without a little ceremony, as it was Sunday, and Hudson first would have delivered the common service, including the prescribed lessons from the Old and New Testaments for that day. The little boat and its five occupants then took to the sea, first passing Pelican Beach, then Plumb Inlet and Coney Island.

The ever observant Danckaerts and Sluyter would visit Coney Island when it was being used as a pasture and note in their 1679–80 journal: "The outer shore of [Long Island] has before it several small islands and broken land, such as Coninen [Coney] Island, a low sandy island of about three hours' circuit, its westerly point forming with Sandy Hook, on the other side, the entrance from the sea. It is oblong in shape, and is grown over with bushes . . . [O]n the sea side, is a meadow or marsh intersected by several kills or creeks. It is not large, being about half an hour or three quarters [walking] long, and stretching nearly east and west. It is sandy and uninhabited. They generally let their horses run upon it to feed, as they cannot get off of it. We found good oysters in the creek inside, and ate some of them."*

Nothing about the island, save its sand, would survive the coming urban sprawl, the resort hotels, midways, roller coasters, burlesque halls, boardwalks, piers, film houses, and freak shows. Plumb Inlet would be filled in, Pelican Beach wiped from the map, and the extremities of the greater, remolded Coney Island (now fixed to the rest of Long Island) resculpted with rectilinear perfection.

Once past Coney Island, Colman's survey party skirted Gravesend Bay. The Narrows between the headlands of western Long Island and Staten Island were before them. They had reached the point where a great glacial moraine had once joined the continental mainland with Staten Island and Long Island. This was the leading edge of the last great glacial period, a repository of rock ground into fine sand by the same ice field that performed the final carving of the Hudson River Valley. Behind the moraine had been a freshwater sea. About twelve and a half thousand years ago, the Atlantic Ocean broke through the moraine at the Narrows, flooding the river valley. The passage through the Narrows by the men in the *Half Moon*'s boat was far less visually dramatic but had its own momentous consequences.

Upper New York Bay had been breached, and this would be no brief inspection as had been the case with Verrazzano. The European colonization

---

* Seventeenth- and eighteenth-century charts reveal major changes in the coast of western Long Island. The hand-painted Vinckeboons map of 1639 shows Coney (Conyne) Island as the broad end of a peninsula extending into the East Bank, which agrees somewhat with the description of Danckaerts and Sluyter that it formed a complementary point to Sandy Hook. A 1656 map by Nicholaes Visscher shows the end of the point having broken away into a distinct island. Perhaps it was mostly reattached by the time Danckaerts and Sluyter came along, but in a 1732 English pilot's chart a westerly Coney Island is again an island in fact, its peninsular bridge to Long Island having been submerged. This configuration is essentially repeated in a 1778 French chart as well as a 1781 English chart. At some point in the early nineteenth century, this small offshore Coney Island was absorbed into East Bank, and the name was again applied to the island close along the Long Island shore.

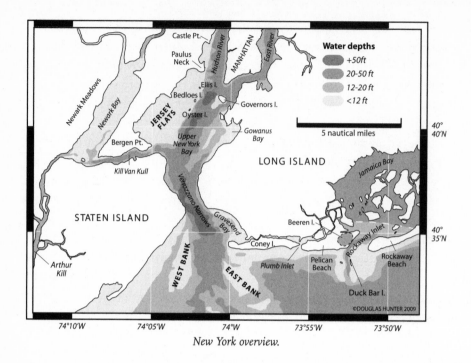

New York overview.

now began, with the dipping of oars, possibly a gentle ruffle of a small boat's sail, and an odd murmuring mixture of Dutch and English words carrying across waters that would never be the same. The Dutch, following hard on Hudson's heels, would start the settlement process in fits and starts in 1624, but Anglo-Americans would not be far behind, fleeing religious persecution in the New England colonies in the mid-seventeenth century for the freedom of worship in New Netherland.

The landscape would be so radically altered as a result of the arrival of these five newcomers that it is not enough for us to travel back in time to them in order to understand their experiences: we also have to travel forward in time from them to understand how much of what was there, then, is no longer here, now. The hyperkinetic terraforming that lay ahead would have so great an impact on landscapes and ecosystems that its scouring, reshaping, and repurposing deserves to qualify as a special glacial period of its own.

JUET REPORTED THAT Colman's survey party found depths of eighteen to twenty fathoms "and very good riding for ships," which they could only have located in the center channel of the Narrows, close to the span of the Verrazzano Bridge.* They were promptly turning the corner at the ferry terminals and the minor-league ballpark on northeast Staten Island and entering "a narrow river to the westward, between two islands."

They had entered the tidal strait of Kill Van Kull. They were right in that Staten was an island, but modern readers of Juet's account will be puzzled by where the second island could have been, unless they appreciate that Bergen Neck, on the north side of Kill Van Kull, has been more than doubled in width by New Jersey's mammoth port lands. The Jersey Flats on the east side of the neck have been largely consumed by piers that extended the shore as much as two miles from its natural limit in Hudson's time. The men in the boat were skirting the bulge at the lower end of the neck, which began south of West Thirty-second in Bayonne, and seeing the possibility of an island.

Samuel Akerly, in "An Essay on the Geology of the Hudson River," a paper he delivered to the New-York Lyceum of Natural History in August 1819, would note that Bergen Point, as he called all of Bergen Neck, rose only eight to ten feet above the water. It was "a low sandy alluvion . . . [that] extends northwards for four or five miles, till the trap or greenstone formation commences opposite the city of New-York . . . In sailing up or down the bay, the view is extended over this low point, and the mountains of Newark are seen at distance."

The lands "were as pleasant with grass and flowers and goodly trees as ever they had seen, and very sweet smells came from them," according to Juet. Tradition would have it that part of a contingent of thirty Walloon families—French-speaking Protestants seeking a place to practice their faith free of persecution—would establish themselves initially on Staten

* A depth of 18 to 20 fathoms, or 108 to 120 feet, is significantly deeper than what is charted now in the Narrows, where maximum depth is shown to be 96 feet, or 16 fathoms. But Colman's survey was not mistaken, as a circa 1750 chart of New York Harbor would give a maximum depth of 19 fathoms in the Narrows, and a 1778 French chart depths of up to 20 fathoms. Much sediment plainly has been deposited in the Narrows, and such changes underscore the challenges in correlating historic observations with modern charts.

Island in 1624, as part of the first modest wave of colonists introduced by the Dutch West India Company.* Bergen, to the north, would become part of Pavonia, one of the feudal *patroon* manors established under a new settlement charter in 1629.

The visit by the *Half Moon*'s boat was the initial European experience of the greatest commercial seaport in eastern North America, a terminus for container ships, cruise liners, oil tankers, and naval vessels. This quiet tidewater channel would become a main thoroughfare of the Port of New York and New Jersey, which would rank in the early twenty-first century as the largest port in the eastern United States (and be the nation's largest landing point for imported oil). It would be the twentieth largest port in the world by cargo tonnage and eighteenth by container traffic. Where a handful of men glided along in a small boat, savoring the fragrance of wildflowers, 143 million metric tons of goods would load and unload in a single year on a tableau of steel, asphalt, and concrete. And while the Dutch would launch the development of this mercantile center within a little more than a decade, less than 4 percent of its trade tonnage would involve their nation by 2007. China, the country Hudson was trying to reach by finding a way through or around America, would account for about one quarter of it.

After only a few miles they were at the point where vehicles vault the kill on Bayonne Bridge, the world's third largest iron suspension bridge, hard by the neighborhood Steven Spielberg would choose to have spindly-legged alien craft erupt from beneath the pavement in his 2005 remake of *War of the Worlds*. They were looking upon "an open sea," a tolerable exaggeration of Newark Bay, with the expansive marsh of Newark Meadows extending westward. The marsh would disappear beneath the Port Newark–Elizabeth

---

*The arrival of the first colonists was long reported as having occurred in 1623. But Jaap Jacobs, in *New Netherland: A Dutch Colony in Seventeenth-Century America*, shows that the first ship arrivals carrying colonists were in 1624. The *Nieu Nederlandt*, the ship carrying the Walloons, sailed in March 1624. The earliest departure is a vessel called the *Eendracht*, which cleared Texel in January 1624. Rather than the initial colonization being focused exclusively on Upper New York Bay, Jacobs suggests that the *Eendracht*'s colonists "were divided over four locations: the Fresh River [Connecticut River], the South River [Delaware River], Nooten Eylandt [Governors Island] near Manhattan, and the upper reaches of the North River, where Fort Orange was founded. No doubt the reason for the dispersion of the colonists was to lay claim to the whole area."

Marine Terminal for container ships and Newark Liberty International Airport. Had they been able to wait four centuries, KLM Royal Dutch Airlines would have been able to get them back to Amsterdam, nonstop, in seven hours and forty minutes aboard a Boeing 757.

They seem to have gone far enough into Newark Bay to detect Arthur Kill and correctly conclude that Staten was an island. And having traveled about fifteen nautical miles from the *Half Moon*, they had seen enough for one day. The future of these wildflower-dappled shores and tidewater wetlands was now firmly charted.

When they turned back along Kill Van Kull, the Department of Homeland Security was waiting.

THE MEETING BETWEEN the five Europeans in the ship's boat and the twenty-six native men in two enormous dugout canoes could not have been a chance encounter. The boat's leisurely progress under sail and oars would have been obvious for hours from any decent vantage point, especially the moraine heights of Staten Island. The *Half Moon*'s men already were being stalked by the time they turned around.

Juet (who wasn't there) avowed the men were "set upon" by the two canoes. Even if the encounter had been initially peaceful, both sides would have been warily on edge. The five Europeans were a very long way from the support and shelter of the *Half Moon*, and badly outnumbered. And while the natives had the numerical advantage, they only brandished Stone Age weapons, where the *Half Moon*'s party would never have set out without arming themselves with pikes and muskets. And unlike the men in the boat, who had already met with (and at La Have attacked) native Americans, the men in the canoes had assuredly never seen anything like the *Half Moon*'s sailors.

We will never know how far the extensive native trade networks had carried tales of encounters with such strangers, which had been occurring up and down the eastern seaboard for about a century. Sometimes, to be sure, they had wonderful things to trade. Sometimes they loosed their horrible dogs on you. Sometimes they pretended to be friendly, then abducted your friends and family, your children. And sometimes they killed whoever got in their way as they stole whatever they wanted.

This was a first contact no oral history would preserve. The natives likely were Lenape, specifically Munsee, whose territory may have entirely encompassed the upper bay, including Manhattan Island. Who shot first is moot, but something as simple as a native attempt at minor pilfering—a hand reaching to grab at a button or a knife—could have set off the melee. That the *Half Moon*'s men escaped at all must mean they had enough time to load and discharge powder weapons and inflict enough damage to terrify their opponents into retreat. Otherwise they never would have been able to outpace two heavily manned canoes. Danckaerts and Sluyter would describe the sort of craft the *Half Moon*'s men likely were up against on a visit to a small band at Najack on the east side of the Narrows: "for fishing, [they use] a canoe without mast or sail, and without a nail in any part of it, though it is sometimes full forty feet in length, fish hooks and lines, and scoops to paddle with in place of oars."

In the fight, several native arrows sang home. Two Dutchmen were wounded, and John Colman was pierced through the throat and killed.

Darkness was soon upon them. Under a quarter moon in an overcast sky, darkness was truly dark, and it got even darker when the boat's sole light ("match") snuffed out as rain began to pelt them with further misery. Colman was dying if not already dead. Where their course took them that night is unrecorded, but as they groped their way back toward the *Half Moon*, they managed to find a current so strong during a neap tide that they could not get their anchor to hold, and so had to drift on the tidal stream.

At ten o'clock the next morning, the ship's boat reappeared in Rockaway Inlet, bearing Colman's body, with only two surviving occupants untouched by arrows.

Colman was carried ashore for a proper burial. In accordance with his ingrained duties as an English ship's master to maintain proper religious observances, Hudson would have read the Order for the Burial of the Dead from the Book of Common Prayer, as last revised in 1559.

"I am the resurrection and the life, saith the Lord," Hudson would have begun, quoting from the story of Lazarus in John 11, as Colman's body was carried to the burial place, which was probably a trench cut into a dune. Hudson proceeded through the further prescribed readings, until the point where earth was to be tossed upon Colman's corpse, which was probably wrapped in old sailcloth. As a shovel—wielded by

Juet or Hudson's son John?—began to dump sand over the body, Hudson would have been reading the prescribed selection from Job 11: "for as much as it hath pleased almighty God of his great mercy to take unto Himself the Soul of our dear brother, here departed, we therefore commit his body to the ground, earth, to earth, ashes, to ashes, dust, to dust."

As John Colman was the first man known to have died on a voyage commanded by Henry Hudson, this was also the first time Hudson was called upon in his exploration career to deliver the 1,600-odd words of the Order of the Burial of the Dead. The simple ceremony would have been over in five or ten minutes. From Timothy, Hudson was prescribed to read, "We brought nothing into this world, neither may we carry any thing out of this world." Back at the ship, Colman's personal effects, including whatever clothes and boots he had been wearing that were not hopelessly bloodied, would have been secured for return to his next of kin, or alternately sold by auction at the mainmast to the highest bidder, as custom permitted. Colman's pay, prorated to the day of his death, would go to his heirs—provided that he had any, and that the VOC could be persuaded to cough it up when this rogue voyage was over.

Hudson named the burial place Colman's Point, but nothing from the voyage survives to locate it, and the coast underwent so many changes through natural processes before the man-made ones took over in the coming centuries that we will never know for certain where it was. Hudson may have chosen to bury Colman on Rockaway Beach, on the point at the mouth of the inlet, where a lifeboat station would be established in 1849: close to the *Half Moon*'s anchorage but away from the Canarsie, who may have been suspected as being complicit in the assault. Wherever it was, Colman's grave was long ago lost in the ever shifting sands, or dredged away.

Even if no chart by Hudson indicating Colman's Point endured, the memory of the burial place must have, among the *Half Moon*'s Dutch crew. Some of them surely returned to serve as guides when independent Dutch traders followed up on Hudson's discoveries as early as the very next year. For Colman's name evidently became fixed to a nearby island during the early years of the New Netherland settlement. Just as the English settlers who succeeded the Dutch on Long Island turned Beeren into Barren Island, so the Dutch probably corrupted Colman variously into Coninen, Conyen, and Conyne, with English colonists then corrupting it back, into Cunny, then Coney, as if the island were a hare sanctuary.* John Colman's unlikely legacy would be the name of the world's first amusement park.

*Neither Adriaen Block (1614) nor Cornelius Hendrickson (probable cartographer, 1616) drew or labeled the island, although the scales of these maps are rather large. Conyne Island appears in the hand-painted circa 1639 map *Manatus gelegen op de Noot Rivier* attributed to Joan Vinckeboons. Coninen was the name used by Danckaerts and Sluyter in their 1679–80 journal.

Nicholaes Visscher's 1656 map *Novi Belgii Novaeque Angliae* left the label *Conyne Eylant* floating vaguely in the Atlantic, east of Sandy Hook, which Visscher called Sant (Sand) or Godyns Punt (Point). This may have encouraged a misidentification of Sandy Hook as Colman's Point. Another tradition places Colman's Point at Keansburg, west of Sandy Hook, on the south shore of Raritan Bay, and sometimes makes it synonymous with Comfort Point on that shore, but Colman most certainly was not buried there.

CHAPTER 17

THE NIGHT THAT FOLLOWED JOHN Colman's burial, the *Half Moon* was a different ship. Contentment with their safe anchorage, its bountiful supply of fresh fish, and its friendly natives had been traumatically undermined. The ship's boat was hoisted on board, and a defensive wall of waistboards was fitted along the perimeter of the *Half Moon*'s main deck. "So we rode all night," wrote Juet, "having good regard to our watch."

That single death also had a profound effect on the dynamics of the crew. Losing Colman reduced the number of English on board to just three: Henry Hudson and his son John and Juet. And if Colman had been brought along by Hudson because he could speak Dutch, his death would have exacerbated the already tense shipboard relations by choking off communications.

While his specific views on Colman's loss went unrecorded, Hudson was inclined to forgive natives for pilfering indiscretions, and to blame his own people when relations soured. Juet was temperamentally inclined to consider natives treacherous by nature, and thus was more likely to side with any ideas of punishment or retribution the Dutch majority might have had in mind.

Hudson could not be careless with natives where everyone's safety was concerned. Neither could he allow a serious disagreement over how to treat the natives, and especially how to avenge the attack in the Kill Van Kull, to compel the Dutch to reject his leadership and seize control of the vessel. The fuse to the powder keg of insubordination last lit at La Have was in danger of being touched off again.

They waited all night, and into the next day, September 8, for an attack. The new day brought "very fair weather" but nary a sign of menace. "We rode still very quietly," wrote Juet. The *Half Moon* was frozen in apprehension, uncertainty, and perhaps more than a little internal disagreement over what to do next. It fell to the natives to jar the *Half Moon* out of the inertia. They did so simply by showing up to trade.

An untold number appeared. Juet gave no indication of who they were or where they came from: if they were Canarsie or more distant visitors. They could have been another Metoac people—the Rockaway tribe from the east side of Jamaica Bay—or even Munsee from around Upper New York Bay. The visitors "came aboard us." Juet generally used "aboard" (or in his spelling "aboord") in the strict nautical sense of visitors coming *along-side* a ship. It didn't necessarily mean that they then all came *on board*, and this was certainly one of those times. They had tobacco and maize to trade for glass beads and knives—more of the barter stockpile stolen from the Mi'kmaq. Someone had the bright idea of putting the ship's boat on prominent display, so that the visiting natives would come right alongside it in their canoes. The *Half Moon*'s men then watched the natives to see if any of them viewed the portable crime scene with guilt or unease. As Juet conceded, none was seen to "make any show of the death of our man." Furthermore, the trading was amicable and uneventful, as they "offered us no violence."

It was possible that some of the men aboard the *Half Moon* suspected that the local Canarsie were complicit in the attack on the boat. These European newcomers as yet knew nothing about the many different indigenous groups around the Hudson River estuary. But as the Jamestown colonists well understood that a few miles of travel could introduce them to a complex world of warring and allied tribes, perhaps it wasn't beyond the grasp of the *Half Moon*'s men that the Canarsie might have had nothing to do with whoever killed Colman. At the same time, it was perfectly logical, in a worldview dominated by treachery and double-dealing (and consistent with the view of natives emanating from Jamestown), that the Canarsie might show abundant goodwill and trade so congenially while at the same time be scheming to kill them all.

Hudson seemed unconcerned with the Canarsie, as he was in no apparent hurry to leave Rockaway Inlet. But a profound dissatisfaction with the Canarsie, with an infuriating incapability of showing the slightest guilt or even awareness of Colman's loss, also could have kept Hudson mired in the anchorage until his crew was satisfied.

He was still there on Wednesday, September 9. That day, "two great canoes came aboard full of men," wrote Juet. Again, we don't know who they were or where they came from. Their approach must have set off alarm bells, as their appearance so clearly recalled that of the assailants in Kill Van Kull. One canoe carried men armed with bows and arrows, while the other transported traders. Juet expected the worst of them. They were "in show of buying knives to betray us; but we perceived their intent."

This time the visitors were motioned on board. The first two to reach the deck were seized, and the rest, still in the canoes alongside, were driven off, as the *Half Moon*'s men "would not suffer the others to come near us."

Juet wrote that we "put red coats" on the two captives, a sign that they were well treated according to the prescriptions of Cabot. These were the "red gowns" or "cassocks" Juet had reported that the French traded with the Mi'kmaq. They were prized goods in the fur trade, yet more items snatched by the *Half Moon*'s men in their pillaging of the La Have village. But putting red coats on the captives also could have been Juet's clever way of saying they were beaten bloody in vengeance for the death of Colman.

Hudson's crew watched the repulsed visitors make for shore. Bewildered by the fact that two of their companions had been kidnapped in the midst of a trading visit, the natives sent back two emissaries to the *Half Moon*. Hudson's men responded by deciding to keep one of them as well after permitting them on deck, but this third captive leapt overboard. "Then we weighed and went off into the channel of the river, and anchored there all night," wrote Juet. The *Half Moon* was probably still in Rockaway Inlet, staging to depart with its two abductees.

Juet relates too little for us to know the purpose of the abductions. Were the captives hostages, held as an assurance of good behavior by the natives? Or had Hudson backslid into the methods of George Waymouth, grabbing these trusting shipboard guests because he needed interpreters?

If they were seized as interpreters, one must wonder how Hudson expected them to be useful when no one on board could speak Algonquian and no local native could speak English or Dutch. A major disadvantage for Hudson was the lack of a trade creole. As he had already discovered at La Have, there were natives on the eastern seaboard with some mastery of French. But the local people around greater New York had no known living experience of outsiders. Hudson, however, may have had something of a head start in establishing basic communications. The English had begun building Algonquian lexicons in the Chesapeake and Norumbega. John Smith would include one (as well as phrases) in *A Map of Virginia*, and among its entries were *mattassin* (copper) and *usawassin* (iron, brass, silver, or any white metal), which Hudson, in his persistent query of natives on the subject of lucrative natural resources, would have tried out had he known them. James Rosier in the preface to his account of the 1605 Way-mouth voyage asserted he had assembled a vocabulary of five hundred words, but only a selection was included in the published work, and none was for metals or ores. A copy of the complete Rosier vocabulary (which, like so many other documentary items from this period, has never been found) would have been highly useful to Hudson, even if the Algonquian language group spoken on the eastern seaboard had innumerable distinct dialects.

There is another possible explanation for why the two natives were taken: the majority aboard, with or without Hudson's blessing, were bent on retribution. They took the men because they felt like it, because they would not suffer anyone to cross them without having to pay a price.

SEPTEMBER 10 WAS the sixth consecutive day of fair weather. But for the single reconnoiter by the ship's boat, the *Half Moon* had been holed up in Rockaway Inlet the entire time. A ship's day as recorded in the log formally begins at noon, after a sun sight is taken (although Juet's journal is written according to normal calendar days), and it was Hudson's habit while at anchor, if he was not feeling hurried, to wait until the noon sight was made on a stable, anchored ship before moving ahead. Observational margins of error were so endemic to navigation that Hudson and Juet would have taken every opportunity to get fixes and compare their individual results, even when the ship had not actually been moved in the past twenty-four hours.

They departed Rockaway Inlet around noon, sailing over to the approaches to Verrazzano Narrows. They felt their way gingerly over the East Bank, the broad sweep of shallows south and east of Coney Island, and when the soundings recovered to seven fathoms, they anchored for another night.

"The bank is sand," Juet wrote, by which he may have meant the shoaling water of East Bank rather than the shore. The *Half Moon* was probably just west of Coney Island, with the Narrows right ahead and the sandy coast of Coney as well as Gravesend Bay to the east. Dutch settlers named this place Grave Sant, or Grave Sand. Colonists would recover stone tools at Gravesend by the wheelbarrow load, and it was also said to be a place where the Canarsie made wampum, the shell beads that served in part as currency. A 1639 Dutch map placed a longhouse here denoting a native settlement labeled *wick Quawanck*. If the men Hudson had snatched were Canarsie, one imagines that people gathered on the shore, to gaze in anguish on the anchored vessel in which two of their number were imprisoned and unlikely ever to be seen again.

Perhaps Hudson waited for another day because the tide had turned against him, with the ebb (a current stronger than the flood) surging through the Narrows. Later in his journal Juet would indicate that the approaches to the Narrows were extensively sounded, and so the *Half Moon* also could have paused while the ship's boat heaved the lead line and probed the depths in and around the channel, and over to the West Bank at Staten Island. In any event, they were content to wait before seeing the upper bay.

The eleventh was again fair, but the weather "very hot." There was another protracted wait to get under way. More soundings could have been made in the meantime. Beyond the need to make the daily sun sight, the timing of the tide would have been important in tackling the Narrows, as the wind was faint, out of the south-southeast. Riding the flood would have made sense, and at one in the afternoon they began to sound their way forward, finding as many as fourteen fathoms. Then the soundings retreated to five fathoms, and the upper bay opened before them between today's ferry docks on Staten Island and Owl's Head over on the Brooklyn shore.

They anchored, possibly right where this vista struck them. Thomas Pownall described the view on passing through the Narrows in the mid-eighteenth century as that of "a kind of Amphitheatre, to appearance circular, about 12 miles in diameter." As Juet observed, "We saw that it was a very good harbor for all winds, and rode all night." In that entire Friday—the first September 11 in New York's history to matter—they might have progressed five miles. The scale of their discovery, now shared by all on board and not just the four men who had survived the Colman survey jaunt, had veritably stopped them in their tracks.

As THE HEART of one of the world's great commercial ports and urban centers, today's upper bay bears only the slightest resemblance to the one Hudson entered. Were Hudson resurrected and taken back to the Narrows, by squinting hard he might just barely be able to recognize where he was. A major distraction for Hudson would be the architectural skyline, which obscures the natural features—in F. Scott Fitzgerald's oft-quoted words in *The Great Gatsby*, the "fresh, green breast of the new world" that had "flowered once for Dutch sailors' eyes." The skyscrapers would rob him of his perception of the place as much as tearing down all the buildings would ours.

New York City has about 8.3 million residents today (which doesn't include all the commuters who cram into Manhattan on a weekday, or the tourists). There were about 8 million people in all of Spain, circa 1600. Queens and Bronx counties together have 3.6 million, with another 1.4 million in two of the counties (Hudson and Essex) over on the Jersey shore. Together, these four counties eclipse the number of people alive in England (about 4.5 million) at the time the *Half Moon* visited. Staten Island, with a population of around 450,000, has twice as many residents (200,000 to 250,000) as were living in Hudson's great metropolis of London.

Beyond the sheer scale of humanity, Hudson would be struck by how much smaller the upper bay had become in his four-century absence.

Until the late nineteenth century, and in some respects well into the twentieth, Hudson would have had an easy time recognizing where he was. For despite the urbanization, the upper bay's essential contours were not radically changed before the First World War. Manhattan, to be sure, had undergone significant waterfront changes, with piers, especially on the East River, and infilling in lower Manhattan, expanding the island's shoreline.

The shore of lower Manhattan when Hudson arrived was about a quarter mile inland from its present limits, extending only as far west into the Hudson River as Greenwich Street (the shore road of the seventeenth century) and about as far south as State Street, where it follows the general curve of what was once the island tip and becomes Water Street, which in turn was about as far as the island extended into the East River. The Kapsee (Copsey) rocks, glacial erratics that the *American Coast Pilot* of 1822 warned of, a hundred yards off the Battery (and on which Danckaerts and Sluyter ran aground after descending the river from present-day Albany), have long been built over. Essentially all of today's Battery Park was river bottom when Hudson visited; Castle Clinton, in the heart of today's park, was a fortification placed well into the river, on the end of a causeway, when completed in 1811. The major changes over on the New Jersey side were much later to arrive, with many occurring only since the 1950s in the tremendous expansion of the port lands.

The upper bay as Hudson found it spanned about five miles from the upper Narrows in the south to the Battery on lower Manhattan Island in the north, and five miles again (at its greatest width) from Bergen Neck in the west to Gowanus Bay on the Brooklyn shore in the east. The major change has been the bay's tremendous east-west narrowing, with the expansion of essentially every shoreline in some fashion. Gowanus Bay and the waterfront around Red Hook would be largely claimed by Erie Basin and the Brooklyn docklands. On the west side, development of the New Jersey port lands would obliterate much of the Jersey Flats.

The islands of the future harbor would expand as well. The Dutch in the early seventeenth century learned that Governors Island was called by the natives Pagganck, or Nut Island, because of its hickories, oaks, and chestnuts. Long an important military facility, it was massively expanded shortly before the First World War, as the U.S. Army Corps of Engineers dumped almost five million cubic yards of stone excavated in the construction of the Lexington Avenue subway to add more than a hundred acres to its south side, thus more than doubling its size, to 172 acres.

Over on the New Jersey shore, running south from the sand spit of Paulus Neck (which has been absorbed by waterfront expansion), were three small islands, hummocks set within the Jersey Flats. The two northernmost, Ellis and Bedloes (or Bedlow's), became important fixtures of the upper bay in the late nineteenth century through major reengineering.

Before the harbor was properly charted and marked with navigational aids, Bedloes Island was an important guide to pilots entering the harbor at the Narrows. The *American Coast Pilot* of 1822 cautioned to "steer up for Bedlow's Island to avoid the Mud flat, which you leave on your starboard hand; this flat is a kind of oyster bed, or bank of mud and shells, and has not more than 11 feet on it at low water." The mudflat, safely corralled today by buoys, is now known as the Bay Ridge and Gowanus Flats, and Bedloes has become the site of the most prominent navigational aid anywhere in the upper bay, if not the western hemisphere. It was transformed into Liberty Island, as the Statue of Liberty, newly arrived as a gift from France, demanded a pedestal base in 1886. Ellis was turned into New York's federal immigration center in 1892, with a causeway linking the much expanded, now rectangular island to Bergen Neck.

Only the southernmost of the three islands, Oyster, endures, albeit as an unnamed "foul area" in the nautical chart of the upper bay, on the edge of the surviving flats south of Liberty Island. The vanishing of its name is a reminder of the concomitant loss of a highly productive oyster fishery in the greater New York area. Pearl Street on lower Manhattan was so named by the Dutch because of the enormous midden of oyster shells left by native peoples. Relict oyster beds have been discovered upriver in the Tappan Zee, with shells up to 5,500 years old. Upward of half a million barrels of oysters a year were being harvested from local waters in the early nineteenth century, before the fishery was ruined by excessive harvesting, pollution, and habitat loss.

Juet repeatedly mentioned the *Half Moon* receiving oysters from natives, and the Dutch turned Gowanus Bay into a prized source of them for export. The mudflat that the *American Coast Pilot* of 1822 mentioned being "a kind of oyster bed" was part of this bountiful resource. "Oysters are very plentiful in many places," Van der Donck assured his readers in 1655. "Some of these are like the Colchester oysters, and are fit to be eaten raw; others are very large, wherein pearls are frequently found, but as they are of a brownish color, they are not valuable. The large oysters are proper for roasting and stewing. Each of these will fill a spoon and make a good bite. I have seen many in the shell a foot long, and broad in proportion."

Danckaerts and Sluyter described a feast of oysters at a home at "Gouanes" Bay, proclaiming them to be "the best in the country. They are fully as good as those of England, and better than those we ate at Falmouth. I had to try some of them raw. They are large and full, some of them not less than a foot long, and they grow sometimes ten, twelve and sixteen together . . . They pickle the oysters in small casks, and send them to Barbados and the other islands."

The sheer scale of natural resources that once existed in the Hudson River and its coastal estuary is difficult to overstate. Even in writing so as to encourage immigration to the colony, Van der Donck was hard-pressed to exaggerate the bounty. Among his long list of fisheries resources, he noted the following: "Outside at sea, and in some of the bays of the East river, the cod-fish are very plenty; and if we would practice our art and experience

in fishing, we could take ship-loads of cod-fish, for it can be easily accomplished. There are also shell-fish, weekfish, herrings, mackerel, roah, halibut,
scoll, and sheeps-heads."

Danckaerts and Sluyter praised the river's generosity. "The North River
[aka Hudson] abounds with fish of all kinds, throughout from the sea to the
falls, and in the branch which runs up to the lake [believed to be its source].
To relate a single instance: some persons near Albany caught in a single
haul of a common seine between five and six hundred fine shad, bass,
perch, and other fish, and there were, I believe, over five hundred of one
kind. It is not necessary for those who live in the city [of New York], and
other places near the sea, to go to the sea to fish, but they can fish in the
river and waters inside; or even to the Great Bay [Raritan Bay], except such
as live upon it, and they can by means of *fuycks* [truncated cone-shaped
nets] or seines not only obtain fish enough for their daily consumption, but
also to salt, dry, and smoke, for commerce, and to export by shiploads if
they wish, all kinds of them, as the people of Boston do; but the people here
have better land than they have there, where they therefore resort more for
a living to the water."

The waters yielded Atlantic sturgeon (which Hudson's men caught with
a seine) and shad in huge quantities. The Dutch didn't think much of sturgeon, but the English prized the meat and caviar. Both sturgeon and shad
would be seriously overfished in the 1890s (with sturgeon being sold as
"Albany beef"). Striped bass were once a significant commercial catch.
Other fish species like black drum and sheepshead ("an excellent fish,"
wrote Van der Donck) disappeared from the Hudson River estuary in the
twentieth century. Blue crabs, which migrate from the estuary as far north
as Troy, remain a viable commercial catch.

The diversity of the natural environment, with its freshwater and saltwater wetlands, ocean resources, and river habitats, not to mention the forests
and meadows, had offered such a densely varied food resource that it was
little wonder humans had been living there for at least ten thousand years,
judging by archaeological finds on Staten Island, and that the people could
be so generous in their offerings to newcomers when the *Half Moon* arrived.

CHAPTER 18

M ORE VISITORS PADDLED TO THE *Half Moon* on September 11, "making show of love," according to Robert Juet. The natives gave them tobacco and maize, but, Juet related in his usual monotone of suspicion, "we durst not trust them." The *Half Moon* was still near the territory of the Canarsie, which extended at the minimum west into Brooklyn and may have reached the eastern shore of the upper bay, around Gowanus Bay. The people may have been desperate to show their kindness and retrieve the two abducted men, but there was no gaining their release.

The following morning, September 12, an armada of canoes turned out, bearing oysters and beans. These visitors seemed to be a new people, given the size of the greeting party and how Juet took care to note that "they have great tobacco pipes of yellow copper, and pots of earth to dress their meat in."

Who they were is anyone's guess. It doesn't help matters that Juet didn't say precisely where the *Half Moon* was, or from what direction the visitors came. And the early history of European contact and settlement around New York is a confusion of tribes and names, which spoke different Algonquian dialects. Disruption of the indigenous population would be rapid and massive, caused by an overwhelming combination of factors. Pathogens (influenza, measles, and smallpox) would radically reduce their numbers. War with the Dutch and other tribes (often arising from trade) would cause death and displacement. Colonization, which involved the purchase of land for pitiable sums, would rapidly move the survivors off their land. By the 1630s, all of the land around Upper New York Bay was essentially in the hands of colonists, with some natives still living on land they had once occupied without any notions of private real estate by paying rent to remain there. Particularly disputed is who was occupying Manhattan Island, as their descendants (if there were any) would ultimately live with the shame of the island having been sold to the Dutch West India Company in 1626 for sixty guilders' worth of trade goods.*

Van Meteren reported Hudson to have entered "as fine a river as can be found, with good anchoring ground on both sides" on September 12. Hudson more than likely, then, was into the first miles of the Hudson River above the Battery that day, and so the people he encountered on September 12 and 13 probably were from Manhattan Island. They would be called the Manhattan, or some variation thereon. In the portion of his journal relating the downbound leg of the Hudson River journey, Juet would state that the land on one side of the river was called Manna-hata, but he seems to have mistakenly applied it to the west side, where Hoboken is.†

The historic affiliation of the Manhattan—if there ever was such a group—has been passed among different confederacies whose territories converged on the upper bay. Historians and anthropologists have sometimes assigned them to the Metoac. Others have placed them in the Wappinger confederacy, which occupied the east bank of the Hudson north to present-day Poughkeepsie and lands east to the Connecticut Valley.

It has also been argued that Manhattan Island was specifically not part of Wappinger territory, and that the island was home to at least one settlement of the Munsee people of the Lenape at the time of Dutch colonization. In present-day north Greenwich Village, where West Fourteenth Street,

---

*The amount for which Manhattan was said to be sold by the natives to the Dutch is routinely reported to have been twenty-four dollars, but this derives from nineteenth-century histories. Relative purchasing power of currency over many centuries is anything but exact. However, the sixty guilders in trade goods was the modern equivalent of about eight hundred dollars—still a shockingly small sum for what would become some of the world's most expensive real estate. The payment would cover one month's rent on about four square feet of commercial real estate in lower Manhattan in the early twenty-first century.

† Further complicating the matter are the labels on the so-called Velasco Map, which must have derived its portrait of the region from materials from Hudson's voyage. It labels the west side of the lower Hudson River *Manahata* and the east side *Manahatin*. See page 256.

Greenwich Avenue, and Eighth Avenue converge, was a shoreline settlement called Sapokanikan. Now about half a mile inland from the river, it was set on a trout stream and surrounded by agricultural plantings. A Dutch tobacco plantation would be established at Sapokanikan in 1629, after the people moved west of the Bronx River in 1626. This new Dutch settlement was called Noortwyck, but in the 1670s a man named Yellis Mandeville acquired the property and gave it the name of his former home on western Long Island: Greenwyck. The name in turn would be anglicized to Greenwich.

Recent analysis has argued that the people specifically of lower Manhattan were a group of Canarsie, the Marechkawieck, who also controlled the islands of the East River as well as Brooklyn, and that the Canarsie themselves were related to the Munsee, who (to complicate matters) ought be viewed as a dialectic subgroup of the Lenape. Furthermore, this approach to historic ethnography holds that the Lenape should be defined more as a language subgroup of Algonquian rather than according to European conventions of territory, politics, or even clan.

According to this version of ethnohistory, the Marechkawieck (long gone) draw the short straw in the unhappy contest to decide which local native group unloaded the entirety of Manhattan for sixty guilders in trade goods in 1626. They were occupying Governors Island when the first contingent of colonists arrived in 1624, and they had a settlement on lower Manhattan at present-day Foley Square, where two ponds fed by freshwater springs, the Collect and Little Collect, existed at the time of New Amsterdam. A trail ran from their settlement at the springs to the lower Manhattan waterfront; the Dutch would turn it into Brede Way, today's Broadway. They also sold the land around Hell Gate to the Dutch in 1637.

The very origin of the name Manhattan is in dispute. It might have meant "people of the island" in an Algonquian dialect. Others have argued that *mannahata*, as Juet essentially recorded it, was a Lenape word meaning "hilly island." And Heckewelder, in recording the first-contact stories of the people he encountered in 1760, asserted that *Manahachtanienk* meant "the island where we all became intoxicated." Van der Donck, who acquired some facility with native languages (and asserted that natives had no specific word for intoxication, instead equating it with foolishness) applied "Manhattan" to all people who spoke one of four native language groups known to the colonists. In addition to natives actually living on Manhattan

Island, he wrote in *A Description of New Netherland*, "we include those who live in the neighboring places along the North river, on Long Island, and at the Neversink." But by the time Van der Donck arrived in New Netherland, in 1641, the disruption of native groups was so profound that his observations may not bear the slightest resemblance to the distribution of peoples in 1609.

Whoever the people were who appeared en masse to greet Hudson with oysters and ceramic pots of meat on September 12, they were not allowed to board the *Half Moon*, although trading occurred. Juet's hostility reached absurd levels when he recounted how "there came eight and twenty canoes full of men, women and children to betray us." More visitors appeared on the thirteenth, only four canoes now, bearing a "great store of very good oysters." And while some were purchased, no one was again allowed to board.

De Laet preserved one valuable journal entry by Hudson that described the land and the people at latitude 40 degrees, 48 minutes. As de Laet also mentioned that the natives brought "very fine oysters to the ship" and Hudson further took note of copper tobacco pipes, this appeared to relate to Juet's events of September 12 and 13. A literal interpretation of the latitude fix would place Hudson in the river around West 100th Street, opposite the ten clay tennis courts of Riverside Park; the usual margins of error in fixes would have him at least five miles up or down the river from there. That was well within paddling distance of Sapokanikan, but as even sedentary agricultural groups of natives tended to relocate villages every twenty to thirty years to allow the land to lie fallow, there is no guarantee that anyone would have been living at Sapokanikan specifically when Hudson was in the area.* There is also the matter of the Marechkawieck to consider.

"It is as pleasant a land as one need tread upon," Hudson opined of the land in de Laet's account, "very abundant in all kinds of timber suitable for shipbuilding, and for making large casks or vats. The people had copper tobacco pipes, from which I inferred that copper might naturally exist there; and iron likewise according to the testimony of the natives, who, however, do not understand preparing it for use."

---

* As no archaeological resources survive in the area of Sapokanikan, it's impossible to say who lived there when, in what numbers, and for how long. The only precontact archaeological sites on Manhattan Island are at the northern end, and in the east and southeast. We're otherwise reliant on Dutch colonial records in identifying peoples at the time of contact, and the difficulties therein by now should be apparent to the reader.

Hudson would have questioned the natives who paddled to him with their oysters about the noted metals—if not shouting out queries of the availability of *mattassin* and *usawassin*, then pointing to objects (the copper pipes of the natives, the iron of his own hardware) and attempting to secure pantomimed answers about where one might find more.

Hudson's reference to land "tread upon" doesn't mean he stepped on it himself. There is no indication from Juet that Hudson or anyone else actually left the ship on these days, and it's doubtful they did so. In fact, once through the Narrows, Juet does not report the ship's boat being deployed, and it would have been unusual for him to repeatedly overlook such a key operation. Hudson instead would have casually observed the wooded cover of Manhattan from the vantage point of the *Half Moon*'s deck and drawn his own speculative if obvious conclusions about the timber resources. There hasn't been an explorer worth mentioning who could not gaze upon a virgin forest and come up with a valuable natural resource. Hudson's fail-

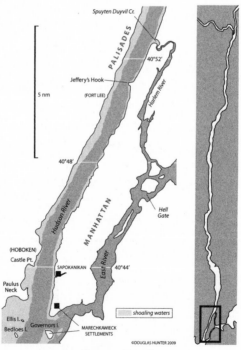

Spuyten Duyvil.

ure to point out any particular species may be considered a further indication that he went nowhere near any particular tree on those days.

HUDSON CONCLUDED SUNDAY, September 13, at anchor somewhere off Manhattan's West Side. His progress had been outwardly slow, as it had been three days since he had gained the Narrows, but the pace was actually strikingly quick—because Hudson was not taking the time to properly investigate and survey the upper bay.

The East River went unnoticed. Manhattan was never recognized as an island. Hudson never sounded around Governors Island, much less identified it or any other island in the upper bay. And because the ship's boat was not sent out after passing through the Narrows, no one went ashore or attempted a rudimentary survey based on triangulation—observing key landmarks from different vantage points, and using the angles (or compass points) of observation to then map out the basic dimensions of the upper bay. A grand mythopoetic scene of Hudson planting perhaps the first European footprint on Manhattan Island before a crowd of awestruck natives most certainly never happened. And while Colman's party intriguingly had reported a "sea" at the western end of Kill Van Kull, there was no second look.

Fear of another attack probably dissuaded Hudson from again deploying the ship's boat on any assignment. Having lost Colman, the first person Hudson would have turned to for future surveying was Juet, whose suspicion of and hostility toward even the most welcoming natives was at fever pitch. And even if Juet had been willing to lead a party in the ship's boat, Hudson would have been left to calculate the risks of being left with his son on a ship full of Dutchmen who might view Juet's absence as an opportunity to seize command.

Even when he had a ship full of Englishmen on his other voyages, Hudson was careful about managing the risks his own crew could pose. He appears never to have left the ship in 1607, when the *Hopewell* called at Spitsbergen. On the 1608 *Hopewell* voyage to Novaya Zemlya, he never joined any of the shore parties, nor apparently did his son John. When Hudson sent out the shallop to kill a walrus at Novaya Zemlya, he ordered the entire crew to go with Juet, leaving only himself and his son aboard the

Hopewell. Hudson avoided being in a position in which the crew could strand him ashore or a hostile faction could overwhelm him on the ship. While he had gone ashore with the crew in the Faeroes, he had otherwise stuck close to his command on the *Half Moon* voyage. Juet gave no indication that Hudson went ashore at La Have. Men were sent ashore in the shallop at Cape Cod, and Hudson evidently didn't join them, instead having the lone native brought aboard to be entertained. At Rockaway Inlet, Hudson stayed so close to the ship when he went on dry land that he did not know the Canarsie lived in any kind of shelter.

Security, then, in all its permutations, would have been an important factor in Hudson's failure to make any effort to assess the upper bay. But it may not have been the most important one. While he would not have relished sending the ship's boat back into Kill Van Kull (and volunteers would have been in short supply), he could have investigated in the *Half Moon* (as the Dutch would quickly learn to use Arthur Kill, Newark Bay, and Kill Van Kull as an alternate route into and out of the upper bay area). And nothing was preventing him from using the ship to see the many other aspects of the upper bay.

The truth was, Hudson was running out of time. The equinox, which then fell around September 29, was only about two weeks away and would mark the astronomical end of summer, as total daylight hours then became fewer than those of night. The crew would have been most sensitive to the coincidental approach of Michaelmas, or the Feast of St. Michael, on September 29. As one of the "quarter days" in the calendar that marked the beginning of a season, it would herald the arrival of autumn. Fishermen who ventured across the North Atlantic and dried cod at shore stations knew it as a cue to begin packing up to return home.

Hudson needed to finish up with his explorations soon if he was to safely recross the Atlantic—or not be forced to do so by his crew. Given the choice between making a thorough investigation of the upper bay and probing the river course leading north to the west of Manhattan, Hudson plainly chose the latter. It was the river that captivated him, rather than the future site of New York City, which was in so many ways superior to Jamestown's location. As soon as he could be through the upper bay, he was.

The question, of course, is: why? And the answer lay in the history of the river itself. Not as a place explored by Verrazzano or anyone else but as a possible passage of great significance, whose nature had been debated for decades. In turning aside the opportunity to assess the upper bay, Henry Hudson was back sailing through the literature of exploration, an evidentiary journey that logged as many miles in France as it did in England and North America.

CHAPTER 19

I N 1535–36, THE FRENCH EXPLORER Jacques Cartier made his second voyage to the St. Lawrence River. About fifty miles downstream from present-day Montréal, he inspected the mouth of another river that flowed into it from the south. Native guides informed him that it provided a passage all the way to the Atlantic coast of "Florida," which for Cartier (and the Spanish) was a highly flexible geographic label that reached well up the eastern seaboard.

Cartier never investigated this river or the passage it promised. But his sidelong consideration proved highly influential in the emerging perception of eastern North America, in no small part because his exploits were revered in England. In the late sixteenth and early seventeenth centuries, his three voyages were better known there than they were in his native France.

Cartier's legacy had Richard Hakluyt to thank for that. The accounts of his first two voyages were known only from Italian versions published by Ramusio in 1556. (Manuscript versions survived in France but would not be discovered until the nineteenth century. The royal geographer, André Thevet, who claimed to have known Cartier personally, wasn't even aware of them.) Hakluyt had the Ramusio accounts translated and published in English in 1580. A French translation from Ramusio would not be published until 1598. And in his second edition of *Principal Navigations*, Hakluyt published a partial transcription of an account of Cartier's third and final voyage to the St. Lawrence of 1541–42, which remains the only known version, as the original manuscript has never been found.

Hakluyt was a dedicated Francophile where exploration lore was con-cerned. As a young ordained priest in the Church of England, he had been assigned to the Elizabethan court's Paris embassy, where he served in the 1580s. By then he was already devoted to the possibilities of passage-making and overseas colonization, and his appointment was an official excuse for him to be in France, rummaging in that country's exploration memories.

France was losing serious momentum in overseas ventures, due to de-bilitating wars of religion that came to include a protracted armed struggle by Henry of Navarre to claim the throne as Henry IV. Hakluyt meanwhile was learning whatever he could about French overseas activities during his time in Paris and in the years following.

He tracked down Étienne Bellenger, who had tried unsuccessfully to es-tablish a New World trading base in 1583, exploring Acadia, the Bay of Fundy, and Norumbega. No account in France existed, and Hakluyt gathered di-rectly from Bellenger (whose name he anglicized to Stephen Bellinger) everything that survives. In the process Hakluyt secured a map of Bellenger's explorations drawn by Jacques de Vaulx, which he gave to Edward Hayes, and which has never been seen.

Hakluyt also secured letters written by a trader named Jacques Noël, a nephew of Cartier who had been active in eastern North America in the 1580s. Among other things, Noël asserted that up the St. Lawrence, beyond the Lachine Rapids (as we now call them), there was a great lake around lat-itude 44. That latitude agreed with the source of the St. Lawrence in eastern Lake Ontario, which no one otherwise was known to have seen. Hakluyt also gathered evidence about the nature of the St. Lawrence and the waters beyond from a Basque named Stevan de Bocall, whose experiences were highly respected in England in the 1590s.

This industrious fact-finding by Hakluyt was forming the body of knowl-edge that would underpin English ambitions in eastern North America in the first decade of the seventeenth century and ultimately help explain what Hudson himself never would: why the river flowing into Upper New York Bay so gripped his attention.

SOME OF HAKLUYT'S French and Basque intelligence made it into print, but much of it did not, as he preserved the most sensitive material for sharing with men like Edward Hayes, whose theory of a midcontinental passage was evolving. This ferment of ideas and observations could not be entirely contained. The treatise of Hayes as expressed in Brereton's *A Briefe and True Relation* of 1602 plainly tapped into it. But the ferment had also bubbled forth in Edward Wright's influential 1599 world chart, which Hakluyt reproduced in volume 3 of the second edition of *Principal Navigations*, in 1600.

Wright's vision drew on England's first globe, created by Emery Molyneux in 1593, for which Jodocus Hondius—the same Hondius who advised Hudson on his VOC contract—did the engraving. Wright's chart featured two noteworthy passages in eastern North America. One indicated that the St. Lawrence originated in a single, protean Great Lake, called Tadouac, which in turn was connected to the Northern Sea. The other passage, derived from Cartier's 1535–36 voyage report, connected the St. Lawrence and the Atlantic coast. It had first appeared as the Norumbega River in a 1556 map that accompanied Ramusio's publication of Cartier's first voyage account, with its northern end near present-day Montréal, and it also appeared in maps by John Dee and Michael Lok in 1582. Wright called it Rio da Gamas. Ironically, despite its Hispanic name, the Spanish considered it to be a notion of the French and the English.

It was impossible to look at Wright's chart and not recognize that the passage reported by Cartier might reach the Atlantic right about where Verrazzano had found the excellent harbor and river mouth at Angoulême. Four years after Wright's chart was reproduced and popularized by Hakluyt in 1600, fresh intelligence on the matter of both passages emerged in France. To secure it, all one had to do was read a revealing book that had just been published in Paris by a new face in exploration: Samuel de Champlain.

CHAMPLAIN MIGHT HAVE been in his early thirties, about the same age as Henry Hudson, when he appeared in northeastern North America for the first time, in the summer of 1603. He had been attached to a new fur trade monopoly for the St. Lawrence, without any authority in the enterprise. His personal history was complicated and ambiguous, but he had appeared in military records for the first time in 1595, serving in Henry IV's army in Brittany, where Spanish forces were resisting Henry's claim to the French throne. A payroll notation saw him compensated for a "secret" voyage or

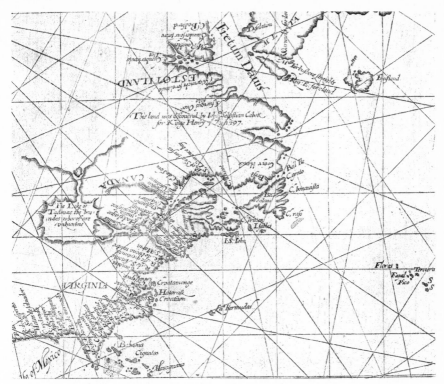

Eastern North America, as it appears in Edward Wright's world map of 1599.
Note the protean Great Lake, Tadouac, with a passage northward as well as a
further passage leading from the upper St. Lawrence to the eastern seaboard.
(Image courtesy John Carter Brown Library.)

journey made for Henry. We don't know what that assignment entailed, but it set a pattern for Champlain for the coming years. He was something of a spy, an intelligence officer of Henry IV.

After the Treaty of Vervins secured a fragile peace between France and Spain in 1598 and acknowledged Henry's claim to the French throne, Champlain made his way to the Spanish Caribbean, where he spent the better part of two years skulking around. After returning to France in 1601, he made a report to Henry on what he'd seen and at this time was probably awarded the pension that also made him a captain-in-ordinary of the French navy, even though he never commanded a naval vessel; France in any case scarcely had any naval vessels to speak of at the time.

By early 1603, he was ready for a new assignment, the trip to the St. Lawrence in the company of the new trade monopoly. While Champlain had no official role, it would become clear that he had been attached to the trade venture so that he could report back on any evidence of a passage to the Orient beyond the Lachine Rapids at present-day Montréal. While Champlain would never admit as much, and the limited French documents relating to the venture are equally silent, the circumstantial evidence in Champlain's own reportage points to the publication of the bestselling *A Briefe and True Relation* the previous autumn as a prime motivator not only for his inclusion in the 1603 journey but for the new trade monopoly's marching orders.

There was much in this popular new English work for the French to absorb, especially since so much of the geographic intelligence contained in the materials contributed by Hayes (and likely with the participation of Hakluyt) had a French (or French Basque) source and dealt with geography the French considered to be New France. However it got there, by early 1603 the information in *A Briefe and True Relation* certainly was in circulation at the Fontainebleau court of Henry IV.

The Hayes materials had such an impact because, in his convoluted effort to support the English colonization and exploration of Norumbega, Hayes first had to make the case for what lay beyond the Lachine Rapids, and why he no longer thought the St. Lawrence should be a focus of English ambitions. In the process of explaining why the route beyond the rapids led to the Northern Sea, which he now argued should be avoided, Hayes brought to bear the hitherto confidential materials gathered by Hakluyt from his French and Basque sources. France had lost so much momentum in its overseas ventures during the wars of religion and succession that the information brought to light by Hayes was of profound interest to the new king and the merchants and nobles he favored with the new trade monopoly.

At the time the book was published, Henry was trying to broker a deal between bickering merchants in his country over rights to the fur trade in Canada. As soon as the information in *A Briefe and True Relation* became available, there was suddenly a trade monopoly with verve and direction, and particular goals in determining a route to the Orient beyond the rapids. Champlain was tasked to the St. Lawrence, to travel up the river and see for himself what was there, and what might be beyond the rapids.

When he returned at the end of the trading season, Champlain published his first book, *Des Sauvages*, a slim volume of about four thousand words, relating his summer of adventures and observations. The book revealed that he was a veritable disciple of Edward Hayes, in the way he articulated his findings from 1603 and argued what the French should do next. Champlain may never have read *A Briefe and True Relation*, instead absorbing its findings and arguments secondhand, as part of his 1603 assignment. But he appears to have fudged his most crucial findings from 1603 in order to concur with the evidence put forth by Hayes for some kind of passage beyond the rapids.

When Champlain was unable to get past the rapids, he questioned native guides about what lay beyond them. Champlain came away with the most detailed word-picture yet of the Great Lakes system, including Lake Ontario, Niagara Falls, Lake Erie, and a great body of water beyond that would have been Lake Huron. Those findings were genuine. But Champlain also included an odd bit of testimony from a young Algonquin on the way back downriver from the rapids, who allegedly described for him a peculiar, and suspiciously familiar, hydrological phenomenon.

As a new translation by Janet Ritch relates, according to this young Algonquin, after proceeding beyond the rapids and several lakes, a traveler entered "a very large lake, which may extend some 300 leagues in length. Proceeding some hundred leagues into the said lake, they encounter an island which is very big where, beyond the said island, the water is drinkable. But he told us that, continuing on some hundred leagues further, the water is still worse. Arriving at the end of the said lake, the water is totally salty. He told us that there is a fall which may extend for a league in width, from where an exceedingly great current of water descends into the said lake. Past this rapid, one no longer sees any land, either on the one side or on the other, but a sea so great that they have not seen the end of it, nor heard of anyone who may have seen it."

This third interview closed the deal for Champlain. The distance from the rapids "to the salt sea, which is possibly the South Sea, is some 400 leagues," he wrote in *Des Sauvages*. "It is not to be doubted, then, according to their statement, that this is none other than the South Sea, the sun setting where they say."

Champlain's proof for a route to the South Sea beyond the rapids hinged on this final interview, which was fundamentally different from the credible information he had already gathered from guides at the rapids. In describing a strange lake with freshwater at one end and saltwater at the other, with a sea beyond of which no one had seen the end, Champlain was parroting a fundamental observation by Hayes in *A Briefe and True Relation*.

Hayes had written that, according to Jacques Noël, the rapids "did lead into a mighty lake, which at the entrance was fresh, but beyond, was bitter or salt; the end whereof was unknown." No such statement had been attributed to Noël by Hakluyt in *Principal Navigations*, which meant that either Hayes was privy to unpublished Noël intelligence provided to him by Hakluyt or that Hayes's information had been cross-contaminated by intelligence gathered from the Basque informant, Stevan de Bocall. Either way, Champlain had no known source of his own for this material, and so must have copied the Hayes evidence that had just been published in *A Briefe and True Relation*. He had done so in order to make the case for a midcontinental passage that suited the purposes of powerful Frenchmen. Champlain's reportage was the key to justifying a trade monopoly bestowed by his king that was supposed to finance the proving of a route to the Orient but above all permitted a select group of merchants and nobles to profit exclusively from the local fur trade. Champlain had also done them a major favor in bending the passage route away from the Arctic, as Hayes and Wright had described it, and instead pointing it at the balmy Pacific.

Champlain's evidentiary shenanigans had repercussions beyond France. Richard Hakluyt acquired a copy of *Des Sauvages* and produced an English translation, either on his own or by farming out the job. It was in his papers, unpublished, when he died in 1616 (and would be included in *Purchas His Pilgrimes* in 1625), but Hakluyt most certainly didn't allow it to collect dust. *Des Sauvages* was too important a work not to share with Hakluyt's fellow investors and promoters of the new Virginia scheme of 1606. Its influence was enhanced by a major mistranslation: as the new Ritch translation affirms, all of Champlain's references to "healthy" (*salubre*) water, meaning freshwater, were misread (or deliberately misstated) as "salty" (*salé*), thereby making a more forceful claim for a passage to the Pacific beyond the rapids than even Champlain had.

There is an unmistakable echo of Champlain's fact-finding results in the instructions given to leaders of the flotilla of the London wing of the Virginia Company when it set out to found Jamestown in December 1606. As we've already seen, they were to choose for the colony site a river "which bendeth most toward the North-west for that way you shall soonest find the other sea." There was no previous recorded English expedition to the

Chesapeake, so the idea that the river should bend northwest if the "other" sea was to be reached must have come from careful study of the available evidence. And the recent hard evidence resided in *Des Sauvages*.

Henry Hudson's friend Captain John Smith seemed explicitly indebted to *Des Sauvages* in discussing the passage-making potential of the Potomac River in his *Map of Virginia*, published in 1612. Its headwaters, he asserted, were in nearby mountains, beyond which was "a great salt water, which by all likelihood is either some part of Commoda [Canada], some great lake, or some inlet of some sea that falleth into the South sea."

Another connection to *Des Sauvages* turned up in a delirious letter to James I written in December 1607 by George Popham, president of the Sagadahoc colony of the West Country wing of the 1606 Virginia Company. Popham had written that the Kennebec River led inland to saltwater only seven days' journey from the colony, saltwater that "can be none other than the Southern Ocean, stretching towards the land of China which doubtless cannot be far away from this region." Popham's observation was strikingly close to Champlain's conclusions in *Des Sauvages* about the great lake upstream of the rapids: "It is not to be doubted, then, according to their statement, that this is none other than the South Sea."

Champlain's little book resonated so persuasively with the Virginia colonization and passage-seeking scheme because his logic was purely Hayesean. He wrote that on his return he had delivered a report to Henry IV "on the feasibility of discovering the passage to China, without the inconveniences of the ice of the north or the heats of the torrid zone."

The scheme Champlain advocated was precisely the one Hayes had urged on the Virginia venture: establish a colony on a navigable river that led deep into the interior, which would provide via a portage access to another river or passage leading to the Pacific—in his worldview, the passage he claimed to have ascertained above the Lachine Rapids. Champlain argued that the French should move their efforts out of the St. Lawrence (just as Hayes advised his fellow English to abandon the idea of a St. Lawrence base, which he had advocated in the early 1590s with Carleill) and establish themselves on the Atlantic coast, as "it is certain that there are rivers on the coast of Florida, not yet discovered, extending into the interior, where the land is very good and fertile, and containing very good harbours."

Hayes had proposed that the English colonize the coast somewhere between latitudes 40 and 44. In November 1603, Henry IV granted Pierre du Gua, Sieur de Monts, a noble from Champlain's Saintonge region on the Bay of Biscay who had participated in that summer's venture, a ten-year trade monopoly whose lower limit coincidentally was set at latitude 40. While his rights included the St. Lawrence, de Monts followed the Hayes/Champlain advice in choosing a base of operations. Subletting his trading rights on the St. Lawrence, de Monts went looking for a suitable site in Norumbega. In the summer of 1604, Champlain was again in North America, attached in no formal way to de Monts's monopoly, yet mapping Norumbega while searching for the river into the interior that would provide the eastern leg of the passage to the Pacific.

The French and English who were striving to establish colonies linked to passage-seeking in eastern North America at the beginning of the seventeenth century were in a kind of intellectual echo chamber, their ideas reverberating in each others' plans and reports. It was a new, literate age of exploration, with much material that used to be squirreled away in hand-written manuscripts suddenly becoming available for everyone to read, regardless of nationality, as the propaganda potential of voyage reports was seized by promoters as a way of raising merchant capital and currying royal favor.

But it seems the French and English participants in this echo chamber also had been attuned to even earlier reverberations. Decades before Edward Hayes had begun formulating his transcontinental passage theory, a strikingly similar one had been formed in the Spanish New World.

This earlier theory's architect, Pedro Menéndez de Avilés, had begun commanding Spanish treasure fleets in 1554; he would establish San Agustín in 1565 and be named governor of Cuba in 1568. In 1554, Menéndez met a Basque sailor who claimed to have crossed North America in the 1540s with a band of French pirates. After proceeding up what would have been the St. Lawrence River and entering a great bay, on the other side of a portage of only a quarter league they found an arm of the sea leading west to the Pacific. They paused here to build four brigs and sailed on to the far ocean. Menéndez also believed that this great bay, upstream of the St. Lawrence, could also be reached from the Atlantic coast via a river called Salado, which he evidently thought reached the sea in the Chesapeake. He expressed these ideas in letters to Jesuit officials in the 1560s in an effort to encourage a mission on the Chesapeake. When Río Salado began appearing on selected maps, it seemed to be equated with the Potomac or the Susquehanna River.

One has to wonder if Hayes and Champlain had found their separate courses to the Spaniard's notions. Intelligence from Spain could have reached the English by the 1580s, with Menéndez's idea of a great bay upstream of the St. Lawrence helping shape the concept of Lake Tadouac in Edward Wright's map. Indeed, the midcontinental passage concept can be seen in an unpublished 1582 circumpolar chart by John Dee. For his part, Champlain conspicuously had spent more than two years wandering the Spanish Caribbean, where the late governor's notions could have been in circulation—right before *A Briefe and True Relation* was published and Champlain made his first visit to the Lachine Rapids. Champlain's ideas in *Des Sauvages* do seem to be a blend of Hayes and Menéndez, suggesting he absorbed on his own more about the ideas originating with Menéndez than what may have been filtered by Hayes. And the key to success in all of these multinational scenarios was discovering a river that would lead deep into the continent and provide a route to the Pacific.

CHAPTER 20

B Y 1604, THE CAREERS OF SAMUEL de Champlain and Henry Hudson were converging, even if Hudson had not yet made his own appearance in the historical record. From 1604 to 1607, Champlain was active on the Norumbega coast with the de Monts monopoly, which was based initially at Ste-Croix, an island on the modern Maine–New Brunswick border, and then at Port Royal, tucked up into the Annapolis Basin on Nova Scotia's Bay of Fundy shore. Champlain foremost was trying to find the Norumbega River, the first leg of his envisioned midcontinental passage. In the course of four summers of exploration, it was a small miracle that Champlain never ran into his English contemporaries, although he came very close.

In the summer of 1605, Champlain called at the Georges River with a party led by the Sieur de Monts and met a Pemaquid chief named Annasou. "He told us that there was a ship, ten leagues off the harbour, which was engaged in fishing, and that those on her had killed five savages of this river, under cover of friendship," Champlain would recount in his next book, Les Voyages of 1613. "From his description of the men on the vessel, we concluded that they were English."

Champlain now knew for certain that the French would not have this coast to themselves. He had correctly guessed the nationality of the interlopers. The ship was the *Archangel*, and her captain was none other than George Waymouth, the man whose explorations of the Georges River area that season would attract Henry Hudson and the *Half Moon* in 1609.

It turned out that the *Archangel* was gone. About two months had passed since the incident, which was not, as we know, a massacre (although the Pemaquid chief's worst fears were understandable) but a mass kidnapping. Visits by the English to Norumbega were accumulating, as momentum built toward the establishment of the North Virginia colony of Sagadahoc on the Kennebec. Only the accidents of history continued to prevent them from crossing paths with Champlain while ranging up and down the same short stretch of Atlantic coast, encountering many of the same native people and admiring many of the same rivers and harbors.

The Kennebec River was assessed by Champlain in 1605, two years before the Plymouth wing of the Virginia Company established its short-lived colony there. Champlain didn't think much of its settlement potential and correctly gathered from the natives that the river, through portages, would only lead to the St. Lawrence, not the South Sea, as George Popham alleged. Champlain appeared to take heed of an assertion Jacques Noël made, via Hakluyt, that a bay on the Atlantic coast at latitude 42 might "pass through." This location agreed with Massachusetts Bay, and Champlain probed it in July 1605. A river there, which would be called the Charles by Captain John Smith, was named for de Monts. "It stretches, as it seemed to me, towards the Iroquois," Champlain remarked hopefully, and without any evidence at all.

The Charles was hardly the great watercourse that he would indicate on his 1612 map of New France, stretching westward into Iroquois territory. Its headwaters were actually only a few meandering miles away, in what is now the Boston suburbs. Still, Champlain seemed confident that he might have found an important component of the passage between the St. Lawrence and the Atlantic coast, as he understood its configuration. As it turned out, this was a passage both he and Henry Hudson, utterly unaware of one another, would attempt to prove in the very same year.

CHAMPLAIN HAD INITIALLY come at this passage from the north, during his 1603 investigations of the St. Lawrence. He was traveling in a pinnace with a veteran of the fur trade, François Gravé, Sieur du Pont (whom Champlain called Pont-Gravé). En route to the rapids, they paused at the mouth of the very same river flowing into the St. Lawrence from the south that had attracted the attention of Cartier. The River of the Iroquois led into

DOUGLAS HUNTER

the territory of the enemies of the main native peoples with whom the French traded: the Montagnais (Naskapi) people of the north shore of the lower St. Lawrence, the Algonquin of the Ottawa River valley, and the Huron (Wendat) from southern Georgian Bay in the central Great Lakes. In fact a war party of the trading allies had assembled and was about to head upriver.

Champlain and Pont-Gravé were so intrigued that they wanted to join them. But passage on the river, now called the Richelieu, was blocked by the Chambly Rapids. They tried to have their pinnace dragged past the white water but could not force it through the trees, and the current upstream was too much for the smaller skiff they were carrying, which helped convince Champlain of the ingenuity of the birchbark canoe. Unable to accompany the war party, Champlain instead had them describe the route south.

Champlain was informed that at the head of this river was a large lake "some forty or fifty leagues long, and some twenty-five wide, into which as many as ten rivers flow." Beyond the large lake, a portage led to another lake. At the end of that lake was an Iroquois encampment. Nearby was a river "extending to the coast of Florida, a distance of perhaps some one hundred or one hundred and forty leagues from the latter lake."

Champlain's use of "leagues" was erratic and flexible, but his account in *Des Sauvages* proved to be highly accurate. He had just described the essential components of the passage that Cartier had previously heard about and that repeatedly had been drawn as a single waterway between the St. Lawrence and the Atlantic coast, most recently by Edward Wright. Champlain actually knew nothing about Cartier's findings (an impressive level of ignorance for a French explorer), but he must have been aware of the cartographic evidence, especially a map as recent and as famous as Wright's. So he knew that there was a transportation corridor, but instead of being a single continuous passage, it involved the River of the Iroquois, two lakes, and a short portage to another river that ran to the ocean for about two hundred miles.

And as Champlain's description of this corridor was in *Des Sauvages*, which Hakluyt had translated and would have made available to the leading figures in the English colonization and passage-seeking effort, one has to ask: Had Hudson, too, read about this corridor, before making the *Half Moon* voyage? Did he suspect that the river flowing into Upper New York

Bay might be the one of 100 to 140 leagues described by Champlain? Or was he holding out hope that Edward Wright and earlier cartographers were correct and that a passage navigable by ship ran from the coast to the upper St. Lawrence?

As it turned out, Champlain had already embarked on his own quest to solve the matter for himself in early July 1609, while Hudson was still comfortably far removed, approaching the Grand Banks off Newfoundland in the *Half Moon*.

CHAMPLAIN COULD THANK the violent indiscretions of Dutch sea beggars for his chance to investigate from the north the transportation corridor between the St. Lawrence and the Atlantic coast. In May 1607, the Sieur de Monts had his ten-year monopoly canceled, after Henry IV bowed to pressure from merchants in St-Malo and the French Basque region. It forced him to abandon Port Royal and Champlain to end his explorations of Norumbega. But de Monts was pursuing compensation for the losses he had suffered at Tadoussac in 1606, when the sea beggars in the *White Lion* struck at his ships and carted away their valuable furs. Henry IV took up his cause, sending a diplomatic note of protest to The Hague. And in order to help de Monts recover his losses while his legal actions wended through the courts, Henry agreed to a one-year extension of de Monts's monopoly in October 1607.

De Monts now named Champlain his lieutenant in New France, the first formal role Champlain had secured within a trade monopoly. Champlain was to go to the St. Lawrence and establish a new trading habitation, where the city of Québec now stands.

It was almost the end of Champlain. He hadn't even started building the habitation when a plot to murder him by some of his own men was uncovered. When Champlain learned of it through a conspirator who had second thoughts, the plotters were trying to decide whether to just strangle him or to lure him out at night on some pretext and shoot him.

Champlain organized a trial on which he reserved himself a seat on the jury. Three men were condemned to hang but sent back to France for their execution. Champlain chose to make an example of the ringleader, a locksmith named Jean Duval who had been with him at Port Royal. He had the man hanged, strangled, and decapitated and displayed his head on a pike so that anyone approaching the rising habitation would know what happened to those reckless enough to cross him.

The habitation proved to be its own death sentence. Over the ensuing winter of 1608–9, the men suffered terribly from scurvy and dysentery. Hunting was poor, and the Montagnais around them were forced to eat putrid carrion. In the spring of 1609, twenty of twenty-eight Frenchmen were dead, and of the eight survivors, including Champlain, four were in poor health.

Champlain's first formal command was thus far a disaster. For any hope of long-term success, particularly if another monopoly extension could not be secured, Champlain needed a spectacular achievement. When Pont-Gravé appeared in the spring of 1609 to relieve the desperate establishment, Champlain decided to gamble everything on one grand adventure. He would join native trading allies in a raid on the Iroquois. In so doing, he would forge a special relationship with them that would give him and his commercial associates like de Monts and Pont-Gravé privileged status, should the fur trade be thrown wide open after the one-year monopoly extension expired. Champlain also would be able to travel with the war party south, up the River of the Iroquois and into the lake at its head, and from there, as far as the war party could take him. He could see firsthand what this long-discussed transportation corridor was about.

CHAMPLAIN TRAVELED FOR almost a month with his native war party, accompanied by just two other Frenchmen. They paddled almost the entire length of the large lake, which he named for himself. Nearing the southern end of Lake Champlain, they came to a prominent jog in the increasingly narrow lake: Crown Point, where the British would build a fort in 1759. Waiting for them were some three hundred warriors from the Mohawk, the easternmost tribe in the Iroquois, or Five Nations, confederacy.

War between native groups was highly ritualized. The Mohawk were completing a rough defensive works, and emissaries from both sides agreed to wait until the next morning for battle, so that they could recognize their individual opponents. The three Frenchmen were concealed from the Mohawk until the last possible moment. Each donned light armor and loaded a harquebus, a heavy musket that could fire a lead ball through an oak plank.

Champlain's two French companions took up flanking positions in the woods, to either side of the clearing where the battle was to be joined. Champlain held back in the rear ranks of his allies. He could see the Mohawk advancing and would write that they were "stout and rugged in appearance. They came at a slow pace towards us, with a dignity and assurance that greatly amused me, having three chiefs at their head."

The chiefs could be easily distinguished by the plumes they wore on their heads, and Champlain's allies informed him that "I should do what I could to kill them." To that end, he stuffed four balls down the barrel of his harquebus. He was counting on absolute surprise and a devastating first volley to win the battle and the lifelong esteem of his native companions.

When the forces drew closer, the native allies parted and called him forward. Champlain stepped out alone, a single combat warrior. He was twenty paces ahead of his allies and thirty paces from the Mohawk.

The shock of the sight of Champlain brought the Mohawk force to a halt. Nothing like him had ever been seen before. If the engraving by David Pelletier that Champlain included in *Les Voyages* can be trusted, Champlain was wearing a full set of cavalier's armor, including a helmet adorned with an ostrich feather plume. The metal gleamed as he braced his legs widely and brought the heavy gun up to his bearded face. As the Mohawk recovered and prepared to loose their first volley of arrows, Champlain aimed and fired.

To the Mohawk, it must have seemed that Champlain had disappeared in a thunderstorm of his own making as the flintlock sparked a percussive wreath of white smoke. Some of them didn't live long enough to hear the terrifying noise. The only protection the Mohawk enjoyed came in the form of wooden shields and woven body armor. Champlain's opening multiple shot tore easily through the flimsy shielding, killing two chiefs immediately and mortally wounding a nearby warrior. The flanking Frenchmen then opened fire. The third chief fell dead in the crackling assault as two more bizarre thunderstorms plumed in the woods, and the stunned Mohawk turned and fled the battlefield.

"I pursued them," Champlain wrote, "killing still more of them." While fifteen or sixteen of Champlain's allies were wounded, not a single man had been lost.

Champlain had engineered a major victory over the Mohawk. He had also traumatically changed the course of native and European relations.

Until Champlain came along, no European on the St. Lawrence had become involved in the endless cycle of native conflict. But for reasons that were largely commercial and in his own self-interest, Champlain had directly embroiled the French with the Mohawk.

And while Champlain had become a brother in arms of his native trading partners, de Monts's monopoly would not be extended. Champlain would only be able to arrange another one, through the Prince de Condé, in late 1612. He had meanwhile made the French and the Iroquois confederacy deadly enemies for the better part of the next century.

The consequences of that battle would fan out across still unexplored terrain and ultimately travel down the river that Champlain knew led south but still could not visit. There was no real hope, even in the wake of this victory, for Champlain to go any farther. His allies had prisoners to take home with them and put to death through agonizing torture. Champlain was not a de Soto or a Cortés, with an army of hundreds of foot soldiers and mounted cavaliers prepared to carve a swath of pillage through hostile terrain. He relied on the goodwill and cooperation of native allies to take him anywhere and show him anything. He might have hoped to progress at least as far as the end of the second lake, Lake George, where he had been told in 1603 there was a village of the Iroquois. A battle victory there would have put him less than nine miles overland from the upper reaches of the river to the ocean. Instead, they were not going beyond Crown Point, the place the Mohawk had chosen to engage their approaching enemy.

Champlain knew the rest of the route was there before him, awaiting discovery, but as his allies returned to their canoes with their miserable prisoners and began paddling back up Lake Champlain, Champlain had no option but to go with them. He had come within about fifty miles, most of them easy travel by water, of the river to the ocean, but that was as close as he would ever be to reaching it. It was the first and last time he would be here.

It was July 30. Henry Hudson's men had overrun the Mi'kmaw village at La Have, and the *Half Moon* was at sea, en route to Cape Cod. Just as Fernández de Écija was withdrawing from Hudson's path, Champlain too was leaving the way open for Hudson to make his great discovery. But the ideas he had expressed in *Des Sauvages* about the transportation corridor may well have been on Hudson's mind as the Englishman chose to leave Upper New York Bay and devote the last available days of the sailing season to exploring the river leading north.

CHAPTER 21

RIVERS ARE EXPLORED ON THEIR OWN terms. They are never as simple as a line on a map would suggest or promise. They have their idiosyncrasies, their own rhythms and cycles. They are different places at different times of the year. They raise and lower expectations with their changes.

In many ways the Hudson River is not a river at all. While it does perform a river's duty in draining 13,390 square miles of landscape to the Atlantic, except for its uppermost reaches (beyond the present-day dam at Troy), it does not behave like almost any other river. That is because it has very little slope. The difference in elevation between Troy and the Battery, a distance of 145 miles, is only about five feet. And so it does not flow like a normal river. The "lower" Hudson, below Troy, is considered one long estuary, where freshwater and saltwater meet and mix for part of that length, and its movement is essentially tidal. While freshwater does make its way to the ocean, that flow is more incremental, rather than that of a conventional river in motion. When the tide is in flood, the Hudson flows north. When it is slack, the Hudson stands still. Only when the tide is in ebb does the Hudson flow noticeably like a river, toward the sea.*

The Hudson owes its unusual character to its unique formation. The

---

*The etymology of an oft-cited native name for the river, Mahicanittuk, is routinely said to mean "river that flows both ways." It in fact is a Delaware (Lenape) term and appears to simply mean "river of the Mahican."

river valley, already geologically ancient, was most forcefully carved out by two Laurentide glaciations. The first, the Illinoian, occurred 200,000 to 140,000 years ago. The second, the Wisconsinan, began about 60,000 years ago. By 22,000 years before present, the ice sheet's Hudson-Champlain lobe reached its southernmost point, plowing the terminal moraine that endures as much of Staten Island and Long Island.

Behind this moraine, as the ice began to recede, two glacial lakes formed. One was the future Long Island Sound; the other was the valley of the future Hudson River, south of Peekskill. Above the glacial Lake Hudson was a vast sheet of ice, which had overtopped the highest mountains of upstate New York by as much as a thousand feet. As the glacier receded further, the gap that had been carved through the gneiss of the Hudson Highlands was revealed. Ice had scoured away a U-shaped canyon whose flow bed, or thalweg, was 250 meters below sea level, at a time that sea level was depressed 100 meters. Left exposed when the ice further receded were the prominent heights where the river now crosses the path of the Highlands. Northward through this fjord the glacial Lake Hudson expanded above Peekskill, creating one large glacial lake in the valley, Lake Albany.

The single Lake Albany eventually became a series of glacial lakes corresponding with the broader sections of the river today. About 12,500 years ago came the breaching of the terminal moraine and the flooding of the river valley by seawater. Over the next few thousand years, the essential character of today's Hudson River emerged. Sedimentary deposits of silt and clay as thick as one hundred meters filled in the bottom of the glacial canyon, creating a river course often confounded by shallows.

The lower Hudson River remains a drowned glacial river valley. It is very different from a river like the Thames in England, which has spent thousands of years since the last glacial period experimenting with its course to the sea, developing pronounced meanders in the process. The Hudson inherited a deeply gouged canyon and has limited its route changes to small shifts within the bounds of the valley's fairly straight run to the sea.

The elongated nature of the tidewater river valley produces unusual behaviors in tides. We've already noted the wavelike nature of a tide's progression. All estuarine rivers as a result have a lag in the time that a particular tide is marked along its length. Henry Hudson and Robert Juet would have been familiar with lag from the Thames, even if they didn't understand what caused it: the progressive wave theory of tides was still eleven years away, in Francis Bacon's *Novum Organum*.

On the Thames, the difference between the time of high tide at Southend-on-Sea, where the estuary on the North Sea begins narrowing into something riverlike, and at the Tower of London, where Hudson's English voyages departed from St. Katherine's Pool, is about eighty minutes. But the distance between those two points along the Thames's undulating course is only about 35 nautical miles. Because of the highly elongated nature of the Hudson River tidewater and the river's geometry, its tide lag is considerable, even over short distances.

On a typical day, high tide might be marked at Coney Island at 5:30 in the morning but won't reach the Battery on lower Manhattan until about 6:05. (And because of the additional tidal lag of Long Island Sound, which is more than three hours out of sync, high water isn't marked on the East River at Whitestone until 9:30.) Forty miles up the Hudson from the Battery, at Peekskill, the high tide doesn't come until around 8:30, as the broadening of the Tappan Zee absorbs tidal energy. Just twenty miles farther on, at Newburgh, the tide doesn't show up until 9:50 after coursing through the narrower channel of the Hudson Highlands. And in Albany, about 85 miles still farther upriver, this tide won't come in until 3:04 in the afternoon. The total lag—nine and a half hours—is so great that by the time this high tide reaches Albany, 145 miles upstream of the Battery, a low tide will already have come and gone, about three hours earlier, at Coney Island.

The peculiar nature of the tidal cycle along the Hudson River would have posed a real puzzle for Henry Hudson and Robert Juet in figuring out when they could count on high water as they moved upriver, and conversely when they would be confronting low water, particularly when they were contending with shoaling waters. When calculating the expected tides from one day to the next, they knew that the tidal cycle would shift ahead daily forty-eight minutes because of the different lunar and earth calendars. They also would have expected an additional riverine lag as they progressed upstream, but never to the degree that the Hudson produces.

There was also the odd way in which the river's tidal range changes. From the Narrows to Newburgh, the mean range steadily declines, from 4.8 to 2.8 feet. But then it gains a second wind upstream, as the river's narrowing amplifies the tide. The mean range begins to climb again, reaching 4.6 feet at Albany, which is higher than the range at the Battery (4.5 feet).

The strength, direction, and range of tides were considered important clues in the search for a profitable new passage to the Orient and were observed carefully on northern passage-making attempts. Hudson's probing of the river would have been no different. Although no log survives, Hudson would have taken special note of how the river's tides were behaving. What he made of their peculiarities, above and beyond the threats they posed to safe navigation, may have played a role in how far he sailed upriver, and for how long.

There was another aspect to the Hudson River's unusual flow patterns that may have figured in what Hudson thought he would find, in deciding to ascend the river rather than devote precious time to properly surveying the upper bay. It had to do with how freshwater and saltwater intermingle along the Hudson River's length.

Because saltwater is about 3.5 percent more dense than freshwater, the ocean generally sinks beneath the freshwater outflow as a tide moves into a river and raises its levels. Estuarine rivers nevertheless experience a progressive intermingling of freshwater and saltwater, from entirely salty some point out at sea to entirely freshwater somewhere upriver. Along the way the water is brackish to varying degrees. (The tide, however, continues far higher upstream than the upper limits of saltwater, as it behaves as a wave of energy, raising and lowering the surface level.) How far upstream that tidewater is measurably salty depends substantially on changes in freshwater outflows. In a northern climate, the freshwater content of a river is beholden to the change in seasons, as the snowpack melts in spring and the feeder rivers and streams become gorged with freshwater, in a flow surge called the freshet.

The Hudson River's freshwater outflow is much higher in the late winter and spring because of the melting snowpack (and rains) in the Adirondack, Catskill, and Taconic mountains than it is in late summer and fall. This spring freshet produces a typical outflow of about two thousand cubic meters per second. By summer, the freshwater flow has reached its nadir of only one hundred to two hundred cubic meters per second. In early September, when Hudson arrived, freshwater outflows are about the lowest of the entire year.

Because the Hudson is tidewater all the way to Troy, a massive reduction in freshwater volumes doesn't translate into a massive reduction in water levels. What does change dramatically is the location of the "salt front," the point upriver where the river is considered to be freshwater, which is measured as less than 1,000 parts per million (or 1 psu) of salt. During the spring freshet, the salt front typically is pushed all the way downriver to the vicinity of Yonkers, around fifteen to twenty miles above the Battery, although in a heavy freshet the front can move as far south as Manhattan. On a typical late summer day, when freshwater outflow has become minimal, the salt front is far upriver—above the Hudson Highlands, around Newburgh or higher. While the water cannot be said to be "saltwater" behind the leading edge of the salt front, neither is it fresh.

The river's specific character in mid-September, then, could have had a significant influence on Hudson's plans and actions. He was in a river that looked and behaved more like a fjord or a strait, without a discernible grade, and with a flow that appeared entirely tidal. And because of the time of year, the water would have been saline a considerable distance upriver. While there would have been significant changes in salinity in different places along the way, due to vertical mixing and local current patterns, by and large Hudson was entering a river that he could tell was salty, like the ocean, and that would keep reassuring him of that fact for a goodly distance north.

For a while at least—long enough for him to remain committed to pushing forward—he could have been confident that Edward Wright's portrayal of a passage from the Atlantic to the upper St. Lawrence just might be correct.

CHAPTER 22

A T ONE O'CLOCK IN THE AFTERNOON on August 17, 1807, a nameless vessel left a dock on New York's East River waterfront, to round lower Manhattan and head up the Hudson toward the state capital at Albany. Aboard the boxy 150-foot vessel were forty people, and a boiler fired with pine and oak. The boiler was the heart of a twenty-horsepower engine that drove a pair of paddle wheels mounted on either side of the hull.

After an initial breakdown, the vessel made it all the way to Albany in thirty hours, at an average speed of five miles per hour. After modifications, the craft would be registered in 1808 as the *North River Steamboat of Clermont*. Her inventor, a former miniaturist painter from Philadelphia named Robert Fulton, had revolutionized water travel. As ponderous as the vessel's speed was (and as alarming as the black smoke and flames were that emerged from her stack), it was a reliable sort of speed. Until Fulton's spewing and shuddering vessel came along, virtually nothing had changed about navigating the Hudson River since Henry Hudson had done so for the first time.

The main challenge Hudson faced in progressing upriver—which was the main challenge resolved by the *North River Steamboat of Clermont*—was the wind. Unable to make much headway into it, Hudson would be stymied by a breeze with any amount of north in its direction. And if the wind blew across the river's course, the resulting gusts, lulls, downdrafts, and eddies wherever high ground lined the river could make his passage difficult if not dangerous. Hudson might have to wait for days for a useful wind to come along. In the meantime, he could resort to another tactic, a standard practice on the Thames which future navigators of the Hudson before Fulton also learned to apply. He could leave the sails furled on their yards, wait for the tide to turn from slack to flood, then raise anchor and allow the *Half Moon* to drift upriver on the current like a glorified raft.

On September 12, the *Half Moon* spent the entire morning at anchor in the vicinity of Manhattan, delayed in part because of the twenty-eight canoes that turned out to greet Hudson. The visitors all left at noon, but Hudson himself was going nowhere. The wind was against him, between northwest and north. Finally, at two o'clock he raised the anchor. The flood tide had arrived. The *Half Moon* was under way, so to speak, riding the tide upriver until it went slack for perhaps twenty minutes. It was time to anchor again, before the ebb tide pulled the ship back downriver with greater verve than it had just carried her upriver.

They made all of two leagues (six nautical miles) this way on the twelfth, and the thirteenth dawned with the wind still opposing them, out of the north. The lunar cycle moved to full: Hudson had a spring tide beneath him, and he was prepared to hitch a ride on the first flood of the day, which came at seven in the morning. They made only four miles, as the opposing wind resisted the beneficial shove of the current. The four native canoes that appeared sold them oysters while they were anchored, waiting for the next flood. When it came in the afternoon, they drifted two and a half leagues, around eight miles, before anchoring for the night.

The river was wider then: no piers jutted in their way from Manhattan or Hoboken. By now they had drifted past the Upper East Side of Manhattan, past Spuyten Duyvil Creek, the outlet of the Harlem River, which defines Manhattan as an island (but which Hudson did not notice), and on toward and perhaps even past the high bluffs of blue-gray basaltic magma of the Palisades on the river's western shore. Some of their visitors may have been Lenape who lived along Spuyten Duyvil, which they called Shorakapok. Like Spuyten Duyvil itself (which has been spelled many different ways and translated as "Spite the Devil," "Spitting Devil," and "Devil's Whirlpool"), Shorakapok has different translations but generally connoted a gathering place between high ground.

"At a distance of thirteen miles north of the City of New York," remarked Samuel Akerly in his 1819 paper, "the traveler finds himself opposite Fort

Lee, elevated 311 feet above the river; here the rocks, without any interval, approach the water's edge, forming high and mural precipices, and so continue to their termination at Haverstraw, having only at their base detached portions and loose masses, which have tumbled down from their banks above." These rocks were used as fill in extending Manhattan further into the river. "In common parlance, they are called the *pallisado* rocks, from their vertical position and tendency to columnar structure. The rents and fissures in their dark and majestic sides, may be likened to the reeds of an organ upon a grand scale. A fine opportunity to view these sublime prospects is presented to the traveler, when in the day time he can sail close along these perpendicular cliffs from Fort Lee northward."

But Hudson had not come to sightsee. Time was against him as Michaelmas approached. He was making ponderous, awkward progress, and the voyage could not continue this way.

ON SEPTEMBER 14, everything changed. The wind swung in their favor, out of the southeast, and that morning, in "very fair weather," the *Half Moon* at last began to reel in precious miles. They sailed all the way up the broadening of what had once been a glacial lake, the stretch the Dutch would call the Tappan Zee.

Thomas Pownall would describe the Tappan Zee in 1755 with more words than Juet could spare: "The western Banks are perpendicular rocky Cliffs of an immense Height, Covered with Woods at the Top, which from the great Height of the Cliff seem like Shrubs. The Eastern Coasts are formed by a gently rising Country, Hill behind a Hill, of fruitful Vegetation at the back of which lie the White-plains." There were broad shallows to avoid, particularly on the west side, but Hudson stayed clear of them, reached Haverstraw Bay, above Teller's Point, and finally "came to a straight between two points," according to Juet. "The land grew very high and mountainous," Juet later remarked. "The river is full of fish."

The *Half Moon* had arrived at the narrowing of the Tappan Zee between the points of Stony and Verplanck, and at the fjord where the Hudson Highlands, running southwest to northeast, had dared stand in the way of two ice ages. Once part of a mountain range inconceivably ancient and as grand as the Himalaya, successive glaciations had wearied them into great mounds. The highest summits were more than 1,200 feet above the con-

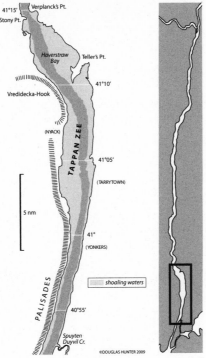

41°15'   Verplanck's Pt.
Stony Pt.

Haverstraw
Bay   Teller's Pt.

Vredidecka-Hook   41°10'

(NYACK)

TAPPAN ZEE

41°05'

(TARRYTOWN)

5 nm

41°

(YONKERS)

PALISADES

shoaling waters

40°55'

Spuyten
Duyvil Cr.

©DOUGLAS HUNTER 2009

Tappan Zee.

stricted river course, which jogged northwest, northeast, then northwest again, as the *Half Moon* continued upstream through the fjord, above Peekskill, where the last retreating ice field had paused long enough to create a river delta as meltwater had poured into what was then Lake Hudson.

Juet had nothing more to say about the most visually spectacular stretch of their river journey, as they entered the Hudson Highlands. The modern reader yearns for more: color and drama, an expression of awe. After all, the *Half Moon* was sailing into the heart of the Hudson River school of landscape painting, which was most active in the middle decades of the nineteenth century and translated river views and promontories into expressions of sublime beauty.

Such descriptive awe would have to wait for later visitors. Pownall drew a word-picture of the river here with the sort of painterly reverence appropriate to an enthusiastic watercolorist. He described the course through the Highlands as "the extraordinary and very singular Passage . . . through a Range of very high and mountainous Lands, about 12 Miles across, called

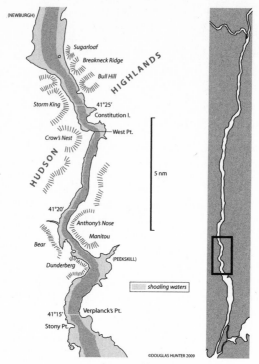

Hudson Highlands.

the Highlands, running directly athwart its Course; for as though a Chasm has been split in this Range of Mountains to make Way for it, it passes in a deep Channel near a Mile broad, with one Zigzag only, through these Mountains piled up almost perpendicular to a most astonishing Height on each Side of it." Pownall would add, "The Reader may imagine that the Scenes on this River must exhibit some of the finest Landscapes in the World; I thought so, and made many Sketches of the different Scenes."

Samuel Akerly, describing the passage up the Tappan Zee in his 1819 essay, likewise foreshadowed the painterly interest of the Hudson River school in the landscape: "On passing the valley of Haverstraw, an enchanting prospect surrounds the beholder. The towering cliffs of Vredideka-Hook [on the western shore] are just behind, and while looking back to retrace the pleasure passed by, the eye is carried downward in the course of the stream to the extent of vision, and when fatigued it turns to the left, and explores a well cultivated country on the eastern bank of the river. Again the eye wanders and meets the towering mountains on the north directly in front, apparently obstructing the further progress; but still inquisitive, and seeking the full enjoyment of the scenery around, overlooking Stoney-point and the valley of Haverstraw, the receding mountains in the west still keep up attention, and are seen afar off 'Steept in hazy distance.' "*

English officers and gentlemen in the diplomatic service were trained as watercolorists, and in Pownall's case the skill was applied with fondness rather than dutiful record-making. No one from the English voyages of the early seventeenth century to eastern North America is known to have at-tempted to create a portrait of the lands (or anything else they saw), beyond crude drawings of how shore features would appear to a ship for piloting purposes. And while Champlain's books were illustrated, based perhaps on sketches he made, the work fundamentally belonged to the engraver David Pelletier, who borrowed elements from other published works and intro-duced palm trees to Lake Champlain.

The Hudson River school painters who followed Pownall and Akerly were transcendentalists, for whom the presence of the divine was infused in every detail of existence. Although they sometimes indulged in fantasy and were not averse to assembling different real-life views to dramatic ef-fect, they strove to capture (even exaggerate) nature untrammeled, un-touched by human hands, so that the presence of God, of the Over-Soul, could be expressed through their pigments.

Their use of *memento mori*—symbols of life's fleeting quality—did have a precedent in the Dutch gilded age of the seventeenth century. Where a Hudson River artist might include a broken tree stump or rotting log in the foreground as a sign of impermanence and the prevalence of the divine, Dutch painters of the Leiden school produced still-life works called *vanitas*. Their high realism was chock-full of symbolism conveying life's ephemeral nature: half-peeled oranges whose spiraling peels mimicked an unwound watch spring, snuffed candles, gutted game, and, when less subtle hints were required, human skulls. Lush ripeness was always on the verge of rot.

The first *vanitas* expressions of the Leiden school didn't emerge until the 1620s, and the movement was most productive around the 1650s, long after the *Half Moon* voyage. In Hudson's time, Dutch commerce was

---

* Akerly's visual enthusiasm sprang from his geological passions, but in concluding this pas-sage he quoted from the ornithologist Alexander Wilson's poem "The Foresters," first pub-lished in *Port Folio* in 1809–10, which recounted his journey through New York state to Niagara Falls in 1804.

ascendant, and the artwork produced for its burghers was derivative of Italian styles. The prevailing Mannerism called for nature to be idealized rather than faithfully represented. It was the inverse of the Leiden school or the less manipulated examples of the Hudson River aesthetic: God resided in buffed perfection.

Adriaen Van der Donck would offer an unabashedly sensual description of Cohoe Falls on the lower Mohawk River near Albany in 1655. He praised it as being "very delightful to the eye. This place is well calculated to exalt the fancy of the poets. The ancient fabulous writers would, if they had been here, have exalted those works of nature, by the force of imagination, into the most artful and elegant descriptive illusions." But the explorers in the decades that preceded Van der Donck composed their descriptions of landscape in language we can easily misinterpret, reading too much into seemingly rapturous descriptions of "fair" and "pleasant" lands and wild-flower scents, mistaking such comments for a later century's enthusiasm for nature's raw beauty. Only so much can be expected of a nautical journal account, but both Juet and Hudson were spare in their subjective observations. They belonged to another time, and responded to other priorities. They were not inclined to embrace reminders of life's impermanence when daily life (as Colman's death had just demonstrated) was more than impermanent enough already.

Nature for them was awaiting transformation: minerals and metals were to be mined, forests to be cleared for planting and timber, wetlands to be reclaimed for agriculture, waters to be fished. Books like John Smith's *A Map of Virginia*, Brereton's *A Briefe and True Relation*, Rosier's *A True Relation*, and Champlain's *Des Sauvages* were all devoted to conveying the economic potential of the lands they visited, as was Van der Donck's *A Description of New Netherland*. In a rare aesthetic outburst, Samuel de Champlain rhapsodized in his *Les Voyages* of 1613 about his summer house at Port Royal in 1606–7, which included an irrigation ditch for a garden that he stocked with trout: "we resorted often to this place as a pastime; and it seemed as if the little birds round about took pleasure in it, for they gathered there in large numbers, warbling and chirping so pleasantly that I think I never heard the like." It was an arcadian pleasure he was expressing: the landscape of eastern North America otherwise left him unmoved, unless it provoked an opinion on its suitability for settlement.

What these explorers described as fair or pleasant, healthy or salubrious, was what they knew their audience would consider to be ripe for exploitation and welcoming to colonists, and so worthy of capital investment, either for an actual colony or a follow-up voyage. Their accounts typically included lists of resources encountered. They did not look upon the New World and consider ways in which its natural beauty could somehow be sheltered from development and mass consumption. They did not express a sense of the divine in untamed nature. There was no supreme Over-Soul, no God in the unvarnished details.

We cannot say that someone like Juet or Hudson was not moved in some pleasurable way by his experience of the Hudson Highlands or any other stretch of their passage. But they were as unlikely to look upon the river's course and ignore its many human potentials as their Dutch carpenter was to stare at a ramrod-straight spruce and not see a ship's spar beneath its bark. They were in the business of transforming nature, not worshipping or delighting in it.

THE RIVER PASSAGE through the Hudson Highlands, which Pownall described as a "puzzled Pass," was one of the most difficult sections for the *Half Moon* to negotiate. Danckaerts and Sluyter would describe their own northbound passage in 1680: "We were at the entrance of the Highlands, which are high and rocky, and lie on both sides of the river. [We were] waiting there for the tide and wind . . . The wind coming out of the south about nine o'clock [in the morning] we weighed anchor, and got under sail. It gradually increased until we had drifted through the Highlands, which is regarded as no small advantage whenever they wish to sail up or down the river; because, if they do not have a fresh breeze aft, they cannot have much favorable wind, as in blowing crosswise over the Highlands it blows above the vessel, and sometimes comes down in whirlwinds which are dangerous."

The southeasterly breeze similarly carried the *Half Moon* through, and would have encouraged Hudson to sail as far as he could while the wind favored him. He must have enlisted the flood tide as well to make such good progress, as the *Half Moon* pressed all the way through the highest ground of the fjord to a fine anchorage around present-day Newburgh, where the river first widens above the Highlands.

At this point the tide—and the river—must have seemed truly strange.

Once at anchor, Hudson and Juet could measure the tidal range, which had reduced considerably: as they were still close to the spring tide of the full moon on the thirteenth, the range would have been about 3.4 feet, having dropped about two feet from what they had experienced around lower Manhattan. The real confusion would have begun when they tried to determine when the next high or low water would be.

They knew that all tidal cycles shift ahead daily forty-eight minutes. But moving through space—upriver—as well as through time would have produced some head-scratching surprises. The river's own natural lag added three hours and forty-five minutes to the time of high tide between lower Manhattan and Newburgh. It was as if the calendar had leapt ahead five days. This was not the sort of confusion Hudson would have welcomed in uncharted waters.

They also may have reached the salt front, which usually extends about as far upriver as Newburgh, sometimes higher, at that time of year. It's difficult to know what Hudson would have made of a noticeable semidiurnal tide on a waterway that was now freshwater, as neither he nor Juet left behind anything illuminating. Hudson's main comparison would have been the Thames. That river being an open sewer, Hudson would have been mad to ever drink from it, and so may not have been that familiar with its changing salinity. The river is considered brackish from Gravesend all the way to London, only changing to a freshwater habitat upstream at Lambeth. There was no salt front on the Thames for a ship's master ever to cross.

Still, Hudson would have at least known that, as on the Thames, the tide can continue to act in freshwater upstream. Of course, he also knew that following the course of the Thames upstream would never lead to an ocean.

So, in finding that the river was becoming fresh, Hudson might have been expected to then turn around, concluding that a river that initially appeared to be more like an ocean strait was a river after all, and that the way forward could never reach another sea. But all was not lost: if the river (or strait, or whatever it was) was connected to the upper St. Lawrence, as Wright drew the passage, Hudson would not have been dismayed by his breaching of the salt front.

Hydrology was not the strongest scientific suit of the early seventeenth century. Hayes had been able to promote the idea of a protean Great Lake upstream of the St. Lawrence that was somehow freshwater at one end and saltwater at the other, and had gotten Champlain to go along with it in his reportage in *Des Sauvages*. Henry Hudson's hydrological puzzle was less of a mind-twister. Breaching the salt front didn't necessarily mean that the river had a typical source in a mountain stream or lake. The St. Lawrence at the point where Wright's passage connected to it was freshwater, and if the two watercourses were so joined, then it would be logical that the water in the Hudson River would become freshwater upstream as the St. Lawrence was approached. And so far, the Hudson River was behaving nothing like a normal river anyway. Perhaps Henry Hudson even considered that the strange nature of the Hudson tides could be explained by the way the two rivers were linked. So long as he had navigable water, Hudson would keep moving upriver.

WITH THE WIND remaining cooperative, blowing from the south on the fifteenth, Hudson carried on. No sailing master over the coming centuries could have been more pleased with his progress, as Hudson ran about nine miles upriver to Wappinger Creek, then entered the die-straight stretch past present-day Poughkeepsie that Juet called the "long reach." Today the cliffs along the west shore are called the Lange Rack, a corruption of the Dutch equivalent of Juet's original description of the river course, *lang rak*.

Not even Fulton could have hoped to outpace Hudson in daylight running in the *North River Steamboat of Clermont*. Twenty leagues were put away, from the morning departure, through the long reach, where the river was typically half a mile wide, and well beyond: sixty miles of uneventful progress through the Hudson Lowlands.

"At night we came to other mountains, which lie from the river's side," wrote Juet. The verdant mounds of the Catskills, an extension of the Allegheny range, had risen on their left and closed with the west bank of the river. The highest summits near the riverside, Sugarloaf and High Peak, topped 3,600 feet; the lower elevations of the range, emerging abruptly from the Hudson Lowlands as the Catskill escarpment, were only about six miles distant.

It was a remarkable performance on this uncharted waterway. Danckaerts and Sluyter would note that on their 1680 passage to Albany, once clear of the Highlands, their vessel's master would not proceed any further upriver from "the Hysopus" because of the hazards. This was an area of settlement the Dutch called the Esopus, situated on the Rondout River; they

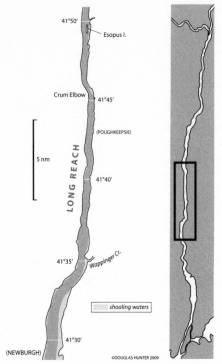

The Long Reach.

established a blockhouse here called the Ronduit. The settlement was chartered as Wiltwyck and was allegedly given to the Dutch by the Esopus tribe
of the Munsee. Friction nevertheless was constant and led to the bloodshed
remembered as the Esopus Wars of the mid-seventeenth century.

While failing light and weather plainly were the main issues holding
back Danckaerts and Sluyter, the journal nevertheless remarked, "In consequence of the river above the Hysopus being difficult to navigate, and be-
set with shoals and passages, and of the weather being rainy with no moon,
we could not proceed without continual danger of running aground, and
so came to anchor."

Above the long reach, the river passage made an easy jog to the west
through Crum Elbow, with the depths still forgiving, often at least fifty feet
and sometimes upward of one hundred. But above the Esopus, the river
began to change dramatically for the *Half Moon*, with shallows extending
from either shore and numerous flats along its center course. About ten

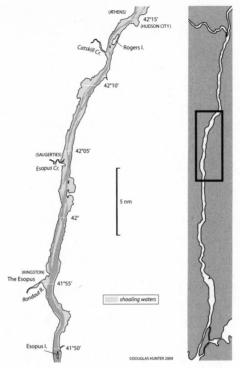

The Esopus.

miles above the Esopus, at present-day Saugerties, navigation became truly harrying.

Conning the *Half Moon* through these uncharted waters, with the helmsman in his hutch, unable to see the river course ahead, was a fair-sized gambit. Today this section of the river is intensively marked by navigation aids to keep traffic in a safe channel. Yet Hudson made it all the way to the vicinity of Catskill Creek. It was a natural place to pause. Hereabouts the Dutch initially would settle about four miles up Catskill (Kaatskill) Creek, adding a port at the river in 1650 for shipping their goods to market. Juet wrote that it was night when they halted. Just ahead the river bent east at Rogers Island, the channel first having to shift hard to the west side near the shore to avoid shoaling waters before swinging to the left above the island.

Henry Hudson's passage north from Manhattan, on a river he'd never seen before and that no one else had charted for him, verged on charmed.

The wind had been perfect for days. He could easily have found himself still trying to make his way up the Tappan Zee when he had instead gotten all the way to Catskill Creek. Small shifts in timing, in his decisions to head where he did when he did, would have made tremendous differences in his voyage's outcome. Beyond perfect wind, he had amplified his good fortune by staying out of trouble with the river's many unpredictable shallows. He ought to have gone aground any number of times. Instead, he had cruised the river without a hitch. Good seamanship, good luck; it didn't matter. Hudson had achieved progress so late in the season that easily could have been denied him.

But there had been one setback: Hudson had lost the two native captives. On the morning of the fifteenth, while the *Half Moon* was still at anchor around present-day Newburgh, the prisoners escaped through a port and swam away. "After we were under sail," wrote Juet, "they called to us in scorn." The captives had been otherwise forgotten in Juet's narrative since their abduction in Rockaway Inlet, and one has to wonder what unacknowledged role they might have played in Hudson's voyage on the ensuing days. Particularly curious is how Hudson's visitors plummeted from twenty-eight canoes on September 12 to just four on September 13 while in the vicinity of Manhattan. Distressing outbursts by the prisoners from within the ship cannot be discounted as a reason so few natives returned to trade with Hudson on his second day in the area.

Now those prisoners were free, shouting insults at the *Half Moon* that Juet could not understand, although he was able to comprehend the general message of "scorn." The pair were heading back downriver: back to their own people, but also able to share with anyone they met along the way what had happened to them, how they had been treated by these strangers that some otherwise would have thought were supernatural. And regardless of whatever notion Hudson may have harbored about being able to reach the St. Lawrence by this route, the natives knew that he would have no choice but to turn around eventually. They would be waiting to remake his acquaintance.

CHAPTER 23

WHILE THE *HALF MOON*'S MEN had lost their prisoners, they gained a fresh opportunity for improved native relations at the end of the long sail north on September 15. Anchored that evening, Juet reported, "we found very loving people, and very old men: where we were well used."

Catskill Creek is considered to have been a dividing line between the territories of the Esopus people of the Munsee to the south and the Mahican to the north, although the Mahican are also thought to have been a Munsee subgroup. The Mahican's historic territory included the river northward and gave the watercourse its Lenape name: Mahicanittuk, River of the Mahican. They occupied palisade villages set back from the river in the hillsides to the west, where they cultivated the land with maize and other crops and came to the river seasonally to fish. One village was still on Catskill Creek when an English settler at Albany, a hatter named William Loveridge, purchased the land in 1682.

Juet never attached a name to any of the peoples they met, but these most certainly were Mahican. The relations were the best that Hudson could have hoped for, as the Mahican from the moment of encountering Hudson were eager to trade profitably and peacefully with the newcomers. Even Juet was able to relax in their company.

Hudson paused here to fish, with the weather scorching, and on the sixteenth the Mahican were welcomed on board. They "brought us ears of Indian corn, and pompions [pumpkins], and tobacco: which we bought for trifles," wrote Juet. Large numbers of Mahican lived in the area, as Juet complained that the fishing was poor that day because "their canoes had been there all night."

While the Mahican were perfect hosts (and the *Half Moon*'s men were at least tolerable guests), the best sailing unfortunately was now behind Hudson. The river ahead was narrowing, with progress becoming confounded by islands, and shoals that would no longer conveniently restrict themselves to the banks and leave the center clear. Setting sail again on the morning of the seventeenth, Hudson twice ran aground near the end of the day as he pressed hard for progress. First he struck near the river's shore as he tried to stay out of the main stream of the ebb that ran in the deepest part of the channel, and he had to use an anchor to haul, or kedge, the *Half Moon* clear. He then went aground on a midchannel shoal and could do nothing but wait for the next flood tide to lift him free before anchoring for the night.

One week after entering the Narrows, Henry Hudson was approaching the future site of Albany. The tidal range now was higher than it had been for the middle part of the passage. But the navigation was becoming more trying, more discouraging, the river less likely to pass through to the St. Lawrence with every mile. If it hadn't already occurred to Hudson, this river was now looking more and more like the one Champlain had described in *Des Sauvages*. The Frenchman had gotten it right. And Wright was wrong.

Unanswered questions arise in the *Half Moon* voyage as consistently as the high tides on the river that would bear Henry Hudson's name. As neither Hudson nor Juet ever explained why they were so determined to explore the river, it is not simple to conclude why they continued to press on, when it was becoming so apparent that they were fast approaching its navigable limits. More to the point, it is far from clear why the Dutch majority was still abiding by this chosen course.

One reason for the Dutch compliance likely was that it had taken Hudson so little time to ascend the river. The river journey had consumed only three days since the southerly breeze first sent them running freely near Manhattan. Impatience may not have set in among the crew, although we cannot be sure that serious friction had not erupted into arguments between the English minority and the Dutch majority. In describing the con-

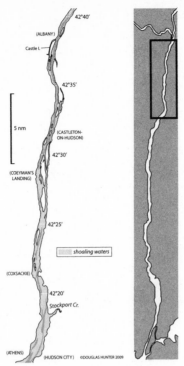

From Athens to Albany.

clusion of Hudson's explorations of the river estuary, Van Meteren would
state that Hudson's crew had been "mutinous" and had "sometimes savagely threatened him," but he did not explain how or when this surliness
began or what ignited the outbursts. It may have been a precarious fact of
shipboard life ever since the two crew factions had squabbled in the waters
of the Barents Sea, beyond Norway's North Cape, its own ebbs and floods
tolerable so long as the animosity didn't turn to flood and stay that way.

Hudson could have been holding the crew together as he approached the
limit of navigation with promises of riches yet unfound, as he continued to
question natives about minerals and ores. And as they were able to trade
agreeably with the Mahican, some of these Dutchmen may already have
been thinking ahead, to the opportunity to return and enrich themselves in
the local fur trade. As for Hudson, his motivations by this point were probably multifold. Having come so far, there was little sense in not pursuing
the river journey to its ultimate conclusion. In the process, he might learn
more about the transportation corridor as described by Champlain in *Des*

Sauvages. And as Hayes was advocating a route to the Orient that was not a direct sea passage but rather a hopscotch of rivers and lakes linked by portages, determining that this river might serve such a purpose would not be without purpose itself.

With Michaelmas fast approaching, Hudson needed to seize on something—*anything*—useful, to take home with him and use as leverage in securing another assignment. The nature of the river and where it might lead was one bargaining chip. But he was also beginning to pay increasing attention to the colonizing possibility of the river, gathering as much as he could about its resources, its settlement potential. Near the end of the 1608 Novaya Zemlya expedition, he had taken the time to kill a walrus and bring home its severed head so that he was not returning literally empty-handed in his failure to prove the Northeast Passage. Now, with no direct passage to the Orient opening for him in North America, Hudson was making sure he noted every possible sign of the river's attractions and advantages.

Falling in among the Mahican amplified his fact-finding. They were unfailing in their hospitality, and as the river journey became more difficult, the *Half Moon* increasingly was forced to stay in one place, which meant spending more time among these people, and so gaining an opportunity to learn as much as possible from them. And on September 18, Hudson went ashore, to meet with Mahican elders.

JUET'S ACCOUNT AS published by Purchas said that on the afternoon of the eighteenth, with the *Half Moon* remaining at anchor, "our master's mate went on land with an old savage, a governor of the country, who carried him to his house, and made him good cheer." Something had gone wrong in the edit, because this was a house call that Hudson himself made. Purchas likely had mistakenly reduced "our master and his mate" to "our master's mate."

Hudson would never have sent the Dutch mate to meet with a native leader in his stead, but he definitely would have taken him with him. In a way, it would have been for personal security: not to protect himself against the Mahican but to ensure that the Dutch majority didn't try to make off with the *Half Moon* while he was ashore. The mate would have been as much a hostage as a companion.

Hudson was beginning to work out the most sensible arrangements for preserving his own neck. When it came time to dispatch the ship's boat to sound ahead, he would give the assignment to the Dutch mate, not to Juet. While Juet might have lacked the fluency in Dutch required to command a Dutch crew, Hudson assuredly was weighing the possibly catastrophic consequence of sending Juet off. Juet could be overpowered in the boat while Hudson was subdued in the *Half Moon*. With survey parties assigned exclusively to the Dutch mate and Dutch crewmembers, Hudson could reduce the number of potentially dangerous men back aboard the *Half Moon* and would have Juet as well as his son John around to help watch his back.

De Laet would quote Hudson directly on his visit to the Mahican chief, which he said occurred at latitude 42 degrees, 18 minutes. It would have been one of the voyage's most reliable fixes, employing not only the noon sight that day but also star sights (if the sky was clear) on the nights preceding and following in the same anchoring place. If dead accurate, Hudson was just upstream of present-day Athens, around where Stockport Creek enters the river from the east.

Hudson didn't say which shore he went to, only that he was taken there in a canoe "with an old man, who was the chief of a tribe, consisting of forty men and seventeen women; these I saw there in a house well constructed of oak bark, and circular in shape, so that it had the appearance of being well built, with an arched roof. It contained a great quantity of maize or Indian corn, and beans of the last year's growth, and there lay near the house for the purpose of drying, enough to load three ships, besides what was growing in the fields."

Such a "tribe" was more of an extended family, and they had all turned out at the chief's wigwam, whose arched roof was constructed from bent saplings, to see this stranger. When Hudson entered the wigwam with the chief, "two mats were spread out to sit upon, and immediately some food was served in well made red wooden bowls." Two men were sent out to bring some fresh game, and they quickly returned with two pigeons they had brought down with arrows. "They likewise killed a fat dog, and skinned it in great haste, with shells which they had got out of the water."

Henry Hudson had his first meal of the New World: pigeon, dog, probably some maize served as an unleavened bread, perhaps a chowder made of the river's fish as well as maize and kidney beans. Tobacco would have been smoked as well in friendship. We have no idea what they attempted to talk about, but the visit was brief; "they supposed I would remain with

them for the night, but I returned after a short time on board the ship."
When the Mahican thought Hudson would not stay because he feared for
his safety, they touchingly broke their arrows and threw them in the fire.
But it was not the Mahican he needed to worry about. Spending a night
away from the ship was too great a risk to his command. He had to return.

THE NEXT MORNING, at eleven o'clock, Hudson began to ride the flood tide
north. He only made two leagues of progress before anchoring and being
swarmed by Mahican eager to trade on this "fair and hot" day. The visitors
brought grapes and pumpkin, and beaver and otter skins. The Mahican
had never before traded with Europeans, but they quickly figured out what
was desired. The *Half Moon* handed over knives, hatchets, and beads in return. With such a volume of clamoring trade, the cache of goods stolen
from the Mi'kmaq could not hold out forever.

Hudson reached latitude 42 degrees, 40 minutes, according to Van Meteren, which agrees with the location of present-day Albany.* He was in the
heart of the main population area of the Mahican. Dutch traders would establish a post in 1613 or 1614 at Castle Island (which has been absorbed into
the port of Albany and alternately has been called Patroon's or Westerlo Island) to do business with the Mahican as well as the Mohawk. This post
would be superseded on the mainland by Fort Orange, and Dutch traders
likely followed the example of Hudson's visit in setting up shop at this point
in the river.

On the twentieth, Hudson remained at anchor while he sent out the
Dutch mate and four men to sound the river course ahead. The ship's boat
was gone all day, and its crew returned to report that the river narrowed and
was initially shallow, not much more than two fathoms deep, only two
leagues ahead, but that it then deepened again to seven or eight fathoms.
Nothing in historic charts agrees with this, but the survey party might have
gotten as far as present-day Troy, six miles upstream, where there is now a
dam and the first lock in the Erie and Champlain canal systems.

When the wind filled from the south on the twenty-first, Hudson de-

---

* Juet's estimates of leagues appear to be reasonably good for the river passage north, and
when they are combined with the latitude reports, we can be confident that the *Half Moon* indeed got as far as Albany, give or take a few miles.

cided to take advantage of it and see how far he could go upriver, but so many Mahican were aboard he could not get under way. While the carpenter went ashore to cut a spare forespar, Hudson and the Dutch mate entertained some of the Mahican leaders, to see "whether they had any treachery in them," as the relentlessly suspicious Juet put it. Hudson was abiding by the advice of Sebastian Cabot to ply a guest with strong drink to "learn the secrets of his heart." But he could not have suspected these elders of harboring malicious plans. Hudson was far more interested in finding out about metals and minerals, and passages to the Orient.

As Juet continued, "So they took them down into the cabin, and gave them so much wine and aqua vitae, that they were all merry; and one of them had his wife with them, which sat so modestly, as any of our country women would do in a strange place. In the end one of them was drunk, which had been aboard of our ship all the time that we had been there: and that was strange for them; for they could not tell how to take it."

Whatever Hudson learned went unrecorded by Juet. Beyond any insights into valuable resources or navigable routes, it would have been plain to him that the natives had no experience of alcohol and were not capable of consuming it in anything close to the massive amounts European mariners were accustomed to, and still function. Sailors generally didn't drink water (although it was used to dilute alcohol). They employed it mainly for cooking, as boiling would kill bacteria and other microbial life. (Landlubbers too avoided water. Beer was the common daily drink of England.) To quench their thirst, mariners drank "strong waters," which included aqua vitae (any distilled spirit, and by which the English generally meant brandy), beer, wine, and cider, and in volumes that would seem to floor most people today.

The provisioning details for the *Dragon*, which sailed in the 1606–7 East India Company flotilla, reveal that each man had a daily ration of a "pottle" (about half a gallon) of ordinary "ship beer," a quart of cider, and a pint of wine, and that was before they got into the "strong beer," a more potent brew that kept better on long tropic voyages and had no specific distribution noted in the *Dragon*'s inventory. The ship also had 150 gallons of aqua vitae, which would have been reserved for the senior ranks. On his 1602 voyage in search of the Northwest Passage, George Waymouth took along more than 375 gallons of aqua vitae, above and beyond an unknown volume of beer, for a two-ship expedition of only 30 men; the *Dragon*'s 150-gallon aqua vitae supply was for a single ship of 150 men.

Hudson's strong-water stores are unrecorded, but he would have had beer for the general crew, and as Juet attested, there was wine and aqua vitae on hand, which he served his native guests. The aqua vitae would have been the *brandiwijn* the Dutch merchants who dominated the coastal (cabotage) trade in northern Europe had introduced from Spain and southern France, a "burned wine" created by distilling wine by boiling it. About half of its volume was pure alcohol. English explorers seemed to favor this potent beverage for plying natives. Gabriel Archer noted how aqua vitae was served by Christopher Newport to a chief on the 1607 expedition up the river James, "showing him the benefit of the water, for which he thank'd him kindly."

While most of the Mahican aboard the *Half Moon* returned to shore, the drunken guest passed out and remained aboard all night, as apparently did others. The Mahican who had left reappeared before nightfall, bearing gifts for Hudson of wampum—"stropes [i.e., strops, or strands] of beads: some had six, seven, eight, nine, ten," according to Juet. Juet's observation is the first ethnographic record of wampum in belt form. Wampum, made from shells, was a form of currency, an item of adornment, and a tool of diplomacy, a gift of complex cultural significance. The intention of the generous presentation is not clear: more than a sign of gratitude or goodwill, it may have been encouraged by a genuine fear for the life of the elder who was out cold in the ship, unable to leave it.

It would occur to nineteenth-century historians that this incident might have been the ur-source of the drinking episode in the first-contact story gathered by Heckewelder, some 150 years later. It might not even have been the first time natives in the Hudson estuary were served alcohol by newcomers, though, and it certainly was not the last time. Alcohol would cause as much devastation among and between the peoples of the New World as any pathogen.

CHAPTER 24

SEPTEMBER 22: THE DUTCH MATE and four crewmembers were again sent out, to see how much more they could discover about the river course. The Mahican reappeared around noon, concerned about the welfare of the untold number of guests who had remained behind. Pleased to see that their friends and relatives were all right, they went back to shore, to prepare for another visit. They returned at three, to give Hudson tobacco and more wampum, "and made an oration, and shewed him [i.e., indicated] all the country round about," wrote Juet. "Then they sent one of their company on land, who presently returned, and brought a great platter full of venison dressed by themselves; and they caused him to eat with them: then they made him reverence and departed, all save the old man that lay aboard." The hangover must have been truly vicious, but no one appeared concerned with his condition.

At ten o'clock that night, the Dutch mate and his four companions returned to the *Half Moon*. It was raining, which could only have further dampened spirits. The mate reported that after making their way eight or nine leagues up the river, they had found "but seven foot water, and unconstant soundings." They had reached "an end for shipping to go in."

If they really did travel that far, they made it at least as far as modern Stillwater, well into the upper river, beyond the influence of tides. But a round-trip of sixteen to eighteen leagues—forty-eight to fifty-four nautical miles—while methodically sounding a river course for a navigable channel seems unlikely. It would have required a steady progress of at least four knots without any stopping, but the river would not have cooperated. While the Hudson has been radically altered by the dams and locks of the Erie and Champlain canals beginning six miles north of Albany at Troy, a circa 1758 property map of northern New York indicates several sections of rapids above the confluence with the Mohawk River, which empties from the west into the Hudson about ten miles above Albany (see p. 290). In addition to seriously impeding the ship's boat, the rapids would have meant the men actually would have found "an end for shipping" after three or four leagues.

At the very least they should have made it as far as the Mohawk confluence. But as the course upstream on the Mohawk from the Hudson is hidden behind Van Shaick Island, they could easily have missed the discovery of the important route into the Mohawk Valley and the lower Great Lakes.

They also apparently managed to not to notice the signs of Cohoe Falls on the lower Mohawk. It is only about two serpentine miles upstream, a little more than a mile due west of the Hudson. Because of significant changes in the Mohawk's flow caused by hydroelectric dams (at times it stops flowing entirely over the Cohoe), it is impossible to say just how unavoidably impressive the falls should have been in 1609, even from the vantage point of a small boat on the Hudson. Historic accounts, however, make the falls sound very impressive indeed at a distance.

Danckaerts and Sluyter visited the Cohoe on horseback from Albany and proclaimed it "the greatest falls, not only in New Netherland, but in North America, and perhaps, as far as is known, in the whole New World." The Frisian travelers knew nothing of the mighty Niagara, 260 miles to the west, which had just been seen by Europeans for the first time in December 1679, by a party led by the French explorer Robert Cavalier de La Salle. The Cohoe nevertheless was awe-inspiring, stretching a thousand feet across the lower Mohawk. While the flow would have been much lower in September, when Hudson's survey boat was near them, than during the spring freshet, when Danckaerts and Sluyter were there, it still would have been much a more forceful presence in the landscape than today.

"As you come near the falls," recounted Danckaerts and Sluyter, "you can hear the roaring which makes everything tremble . . . All this volume of water coming on this side fell headlong upon a stony bottom, this distance of an hundred feet. Any one may judge whether that was not a spectacle, and whether it would not make a noise. There is a continual spray thrown up by the dashing of the water, and when the sun shines the figure of a rainbow may be seen through it. Sometimes there are two or three of them to be seen, one above the other, according to the brightness of the sun and its parallax."

Thomas Pownall was similarly awestruck in describing these falls in 1755. He observed how, in approaching on horseback from Albany, "one begins to hear the *Pouiflosboish* noise of the Tumultuous rushing & dashing of Waters which amidst the stillness of the Woods is like the roar of a Storm at Sea heard from the Land in the dead of night . . . The Vapours which fly off from this Fall disperse themselves and fall in heavy Showers for near Half a Mile round the Place."

Granted, Pownall, like the Frisian travelers, saw the falls earlier in the season, in his case late June. And so we can give the Hudson survey party the benefit of the doubt and say it simply overlooked the signs indicating this natural spectacle was so close at hand. Alternately, whatever the party might have reported was not important enough for Juet to record. But given the incredible distance claimed by the survey party that day, despite the navigational challenges of the upper Hudson River, the Dutch mate and his companions still may have been lying to Hudson about how far they had gone upstream.

It didn't matter. The Dutch mate had delivered the message that the end of shipping was ahead, and he assuredly wouldn't have tolerated Hudson trying to push any farther. Michaelmas was only a week away. The river journey was over. It was time to turn back for the Atlantic.

THE VERY NEXT day, September 23, Hudson was under way. He waited until noon, as there was very little wind, and he also had to offload his remaining shipboard guest, the elder still recovering from the merriment of the twenty-first. With the ebb tide running, the *Half Moon* raised anchor, to travel at the whim of the river.

After only two leagues, the channel divided around a shoal, and the tide carried them aground on the hazard. They waited an hour for the flood to arrive and float them off. A strong breeze came up out of the west, which would have made negotiating any westerly changes in the channel's course difficult. Hudson needed a breeze with a fair bit of north in it, or an ebb tide, to make it back to the Atlantic. The anchor was set; the *Half Moon* retired for the night.

On the twenty-fourth, a northwesterly got them going, and they made it seven or eight leagues downriver, all the way to a spot around Stockport Creek, perhaps a half-dozen miles upstream of Catskill Creek, as another midchannel shoal brought them to an unscheduled halt. They went ashore and gathered chestnuts while waiting for the flood tide to rescue them. At ten that night they were afloat again, and safely anchored.

For the next two days, they went nowhere, as a "stiff gale" blew out of the south, stopping them up in the river as sure as a cork seals a bottle. They inspected the countryside along the western shore; Juet wrote how they found "good ground for corn and other garden herbs, with great store of goodly oaks, and walnut-trees, and chest-nut trees, ewe trees, and trees of sweet wood in great abundance, and great store of slate for houses, and other good stones." Slate indeed could be found on either side of the river and would be quarried in the future.

On their second day at anchor in the face of the strong southerly, the mate and four companions went ashore with the carpenter to keep him company and mind his back as he cut wood. Henry Hudson had no monopoly on impressions or ambitions. While nobody would preserve their observations, these Dutchmen had been taking in the river course that would come to be colonized by their countrymen. New Netherland was already taking shape with every swing of a carpenter's axe and draw of a saw. The first clearing of the river's shore, which would peel back the forest cover for farms, had effectively begun.

While the Dutch shore party was off cutting wood that morning, two canoes came upriver "from the place where we first found loving people," according to Juet. Their visitors thus were from the Catskill Creek area downstream. Aboard one of the canoes was the elder who had spent days laid out in the *Half Moon* after the merrymaking around Albany. He had sprinted (most certainly in a canoe paddled by others) about thirty miles downriver, well outpacing Hudson, to alert an elder from Catskill Creek of the *Half Moon*'s approach. Both elders were now alongside the *Half Moon*; the one from Catskill Creek presented Hudson with wampum and "shewed him all the country there about as though it were his command," according to Juet.

Hudson probably did not leave the ship: he would have been "shewed" all the country with sweeps of the Mahican's arm from the security of the deck. The two visitors were accompanied by their wives and also had "two young maidens of the age of sixteen or seventeen with them, who behaved themselves very modestly." Hudson invited them all into his cabin to dine, and one has to wonder if the modest behavior of the girls wasn't more along the lines of sheer culture shock and fear, as they found themselves in the strange wooden world of the *Half Moon*, while hovering close by were cutthroat men who had not enjoyed the intimate company of any women (unless earlier encounters on the river with the Mahican had been especially welcoming) for months.

Hudson made gifts of knives to the two men, who gave him tobacco in return. They departed at one in the afternoon, paddling back downriver, "making signs that we should come down to them." While Hudson really had no choice but to steer for Catskill Creek, he was determined to reach the sea and wasn't inclined to stop. When the morning of the twenty-seventh brought "fair wind from the north," he had his opportunity, at last, to be under way again.

He raised the anchor and set the fore topsail, enough push to give him some initial steerage as he rode the tide . . . which promptly carried the *Half Moon* firmly aground.

Hudson had spent enough time at anchor around Stockport Creek to at least know the local tide schedule on this perplexing waterway. The *Half Moon* had been halted in the middle of the ebb, and as he could not budge her off the "oozy ground" with an anchor and the river's level was still dropping, he had to wait for the flood to do it for him. Halfway into the flood, Hudson was clear again, with sails drawing. He ran six leagues, past Catskill Creek and perhaps as far as Esopus Creek, but the local elder who had just dined with him on the twenty-sixth reappeared on the river and urged him to anchor and come ashore to eat. Hudson would not give up the fair wind, though, and pressed ahead. The old man "left us, being very sorrowful for our departure," wrote Juet.

The Mahican proved to be persistently agreeable to the presence of the Dutch traders who followed Hudson. But they were soon embroiled in a series of conflicts with the Mohawk of the Iroquois confederacy, vying for preferential trade status, particularly as overharvesting consumed the local fur supply and the Dutch needed middlemen to access more distant resources. The Mahican stood between the Mohawk and the Dutch traders, and the Mohawk chafed at not being able to deal directly with the Dutch and at having to pay tribute or tolls to the Mahican to do so. A truce was

arranged by the Dutch in 1618 that involved the Mahican and all five nations of the Iroquois confederacy as well as the Munsee. Another war
erupted in 1624, however, and the Mohawk began to push the Mahican entirely out of their territories on the west side of the river, to clear the path to
Fort Orange. Selling ancestral lands to the Dutch hastened the Mahican
departure.

While the Mahican would continue to play a pivotal role in the fur trade
and the affairs of New Netherland, the torturously complex conflicts of northeastern North America—involving a multitude of Indian nations as well as
the English, French, and Dutch—saw Mahican numbers further dwindle. By
the eighteenth century, they were unable to hold on to their remaining lands
and were scattering in all directions.

The Moravian missionary John Heckewelder encountered some of these
displaced people in Pennsylvania and recorded their oral history as part of
his first-contact account that may have reflected experiences with Henry
Hudson. Others ended up in western Massachusetts, at a Christian mission in Stockbridge, where they become known as the Stockbridge Indians.
They fought alongside colonists in the French and Indian War and supported the rebels in the American Revolution. They were driven off their
lands as a reward, and the Stockbridge branch of the Mahican—if not the
very last of the Mahican, then as close as one can get in the diaspora
record—ultimately ended up on a small reserve near Green Bay, Wiscon-
sin. Sharing the tiny reserve were Munsee who had once controlled most if
not all of Upper New York Bay and the west side of the Hudson river course
north to the Esopus.

CHAPTER 25

H ENRY HUDSON MADE FIVE LEAGUES of progress downriver on September 28, to the middle of the long reach. A strong southerly wind forced him to use an ebb tide early on the morning of Michaelmas, the twenty-ninth, to complete the final three leagues of the reach. While he was anchored waiting for the next ebb tide, a few natives approached in canoes, "but would not come aboard," according to Juet. As soon as the ebb was again running at three that afternoon, they upped anchor and drifted with it, "down to the edge of the mountains, or the northernmost of the mountains, and anchored: because the high land hath many points, and a narrow channel, and hath many eddy winds."

They had stopped around Newburgh, where they confronted the zigzag passage through the Hudson Highlands to the Tappan Zee. If the wind did not arrive out of the north, they would have to rely on the tide to get them through. A few natives visited them that evening, trading some maize "for trifles." The next morning, the thirtieth, the wind was out of the southeast, "a stiff gale between the mountains." Hudson was not interested in relying on the tide to carry him through the passage in the face of such contrary winds, and so the *Half Moon* stayed put for the day.

Juet admired the location, which would serve as the headquarters of General George Washington's Continental Army in 1782–83. Seven thousand soldiers would bivouac in nearby Vails Gate. Juet called it "a very pleasant place to build a town on. The road [i.e., anchorage] is very near [shore], and very good for all winds, save an east-northeast wind. The mountains look as if some metal or mineral were in them. For the trees that grow on them were all blasted, and some of them barren, with few or no trees on them." Juet must have suspected copper, a natural toxin, was close at hand.

They were approached that afternoon by natives who traded "small skins," and the visitors were questioned about the minerals. "The people brought a stone aboard like to an emery (a stone used by glaziers to cut glass), it would cut iron or steel, yet being bruised [i.e., crushed] small, and water put to it, it made a color like black lead glistening: it is also good for painter's colors," Juet recorded.

Juet had not been shown corundum, the mineral form of emery. He more than likely had examined crystals of magnetite, a type of iron oxide, which will form a yellow-brown coating if washed. It would prove to be plentiful enough in the area to be mined as iron ore and for emery products. Other local iron ores, such as limonite, would be exploited as paint pigments. Magnetite, as its name suggests, is magnetic, a form of lodestone, but the sample Juet examined obviously wasn't magnetized enough (or close enough to the ship's compass) for him to notice. Locally mined iron would form the chains that Washington's forces strung across the Hudson River in the Highlands in an effort to prevent British ships from reaching them.

THE FIRST DAY of October brought fair weather and a moderately coopera- tive wind, out of the northwest. Hudson hitched a ride on the first ebb, at seven in the morning, and he was able to get all the way through the High- lands and into Haverstraw Bay, at the north end of the Tappan Zee. When they emerged from the highlands, the wind was calm, and the flood was setting, so they anchored and waited their next chance to be under way.

They were visited that afternoon by "people of the mountains," by which Juet meant the Highlands. He provided no further description to help iden- tify them. They may have been Wappinger, from the east side of the river, or a branch of the Lenape. They "came aboard us, wondering at our ship and weapons." Hudson traded with them for some small skins, and they may only have come alongside rather than actually stepped on board.

That afternoon, as the visitors gathered in their canoes about the *Half Moon*, one canoe, paddled by a single man, persistently loitered around the ship's tall stern, despite efforts to shoo him away. In a moment the man scrambled up the rudder. The tiller, where it led from the top of the rudder into the stern, would have provided a handy platform to stand on as the man reached into the open window of the master's cabin and snatched an armful of items.

As the thief attempted to escape in his canoe, the Dutch mate leveled a musket and killed him with a blast to the chest.

While the other natives fled, some diving out of their canoes to swim away as quickly as they could, the *Half Moon*'s men launched the ship's boat to retrieve the stolen goods. After they had recovered the items from the dead man's canoe, one of the natives in the water grasped the side of the boat, "thinking to overthrow it," according to Juet. The ship's cook swung a sword and cleaved away the swimmer's hand; they watched him fall away and drown.

It was all over in a moment. Two natives had been killed, over a theft that involved a few items that all turned out to belong to Robert Juet: a pillow, two shirts, and two bandoliers. These were small wooden containers holding the shot and powder for a single musket load, although by "bandoliers" Juet could have meant the sashes that held a dozen of these charges. The shirts could not have been worth much—in outfitting his 1602 voyage, George Waymouth purchased linen shirts for the crew for two shillings, seven pence each. And all of the stolen items could have been provided to Juet by the general account of the vessel. While the loss to the expedition was insignificant, two natives had been killed in the ensuing melee with a casual, reflexive brutality.

Henry Hudson could not have been pleased with the overwhelming response to the pilfering, but there was nothing to be done about it. The action plainly had sat well with Juet, who had his things back and spared no words of consideration for the appropriateness of his shipmates' response. The men who had overrun and plundered a Mi'kmaw village at La Have had now seen fit to summarily execute two natives in a case of petty theft. Some of the savage threats Van Meteren said Hudson received from the crew might have been heard at this time, had Hudson dared to raise any objection. And the extended good relations Hudson had enjoyed with the Mahican, upriver beyond the Highlands, were now very much behind him as he prepared to make the final push for Upper New York Bay and the Atlantic.

They rode the ebb tide two leagues downriver before anchoring for the night. Ahead were the peoples they had first met on arriving in this extended river estuary, and all the attendant unhappy complications: the fight that cost John Colman his life, the kidnapping of the two natives who had then escaped after they had first passed through the Hudson Highlands. Those abductees presumably had long since made their way home, spreading word of their experience as they went. A gauntlet was waiting for Hudson to run—if he had not in fact begun to run it already.

WITH A NORTHWESTERLY coming to his aid, Hudson was able to sail down the entirety of the Tappan Zee on October 2 and into the river's narrowing where it approaches Manhattan Island. They anchored as the flood arrived. The *Half Moon* was near "a point of land," which was probably Jeffery's Hook, on Manhattan's Washington Heights. Fort Washington would be built here during the American Revolution, taking advantage of the constriction in the river and the vantage point of Manhattan's highest elevation. The hook has been absorbed by the base of the George Washington Bridge.

Hudson was about ten nautical miles above the Battery, within striking range of the sea, but he was held in check by the contrary tide. As he waited to move on, a large group of natives approached from downriver.

At least two canoes neared the anchored ship. None of the natives were allowed to board, as they were "thinking to betray us," and this time Juet was entitled to his suspicions. He avowed they had recognized none other than one of their escaped captives among the would-be traders.

Whether the paddlers were Canarsie or Lenape, or some combination, isn't known. Refused permission to board, two canoes at the stern became attack platforms for archers who fired on the *Half Moon*. Six crewmembers responded with musket fire, dropping "two or three" of the attackers. Meanwhile, over at Jeffery's Hook "above an hundred" archers massed on the shore and rained arrows down on them. They may have been Lenape from the settlement area just upriver along Spuyten Duyvil Creek called Shorakapok.

Juet seized command of a falconet and aimed it at the hook. The two-inch iron ball tore into the archers, killing two and scattering the rest. Some of them launched a canoe. Juet reloaded the falconet in time to fire at the approaching craft and its nine or ten occupants, blowing a hole through the hull and killing one man outright, while musket fire finished off another three or four.

The spasm of violence was a brief firefight in which only one side was fighting with fire. More than ten natives had been killed in the exchange. Juet did not report so much as an arrow wound aboard the *Half Moon*, and Hudson was nowhere to be found in his description of the action. Still, the English passage-seeker could now say he had presided over one of the bloodiest exploration efforts in the history of eastern North America. The *Half Moon*'s men had struck out at anyone who crossed them, regardless of nation or tribe, degree of guilt, or appropriateness of response.

Hudson may have come to the river that bears his name as something of a god, if the first-contact oral histories can be believed. But he must have been leaving as a monster to many of its people. The men of the *Half Moon* had turned out to be more than he had bargained for, mastiffs he could not always bring to heel. Henry Hudson's esoteric quest for a passage to the Orient was leaving behind a trail of dead, and his own performance had become a pooling of shame, miscalculation, and impotent leadership. There was nothing more to do but move on. That is, if he could actually escape the place, and the wrath of his own men.

THE HORRENDOUS DEMONSTRATION of the *Half Moon*'s weapons at Jeffery's Hook had, for the time being, driven away the attackers. Hudson moved downriver two leagues, to anchor in a bay on the west side, at Castle Point on the Hoboken waterfront.

And with a swift change of subject in his journal that was almost predatory in its persistent sense of opportunity, Juet dropped the account of the skirmish to praise the mineral potential of the lands by the anchorage. The river might have been freshly bloodstained, but Juet was on to prospecting: "Hard by [the anchorage] there was a cliff, that looked of the color of a white green, as though it were either copper or silver mine; and I think it to be one of them, by the trees that grow upon it. For they all be burned, and the other places are green as grass; it is on that side of the river that is called Manna-hata."

Regardless of Juet's apparent confusion over which direction the land called Manna-hata was, the green-white cliff he described was on the west side. Juet had found one of the world's rare outcroppings of serpentine rock, at Castle Point. Akerly would chip away at it, describing Hoboken as a "little promontory of serpentine," which, "when polished, is variegated with many shades of green . . . Here may be found the fibrous asbestos, of a beautiful olive green, running in thin veins through the serpentine."

Juet may only have seen the green cliff, lustrous in a downpour, from the deck of the *Half Moon*, as it was unlikely anyone left the security of the ship only hours after the fight at Jeffery's Hook. He was wrong about there being copper and silver, although he had found asbestos, which runs through the serpentine of Hoboken, just as Akerly would describe. Some of it is white, and Juet may have taken its gleaming for silver. And it all turned to gray, then black, as night settled upon the vessel and heavy winds drilled rain against the decks. Juet at least still had a pillow for his head.

THE WEATHER HAD been uncommonly good for the September river journey, very often "fair" or "hot" in Juet's account. The morning after the skirmish off Jeffery's Hook, the *Half Moon* was reminded of why Michaelmas was a cue to mariners not to tempt the mood of the North Atlantic. The heavy wind and rain of the night continued into the new day, October 3. It was "very stormy," according to Juet, hammering at them out of the east-northeast. The *Half Moon* was blown aground, then blown right off again as the wind shifted to the north-northwest. They reanchored in four fathoms and chose to go no farther. No natives emerged from the "thick weather" to harass them, much less attempt any trade.

When the weather turned fair on Sunday, October 4, with a north-northwesterly to send them running, they at last cleared the river below the tip of Manhattan Island and were into the upper bay. Where they went next is not easy to follow from Juet's account, but Hudson seems to have attempted a parting inspection of Raritan Bay and the mouth of the Raritan River, grounding in the process along the south shore of Staten Island. They cleared themselves and sounded their way back out to open water.

"Then we took in our boat, and set our mainsail, and spritsail, and our topsails, and steered away east southeast, and southeast by east off into the main sea," wrote Juet. The Hudson River was now behind Henry Hudson. He would never see it again. His foremost concern now was to live to see England.

CHAPTER 26

W HEREVER TO GO NEXT.

No one aboard the *Half Moon* wanted to return to Amsterdam. Yet the alternatives, beyond wandering the seas as fugitives from the VOC to the end of their days, were few. The crew by now was threatening Hudson, and he could no longer trust the Dutch majority in determining where the *Half Moon* should be pointed.

"More could have been done, if the crew had been willing, and if the want of some necessary provisions had not prevented it," Van Meteren would write. "While at sea, they held a council together, but were of different opinions." The Dutch mate suggested they overwinter in Newfoundland and then attempt the Northwest Passage the next season, but Hudson wasn't buying the plan. "He was afraid of the mutinous crew," Van Meteren would explain, "who had sometimes savagely threatened him, and he feared that during the cold season they would entirely consume their provisions, and would then be obliged to return."

More worrying would have been the likelihood that these insolent men would seize control and get rid of Hudson, that the very idea of overwintering in Newfoundland and trying for the strait beyond the Furious Overfall last tested by George Waymouth was a ruse to give them control of the ship. For once, Hudson, a man who never went home until he had exhausted every possibility of discovery on a voyage, wanted to go home.

According to Van Meteren, Hudson proposed that they head for Ireland, which was agreed to. For whatever reason, they never did call there. After clearing the New York bight, they sailed "without seeing any land by the way," according to Juet, for more than a month. Finally, on November 7, Juet concluded his journal account, "Being Saturday, by the Grace of God, we safely arrived in the range of Dartmouth, in Devonshire, in 1609."

DARTMOUTH WAS AN interesting choice of landfall. Hudson had brought the *Half Moon* into a riverine harbor on the river Dart in a prominent West Country fishing port. It was a major activity center for the Newfoundland cod fishery, and a source of political strength for the Gilbert family. Past explorers had routinely called here on their return to England. But it also had a shady reputation, as a port along a porous coast of crannies and coves that was notorious for pirates, smugglers, spies, and other undesirables. It was much closer to France than it was to London—Cherbourg was about eighty nautical miles to the southeast, across the English Channel—and its reputation and distractions made the City's merchants nervous. Five months after Henry Hudson brought the *Half Moon* into Dartmouth, the East India Company would dispatch its sixth trade mission to the Far East. Included in the instructions to its commander, Sir Henry Middleton, was the following: "To prevent disorder either on the outward or homeward voyages, the General is forbidden (unless compelled by necessity) to allow any of his ships to touch at Falmouth, Plymouth, or Dartmouth."

Southern Ireland was similarly disreputable, which may have been why it was the initial choice of landfall, but the disorder-prone Dartmouth would have better suited Hudson. It returned him to his home country, while being safely removed from both loci of power in his life, Amsterdam and London. The Dutch majority in his crew evidently was content with it as well. He could hole up here while planning his next move. But virtually from the moment of his arrival, Hudson was under surveillance.

AS THE MAYOR of Dartmouth, Thomas Holland naturally took an active interest in the comings and goings of his busy harbor. The attentiveness concomitant with his office made him an ideal watcher of the coast, an informant in Sir Robert Cecil's extensive domestic spy network.

The appearance of the *Half Moon* was almost insultingly easy to detect: Hudson had sailed an armed VOC jaght right into his port and stayed there. This was not the sort of arrival Holland would have been accustomed to seeing. The *Half Moon* was like some exotic seabird, blown ashore by distant winds, that was showing no great hurry to be away again. The ship was hiding in plain view, and Hudson moreover was being anything but secretive about where he had been and what he was planning to do next.

After more than a month at sea on the Atlantic crossing, and with seven months having passed since clearing Texel, there would have been much to tend to. Beyond routine shipboard maintenance, there was sickness aboard, according to Van Meteren.* The crew must have come ashore, as Hudson did, and the comings and goings of so many Dutchmen—"Flemings," Holland called them—would have been cause for remark.

Holland befriended Hudson and chatted him up. The ship's master was so breathlessly and unguardedly convivial that Holland had plenty to set down in the letter he then wrote to the Earl of Salisbury. He addressed it to Cecil as Lord High Treasurer, but it was really intended for Cecil to read in his other capacity as secretary of state and chief spymaster.

"My duties to your Honour humbly acknowledged," Holland began his letter, then informed Cecil that a ship out of Amsterdam called the *Half Moon*, "of 70 tons or thereabouts," had just arrived, "whereof one Henry Hudson, an Englishman late of London, is master." In addition to a dozen Dutchmen in the crew, Holland counted two other unnamed Englishmen, who would have been Robert Juet and Hudson's son John. Holland never knew that there had been a fourth Englishman, John Colman, now buried on the American shore.

Holland otherwise was well informed by Hudson of what he'd been up to. The letter explained "that in March last he was set forth out of Amsterdam by the East Indian Company there for the discovery of the North-East passage." Hudson had "proceeded as far as the coast of Nova Zembla and was in 72 degrees [latitude], and that his company (who are all Flemings

---

* Scurvy is naturally suspected, but it wasn't necessarily the case. Hudson did unusually well on his next voyage at prolonging the appearance of the scourge in his crew, and he may have been privy to the rarefied knowledge, demonstrated by Sir James Lancaster on his East Indies voyages, that citrus juice could combat it. The disease otherwise tended to show up on any voyage in which a ship was at sea for more than three months. But Hudson had just spent about a month in the Hudson River estuary, where his men had enjoyed a fresh and varied diet, and the crossing to Dartmouth had only taken a month. If it was not scurvy, then, Hudson may have been dealing with some contagion, an influenza perhaps, although it's not clear where the virus might have been first contracted.

besides himself and two others), being unable to endure the cold, he altered his voyage, and passing by the northern parts of Scotland directed his course for the coast of America."

Holland went on to relate the main details of the voyage, and how after departing the Chesapeake Hudson had "discovered a goodly river, into which he sailed with his ship 50 leagues up and found by his sounding there that the same is navigable with any ships whatsoever."

Now Hudson was in Dartmouth, with his Dutch ship and his mostly Dutch crew. He planned to stay in Dartmouth for ten days, "and upon advice, which he expects from a Dutchman in London, being furnished with some necessaries here, intends to return again to the coast of America."

The "Dutchman in London" was the consul, Emanuel Van Meteren. Hudson had promptly sent him a proposal for the VOC that was almost arrogant, if not typically insubordinate. He must have stewed over it all the way across the Atlantic.

Hudson had no interest in taking the *Half Moon* back to Amsterdam. He wanted to stay in Dartmouth and prepare for a new voyage. While Holland understood it would be to the "coast of America," this was a fairly broad concept. The label *America pars* on charts could and did extend to lands all the way to the presumed location of the Northwest Passage, and this was where Hudson intended to go next. He had no interest in returning to the river that would bear his name, or investigating the coast from the New York bight to Cape Cod that only Verrazzano for certain had seen.

According to Van Meteren, Hudson proposed to the VOC that he replace six or seven of the *Half Moon*'s crew. Illness might have been an issue, but insubordination was probably the greater concern. As someone who had been such a nuisance to the VOC on this voyage, Hudson could not tolerate anyone being a further nuisance to him. The ship's complement would be increased to twenty, probably by adding Englishmen. Hudson further demanded fifteen hundred florins (as the Dutch guilder was also informally known) for supplies, above and beyond the crew's wages, for the new voyage. That was almost twice the eight hundred guilders he'd been paid to provide for himself and his family and outfit the 1609 voyage.

Particularly interesting about Van Meteren's account, is that Hudson was in no hurry to leave Dartmouth under the scheme he proposed to the VOC, despite Thomas Holland's understanding that he expected to be under way in just ten days. The plan put to the VOC called for the *Half Moon* to sail from Dartmouth on March 1, 1610. Hudson would devote April and half of May to fishing and whaling, to relieve the investors' expenses, before investigating the Northwest Passage.

Hudson did not intend to sail right through the passage. He was only proposing to make a preliminary investigation, probably to sort out the highly confusing geography left behind by the English voyages of Frobisher, Davis, and Waymouth that lay between Greenland and the entrance to the Furious Overfall, and if time permitted to probe fully the hundred leagues of the strait Waymouth said existed beyond the overfall.*

Hudson's proposal called for him to end his explorations by mid-September and then—at last—return the *Half Moon* to Holland after sailing over the north of Scotland. In making such a specific assurance of his final course, Hudson may have been implicitly promising not to wander into a West Country port again.

By the time Thomas Holland was able to speak with the voluble Hudson, the rogue master of the *Half Moon* was already waiting to hear back from Van Meteren about his exciting new voyage proposal. But there was much about Hudson's circumstances, behavior, and plans that simply would not square with any single source, or even add up as a logical chain of events.

The timing difference in the accounts of Van Meteren and Holland was one issue. Was Hudson in a hurry to get out of Dartmouth, or wasn't he? Perhaps he had promised the Dutch crew to stay for about a fortnight (although where else they would have preferred to be isn't clear) while actually intending to remain for as long as possible. But the schedule Hudson shared with Holland made no sense. Beyond the fact that Van Meteren was in no position to green-light a new voyage without first delivering the proposal to the VOC and receiving their response (which would require the usual time-consuming consent of the majority of directors from more than one chamber), there was scarcely enough time for Van Meteren simply to reply to Hudson's missive. It took four days for Holland's letter to reach Cecil at his estate, Hatfield House, in Hertfordshire; Hudson could hardly

---

* Among the many confusions yet to be sorted out was the location of Frobisher Strait. It was actually Frobisher Bay, a dead end in eastern Baffin Island, which Davis, unable to recognize it, had given a name of his own, Lumley's Inlet. When the Molyneux globe was created in 1593 with input from Davis, the problem of where to put Frobisher Strait was resolved by running it right through Greenland. Confirming that the strait was actually there would be a worthwhile activity of any new voyage to the northwest.

have expected speedier service for his letter to Van Meteren in London. The time in transit for a message and response was probably eight to ten days, if Van Meteren did nothing but issue immediate approval for Hudson's plan. Van Meteren would do no such thing. And since Hudson did not expect Van Meteren to do any such thing, why would he have told Holland that he expected to be at sea again in ten days, sailing for the coast of America for the VOC?

Complicating matters is Van Meteren's recollection that news of Hudson's appearance in Dartmouth was anything but swift to reach him. "A long time elapsed through contrary winds before the Company could be informed of the arrival of the ship in England," Van Meteren would write. Something or someone had gotten in the way of Hudson's communications with the Dutch consul, if Hudson had indeed sent word immediately, as Holland understood. Or something or someone had prevented Van Meteren's own communications from getting to the VOC in Amsterdam.

Most perplexing was the behavior of Hudson himself. He had been a positive chatterbox with Holland, revealing an astonishing amount about the *Half Moon* voyage and his present ambitions. England was essentially a police state, and saying the wrong things to the wrong people could cost someone his liberty or even his life. Hudson could not have been so naïve as to think that his speaking freely with the mayor of Dartmouth would not result in precisely the sort of letter that Holland immediately wrote to Cecil. Hudson further elevated the strangeness of the exchange by dropping those two prominent names at court and in Cecil's own circle, by telling Holland he was "well known (as he told me) to Sir Walter Cope and Sir Thomas Challener."

And while the mayor was impressed with Hudson's suitability for exploration, "finding him also in my understanding to be a man of experience and fit for such employment," Holland suspected Hudson was holding something back: "it seems to me, by conferring with him, that he has discovered some especial matters of greater consequence which he would not impart."

It is entirely possible, even likely, that Emanuel Van Meteren was not the only person Hudson wrote on his arrival in Dartmouth. He had secrets to share that he would not disclose to Holland. Other letters may have gone out, specifically to Cope and Challener, his contacts or patrons at court, and perhaps to Sir Thomas Smythe as well. If he had not been working for them all along, he was prepared to work for them now.

Given how much Hudson gladly revealed to a total stranger like Holland, he surely knew that the mayor would get word of his arrival and the basic details he had spilled to court, particularly to Cecil. After all, he had just told Holland of how he had taken a VOC ship right into the territory of the Virginia Company, in which Cope and Challener were leading investors, and that he was quite possibly heading right back there again, depending on how someone chose to interpret "the coast of America." That was a red flag that Cecil in particular could not ignore. And Hudson held back just enough about what he'd seen in the New World to set a bit of bait. Because he didn't just withhold secrets—he let Holland understand that he *had* secrets.

The ten-day departure window assuredly was a fiction Hudson had no intention of meeting, as it could never be met, but it did set the clock ticking. Hudson was playing two powerful groups off against each other: the VOC on one hand, and the merchant adventurers and senior figures of court associated with the Virginia Company on the other. Ten days was all the English players had to get back to him. He wanted an early show of interest in what he'd found in the New World, which he could use to leverage the voyage he really wanted, had always wanted, to make. Someone was going to send him to the Northwest Passage. He would sit still in Dartmouth until he found out who.

IT WOULD NOT be the VOC. Perhaps that wasn't much of a surprise to Hudson. He may even have expected it—been counting on it—all along, having made an offer he could be fairly certain they would refuse. The idea of using a jaght like the *Half Moon* for fishing and whaling seemed absurd. And Hudson would have had to be delusional to think the VOC would agree to almost double the funds they'd provided him for the 1609 voyage, a voyage on which he had proceeded to toss his sailing instructions overboard. Not to mention the fact that Petrus Plancius had already told him that searching for the Northwest Passage was a waste of time, or the fact that Hudson was proposing to be sent out a second time without having to first show his face in Amsterdam. But making the proposal bought Hudson some time and gave him an excuse for holing up in Dartmouth rather than sailing directly to Amsterdam.

When word of his return and his proposal did reach the VOC, the response was not welcoming. Surprise: the company had no interest in sending Hudson in search of the Northwest Passage. Surprise again: they wanted their ship back, and the papers from the 1609 voyage. And surprise of surprises: they wanted Hudson to make the delivery, so he could answer for his actions.

But Hudson was going nowhere near Amsterdam, ever again. Why not is yet another element of the strange intrigue of his chosen seclusion in Dartmouth.

According to Van Meteren, Hudson was in fact supposed to leave Dartmouth in January 1610, to obediently return the *Half Moon* to Amsterdam. But on the verge of departure, Hudson and the other English aboard "were commanded by the government there not to leave England but to serve their own country." Henry and John Hudson and Robert Juet had been all but arrested and prevented from serving any maritime nation other than their own in further explorations.

"Many persons thought it rather unfair that these sailors should thus be prevented from laying their accounts and reports before their employers," Van Meteren noted, "chiefly as the enterprise in which they had been engaged was such as to benefit navigation in general." But not everyone in the Dutch republic would be convinced that Hudson was entirely innocent in this affair. When Hessel Gerritsz wrote in 1612 about Hudson's final voyage of 1610–11, he cast a glance back at the *Half Moon* voyage and expressed a suspicion circulating in Holland that Hudson had not been entirely loyal to his employer: "he seems . . . according to the opinion of our countrymen, purposely to have missed the right road to the western passage, unwilling to benefit Holland and the Directors of the Dutch East India Company by such a discovery." More might have been made of Hudson's insubordination by subsequent Dutch writers, had the official line on Hudson then not radically changed in pursuit of greater geopolitical goals, as we shall see.

As for Hudson's January 1610 detention, it is possible that he had overplayed his hand, or had just been recklessly stupid, and that courtly powers indeed forbade him to sail for anyone but England, in no small part because he had been poking around in territories claimed by England in a VOC vessel without first asking anyone's permission to do so. It had only been seven years since Raleigh was able to have Bartholomew Gilbert's ship and cargo seized at Southampton for allegedly transgressing on his charter from Elizabeth I. But while Van Meteren may have sincerely believed Hudson was unwillingly restrained from serving the VOC ever again, there were problems with the scenario. Although this is far from a decisive factor, nothing about Hudson with respect to his detention and compulsory service for England survives in the Calendar of State Papers for the reign of James I, even though such an order also presumably would have required the interest of the Privy Council. The letters and other records of the time are strikingly silent on Henry Hudson.

It also had only been two years since George Waymouth was "arrested" at dockside in Kent, on the way to giving away secrets of the Virginia Company to the Spanish, only to be handsomely pensioned a few months later by James I. One has to suspect that Hudson had just undergone a similar extraction by the court figures he was close to. He was not a double agent like Waymouth, working against the Spanish, but rather was an English mariner with privileged information who did not want to have to answer for his behavior in Amsterdam. And so the "detention" scenario was trotted out and paraded before Van Meteren and the VOC.

The *Half Moon* eventually did make it back to Amsterdam, in July 1610, according to company records. Van Meteren never did elaborate on the nature of the "contrary winds" that delayed the return of the *Half Moon* and the ship's papers, but he surely suspected the same higher authorities that allegedly quashed any possibility of Hudson sailing for the VOC again.

The irony of the situation is that the VOC most certainly did not want Hudson to sail for them again. The purported injunction only prevented Hudson from completing his current VOC voyage. In truth, it handily extricated him from that extreme inconvenience. By the time the *Half Moon* and the papers were back in Amsterdam, Henry and John Hudson and Robert Juet were already at sea, on the assignment Henry Hudson had long yearned for. But never mind Amsterdam: none would ever see England again.

CHAPTER 27

WE CANNOT SAY FOR CERTAIN what the "especial matters of greater consequence" were that Henry Hudson "would not impart," according to Thomas Holland's letter. But the bait Hudson dangled as he set the clock ticking in Dartmouth must have been tailored for the enthusiasms of men like Cope, Cecil, and Smythe. It could have been the information Juet and Hudson recorded about precious metals, ores, and minerals, the sorts of things that had caused so much distractive grief in the first years of the Jamestown colony. Perhaps they felt the information they could impart about the settlement potential of the Hudson River also was of value. All of it was set down in Juet's journal, which was not part of the official ship's papers and would have been written for a privileged English audience.

The evidence Hudson had gathered that bore on the true nature of the passage Wright had drawn from the St. Lawrence to the Atlantic also would have been of considerable interest, and we can be sure that Hudson made available his cartography. It only survives thirdhand and would not surface for more than 250 years, when a map composed of four sheets of letter-sized paper turned up in the Spanish archives at Simanca, in 1887.

Today it is called the Velasco Map, as it is believed to have been sent to Philip III by the new Spanish ambassador to the court of James I, Don Alonzo de Velasco. A letter from Velasco to the king on March 22, 1611, reporting on recent events in Virginia, refers to a map that is no longer attached to the letter, but the so-called Velasco Map, when discovered in the archives, was considered to be the one in question. Velasco explained that James I "sent last year a surveyor to survey that Province [i.e., the Virginia territory], and he returned here about three months ago and presented to him a plan or map of all that he could discover, a copy of which I send Y. M. [Your Majesty]."

Yet no single voyage could have surveyed the entirety of what the map showed, as it stretches from Cape Fear all the way to Newfoundland and far inland, up the St. Lawrence. However, Velasco may have been referring to a different map entirely, one still lost and perhaps produced by Samuel Argall after his 1610 cruise. The cartographic historian R. C. D. Baldwin proposed that the lost original was the work of an elite team, comprised of Samuel Argall, Richard Hakluyt, John Smith, and William Strachey, and that it was a master chart kept in the London headquarters of the Virginia Company. This scenario holds that the work could not have begun any sooner than March 1611, when Argall returned from Jamestown with the Virginia colony's governor, Thomas West, Baron De-La-Warr, who was seriously ill. Baldwin also asserted that the map was not copied by Spanish agents until March 1612. It could not have been created any later than 1613, as by then Samuel de Champlain had published his first comprehensive map of eastern North America, and we would expect elements of it to have been incorporated.

The map is strikingly better detailed than anything commercially available at that time. The team had access to the many charts that we know were made (or would have been made) by English voyagers in the first decade of the seventeenth century but that have not survived. Its makers employed a color scheme for different areas. As these colored zones don't always align with discoveries of particular voyages, they may have indicated a different sort of source, perhaps unpublished regional charts already composed by and for the company. Only one color is explained, by a notation indicating, "All the blue is dune by the relation of the Indians."

The map shows Delaware Bay, the Hudson River estuary, and the Hudson River north to Albany. A single color, a rusty brown, binds together all of the discoveries, except for the oddity of Staten Island being rendered in yellow, the map's dominant color. The color scheme suggests that Hudson was the single source, but we can't be sure how much of the map relied exclusively on his findings, as by 1611 the Dutch were making trade visits to the same area, and Argall had inspected Delaware Bay in 1610. Because of

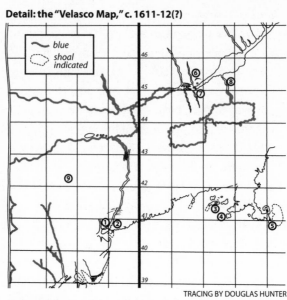

Detail: the "Velasco Map," c. 1611-12(?)

TRACING BY DOUGLAS HUNTER

Selected map labels

1. Manahata
2. Manahatin
3. Elizabethas Ile
4. Marthays Viniard
5. Cape Cod
6. Mont Roiall
7. The first Salt or fall
8. R. Irocois
9. "All the blue is dune by the relations of the Indians"

Velasco tracing.

the drawing's large scale, there isn't much room for detail where Hudson's explorations are concerned. But while place-names (with two exceptions) are not included in the Hudson exploration area from Delaware Bay north, the map shows Raritan Bay, Sandy Hook, the Raritan River, and even Matawan Creek on the south shore of Raritan Bay, which Hudson could have noticed on the very last, confusingly described day of his explorations, before he headed across the Atlantic to Dartmouth.

Staten Island is rendered properly as an island, with Arthur Kill, Kill Van Kull, and Newark Bay also shown. An island to the east of the Narrows, set in a dotted depiction of the east and west banks, is Coney Island. There are several indentations along the south shore of what would prove to be Long Island. Nothing is concretely identifiable as Rockaway Inlet. The map's suggestion of Long Island's southern profile (but not the sound) suggests that a Dutch source was used in addition to Hudson, as the *Half Moon* never saw land between departing Lower New York Bay and reaching Dartmouth.

While the first Dutch traders could have produced maps that informed the Velasco Map's portrait of the Hudson River, it is reasonable to conclude that Hudson was the fundamental source. Once through the Narrows, the map depicts Upper New York Bay so simply that it is indistinguishable from the river course. In perfect agreement with Juet's narrative, there is no East River, no Long Island Sound. (Neither would be discovered until 1614, by Dutch trader Adriaen Block.) Manhattan is not an island. On either side of the unlabeled lower Hudson River is a double label that seems to speak to Juet's confusion about the identity of Manhattan. It calls the west side of the lower Hudson River *Manahata* and the east side *Manahatin*.

Above the Tappan Zee, the Hudson Highlands are sketched in, and the long reach is also identifiable. The river peters out in the north in a way that indicates its source was not reached. Beginning parallel to it at its most explored northern limits in a cluster of dots is another river, which leads northwest. Drawn in blue, it is thus based on native input, and it leads to an enormous body of water stretching westward. That water continues to widen into a veritable ocean until it disappears out of the left margin. But scalloped shoreline along the left margin below it indicates a western sea, and the likelihood that this great inland water is directly connected to the Pacific. From the eastern end of this great water body the St. Lawrence flows.

This blue river can only be the Mohawk. Hudson himself didn't reach it, but the Dutch mate's survey party, as we've seen, would have had to go past its confluence with the Hudson on their way upstream on September 22, had they progressed as far as they claimed. Even if the mate's survey gave no clue to the river's existence, Hudson on several occasions had the surrounding lands pointed out to him by a Mahican elder, and a feature as important as the Mohawk would have been revealed to him. It's also possible that Hudson had a Mahican draw him a map, as Champlain did in questioning native guides, perhaps while serving up aqua vitae in his cabin.

The puzzle is how the Velasco Map's ties in Hudson's discoveries, including the Mohawk, with the St. Lawrence and the great body of water leading to the western sea. The map shows the Mohawk emptying into this great body of water. The river's course seems wrong, as it flows northwest, away from the Hudson, when it actually flows eastward, into it. And the Mohawk never does reach the nearest large body of water.

But for natives, the two rivers were not connected in practical terms. The

Cohoe Falls were such an impediment to travel that a fifteen-mile portage was instead used between present-day Albany on the Hudson and Schenectady on the Mohawk. This would explain the curious dots, which seem to follow a convention used in Champlain's cartography for indicating a portage route. Similar rows of dots appear elsewhere in the Velasco Map, in the upper St. Lawrence, next to "Mont Roiall," the future site of Montréal. (This label is missing from Edward Wright's map but suggests Hakluyt as a source, as he employed the place-name Mount Roiall in his translation of Cartier.) Those circles probably indicated the portage past what the Velasco Map calls the "first Salt or fall," which Champlain called the Grand Sault ("great rapids") and today are known as the Lachine Rapids. The dots overlaying the convergence of the Hudson and the Mohawk likewise indicate the portage. They might have first appeared in a map drawn for Hudson by a Mahican, with their purpose becoming obscured by repeated copying.

The Mohawk does not, as depicted, flow into eastern Lake Ontario. But explorers who questioned natives were known to confuse literal waterways and portage routes. Hudson would have been told about a route to a Great Lake, which we know employs portages, the Mohawk River, Lake Oneida, and the Oswego River. Given how little Hudson and the Mahican shared in the way of a common language, and that the Velasco Map is several times removed from whatever Hudson brought home, this first stab at describing the Mohawk is entirely tolerable and even logical. Even so, the depiction of four small islands leading to a larger island in the large body of water to the north may have been a misinterpretation by the Velasco Map's compilers of what an original native artist intended to depict: a portage route (dots, not islands) leading from the Mohawk to Lake Oneida.

Did Hudson think that the Hudson, the Mohawk, and the great body of water leading to a western sea were linked, and that this great body of water was also the source of the St. Lawrence? That is far from certain.

The St. Lawrence drawn as far upstream as present-day Montréal uses color codes that indicate it had a European source, and many elements would have come from maps based on Cartier's explorations. The river course above the rapids at Montréal to the great body of water is all in blue. Intelligence gathered by Hakluyt from Cartier's nephew, Jacques Noël, and from the Basque informant Stevan de Bocall, could have been used for these blue areas. But it would appear that the map's compilers were also working from a text. For the blue areas other than the Mohawk River portage route reflect the general description that Samuel de Champlain included of the passage to the South Sea beyond the Lachine Rapids as well as the route up the River of the Iroquois in *Des Sauvages*, based on the testimony of natives. The color of the River of the Iroquois (which is labeled *R. Irocois*) even changes to blue, agreeing with how Champlain abandoned his 1603 effort to travel any farther upstream and relied instead on natives to tell him what lay beyond. And Richard Hakluyt knew this material better than anyone in England, having produced an unpublished translation of *Des Sauvages*. The Velasco Map thus illustrates an unappreciated aspect of mapmaking in this period: a cartographer was capable of working from a textual description as much as another source map in rendering a new, comprehensive view.

Studies of the map typically (and understandably) equate the great body of water with Lake Ontario, which is indeed the first Great Lake upstream of the St. Lawrence. But it should not be accepted as a literal rendering of that lake. In its implied relationship with the scalloped shores of the left margin, it is meant instead to depict the great inland sea that led to the Southern Ocean as described by Champlain in *Des Sauvages*. It is no more a true Lake Ontario than was the Lake Tadouac cited by Hayes and drawn by Edward Wright.

The map renders Lake Champlain and Lake George as two large, quasi-rectangular bodies of water, as the mapmakers had nothing more to go on than Champlain's simple description. (Champlain also wrote that ten rivers flowed into the first lake. The Velasco Map appears to randomly distribute about that many around the shores of both lakes.) Such shapes mimic the rectangular outlines cartographers often gave to islands sighted or heard of but not yet properly charted. Of course, by 1610, Champlain had actually visited at least Lake Champlain, but he had published nothing about his 1609 journey and wouldn't publish a map until 1613. The eastern end of the great body of water also has this somewhat angular rendering, which has given it a more explicit, if accidental, similarity to Lake Ontario than the actual evidence in hand would have made possible.

Hudson could have been consulted on the map's planning before he embarked on his next voyage, in April 1610. Its features thus could reflect his own wrestling with the relationship between his recent explorations and the best evidence for what Champlain had determined lay to the north. Therein may have been some of the "especial matters of greater consequence" he hinted at in conversation with Thomas Holland. The portion of the Velasco Map derived from Champlain's writing likely was worked out at a much earlier date by Hakluyt, early enough for its implications to influence the instructions provided to the original Virginia Company on how to choose a river passage leading to the South Sea, in seeking one with a course leading to the northwest of the Chesapeake.

The Velasco Map failed to resolve the relationship between the Hudson River as explored by Hudson and the corridor down through the River of the Iroquois, Lake Champlain, and Lake George as described by Champlain in 1603. While Champlain had indicated that a river flowed to the sea in "Florida" after a short portage from the second lake, the compilers of the Velasco Map didn't know how to sort out the difficult evidence thereabouts. The general thinking was that the desired river to the sea was in Norumbega. As noted, Champlain would wrongly conclude that this river was the Charles in modern Boston. The Hudson River in the Velasco Map is set well to the west of the two rectangular lakes that derive from Champlain's reportage in *Des Sauvages*. The relationship between them eluded definition, no doubt because no one could accurately measure longitude, but perhaps also because Hudson himself never grasped it in questioning the Mahican. And so, while the water course drawn by Wright was now gone, the corridor that would prove to be of tremendous strategic importance was still unrecognized. Henry Hudson was not going back to try to clarify matters, and would not return from the *Discovery* voyage to report if there was in fact a northern passage into the great body of water leading west as well.

CHAPTER 28

WITH THE COMPLETION OF the *Half Moon* voyage, Henry Hudson had become a living omnibus of the passage-seeking effort. No person alive or dead had sought a new Oriental route in as many directions as he had. And despite his blatant disregard for his sailing instructions in 1609 (which, unless they put him up to it in the first place, most if not all of his 1610 English backers probably knew nothing about), Hudson was extremely dependable by the measure of the day. He had made three voyages without losing a ship and had lost only one man, the unfortunate Colman. If you sent him out, you were highly likely to get him back, along with the ship and crew, and to learn new things, or at least to have earlier explorations properly fact-checked by him.

As someone who was supposedly barred from sailing for any other nation than his own, Hudson was hardly downtrodden. He enjoyed enthusiastic support from the leading figures in trade and at court in London for the next voyage. Its patron was Prince Henry, newly vested as Prince of Wales, and the backers included Sir Thomas Challener, Sir Walter Cope, Sir Robert Cecil, Sir Charles Howard (Lord High Admiral), and both the East India and Muscovy companies, which naturally meant a leading role for Sir Thomas Smythe.

The plan Hudson had presented to Van Meteren for consideration by the VOC was essentially the one accepted by his English sponsors for 1610, with the exception that he wouldn't have to do any fishing or whaling in order to defray expenses. No sailing instructions survive, but the voyage was clearly intended to be a single-season reconnaissance, as he was not provided with a pinnace (as Waymouth was in 1602), which would have served as a messenger vessel to bring home an interim report on progress while Hudson either overwintered in the Arctic or pressed through to the Orient. Hudson would reinvestigate the accomplishments of Waymouth as the foundation for a future voyage. To that end, he was given Waymouth's vessel, the *Discovery*, and even the mate from that voyage, William Cobreth. Also included in the crew of twenty-three were Hudson's son John and Robert Juet.

Five days after departing London on April 17, Hudson was back to his old ways. His disobedience was becoming pathological. While anchored off Sheppey Isle at the mouth of the Thames, he dismissed Cobreth, sending him back to London with a letter for the investors "importing the reason wherefore I so put him out of the ship, and so plied forth," according to his voyage journal. As the letter has never been found, we don't know what excuse Hudson gave, and no one else aboard shed any light on the decision.

The explorer Luke Foxe would suggest in 1635 that it was professional jealousy, that Cobreth "was every way held to be a better man" than Hudson. That may have been true, but Cobreth probably posed a more specific problem. Hudson likely had no intention of making a single-season reconnaissance. Cobreth would have known the sailing instructions, and he had his own difficult history. The 1602 Waymouth voyage was supposed to have overwintered in the Arctic, but the crew had refused, forcing Waymouth to return home. Cobreth had supported that respectful but firm insurrection, and while Waymouth praised Cobreth in his journal as a "skillful man in his profession," he nevertheless punished him for his disobedience. In the ensuing inquiry, the voyage's supercargo, the Reverend John Cartwright (who coincidentally had participated with Captain Thomas Hudson in the 1679–81 Muscovy Company expedition to Persia) was blamed for the uprising. Hudson would have known that Cobreth would never abide an attempt by him to overwinter, especially when that would most certainly mean defying the sailing instructions.

In Cobreth's place, Hudson installed Robert Juet as his mate, whose position at departure otherwise is unknown. Hudson must have had this plan in mind from the moment he left St. Katherine's Pool. And there was more to Hudson's crew adjustments. He had paused at Tilbury Hope to bring aboard a young man named Henry Greene, a troubled, highborn fellow with a gambling problem. As the voyage's supercargo, Habakkuk Prickett would note, Greene was not "set down in the owner's book, nor any wages made for him." Hudson explained that Greene was along because he could "write well," according to Prickett, and so would be given the task of composing an official voyage account.

When the *Discovery* reached Iceland, the crew's cohesion began to disintegrate. Henry Greene got into a fight with the barber-surgeon, Edward Wilson, "which set the company in a rage," according to Prickett. Wilson tried to quit the voyage by staying ashore but was talked out of leaving. Hudson declined to discipline Greene and even blamed Wilson for the incident, telling Prickett that the barber-surgeon "had a tongue that would wrong the best friend he had."

Hudson was then wronged by the tongue of Robert Juet. After departing Iceland, Juet got deep in his cups in conversation with the carpenter, Philip Staffe. The carpenter must have been wondering what was so special about Greene that he could be allowed to almost cost them their barber-surgeon. Juet revealed that Greene's true role was as shipboard snitch, to spy on the crew for Hudson and watch for signs of insurrection. When word got back to Hudson, he was so enraged with Juet that he considered returning to Iceland and putting his mate on the first fishing boat returning to England. Relations were patched up, but much damage had been done. Greene's true role had been exposed, and Juet had begun to break with the master who had held him in such esteem.

Perhaps the signs had already been there for Hudson to read on the *Half Moon* voyage: that Juet, in his relentless mistrust of the natives and his involvement in the bloody clashes, would never defer unquestioningly to Hudson's command. They were scarcely beyond the Furious Overfall and into Hudson Strait when Juet began to openly defy Hudson. With the *Discovery* almost trapped by ice in Ungava Bay, Juet agitated for an abandonment of the voyage, instilling fear among the crew about the prospects of overwintering. The irony of Hudson having to contend with precisely the crisis of command that he surely had hoped to avoid by replacing Cobreth with Juet was almost too delicious. Their differences were again patched over, but a showdown was brewing. That September it boiled over, as Juet demanded a hearing to respond to allegations made against him by other crewmembers.

Juet got his wish, as several crewmembers gave Bible-sworn testimony while Hudson sat in judgment. They avowed that Juet had made several attempts to incite a mutiny. One swore that Juet "did threaten to turn the head of the ship home," and another alleged that Juet predicted that there "would be manslaughter" and that the insurrection "would prove bloody to some."

Hudson listened to them all, as well as to Juet, and chose the least punitive course. Juet was demoted, replaced as mate by a crewmember named William Wilson. (The boatswain, Francis Clement, was also demoted.) And while Juet may have been confined belowdecks for a spell, Hudson otherwise took no further action against him, and even held out hope that all could be forgiven if Juet and Clement remained on their best behavior.

By then, the *Discovery* was a long way from both England and her mission to make a preliminary investigation of the Furious Overfall and the strait beyond. Three hundred miles into the strait, Hudson had found an enormous expanse of water leading south. There was still ample opportunity to steer west, which was the most reasonable course, as the Northwest Passage was believed to lie somewhere around latitude 62. Instead, Hudson had plunged south with the *Discovery*, sailing the length of what would become known as Hudson Bay and then into James Bay, toward latitude 52. They were deep in this bay, with no hope of returning to England before winter set in, when Juet's hearing was held.

The lack of information about Hudson's expectations of where the Hudson River would take him on the 1609 *Half Moon* voyage may have been due to the same penchant for secrecy he now displayed aboard the *Discovery*. He surveyed James Bay without telling anyone aboard what he was looking for. A voyage participant, Thomas Woodhouse, would attest to this in a note that explained how, at the time of Juet's hearing, they had "now lately been embayed in a deep bay, which the master had desire to see, for some reason to himself known." Prickett would describe how, after Juet's hearing, they sailed back and forth in James Bay for reasons he did not understand: "up to the north we stood till we raised land, then down to the south, and up to the north again, and down again to the south."

Juet surely knew what Hudson was up to, even if it did not explicitly emerge during his hearing.* Woodhouse's account of the hearing observed that Juet lately had been mocking Hudson's ambitions to reach the Orient,

---

* Hudson's journal, as published by Purchas in 1625, provided no insight into his plans, or anything that happened after August 3, 1610, when he turned south into the great bay that would be named for him. The account in Purchas (the only version that survives) plainly had been terminated at that point to preserve confidential details about the possible location of

"jesting at our master's hope to see Bantam by Candlemas [February 2]." Hudson's persistent interest in James Bay, ten degrees of latitude farther south than where the passage was supposed to be, suggests that he had an alternate route in mind and that he continued to be fascinated with the possibilities in Edward Wright's 1599 chart.

On the *Half Moon* voyage, Hudson had probed from the south a river that promised to be the passage leading from the Atlantic to the upper St. Lawrence on Wright's chart. The chart also showed the upper St. Lawrence draining from the protean Great Lake, called Tadouac, which in turn was connected to the Northern Sea by a passage. The deep indentation that Hudson and James bays made into the continent must have held out to Hudson the promise of that passage. Hudson would have been further encouraged by the unique nature of James Bay. Although it is about two hundred miles long and a hundred miles wide, the bay is quite shallow, and its saltwater is noticeably diluted by the outflow of rivers. The farther south Hudson sailed in the *Discovery*, the less saline the water would have become, suggesting that it would lead toward freshwater in the continent.

If Wright proved correct, Hudson's course would deliver him through Lake Tadouac to the St. Lawrence. But if Hudson truly thought he could make it to Bantam in Java by February, as Juet mocked, then he must have been expecting to find a passage west by this route. And that would be possible if the great lake upstream of the St. Lawrence was as Samuel de Champlain had conceived it, and as the Velasco Map portrayed it: an enormous body of water that was actually an arm of the Pacific. Hudson's obsessive, secretive searching in James Bay strongly suggests that he was hoping to find a geographic synergy between Wright and Champlain: a passage from the Northern Sea to the waters upstream of the rapids on the St. Lawrence, which would then allow him to sail west to reach the Orient.

So determined was Hudson to probe the southernmost reaches of James Bay that he committed the *Discovery* to an overwintering that had not been imagined on departure. The location of the chosen sanctuary—around latitude 52, which was likely Rupert Bay in the southeast corner of James

---

the Northwest Passage. At the time of publication, the search was ongoing, and a passage location somewhere in Hudson Bay had not been ruled out. Prickett's journal account is terse and confused in its geographic details and shows signs that it was heavily edited.

Bay—is farther south than Liverpool. That would have given Hudson confidence of a mild winter and allowed him to deflect the concerns Juet's objections would have raised among the crew.

The winter was anything but kindly, but the crew came through the cold and misery in astonishingly good shape. Only one man died, the gunner John Williams, and that was in mid-November, just a few days after Hudson had the *Discovery* beached for the winter, and due to an unreported cause. It was such an exceptional performance that Hudson must have been privy to the rarefied knowledge of how to prevent scurvy with citrus juice. But while the men endured, Hudson's reputation did not.

His downfall, if the account of Prickett can be trusted, began with the simple matter of what to do with the personal effects of the dead gunner. As we've noted with the death of John Colman in 1609, auctioning the effects at the mainmast was an established option. Rather than hold a proper auction, however, Hudson promised the gunner's gray cloth gown to his shipboard snitch and favorite, Henry Greene.

Hudson next asked the carpenter, Philip Staffe, to go ashore and build a cabin for the winter. Staffe refused, believing the season was too far gone for him to do a proper job. Hudson was furious and "ferreted him out of his cabin to strike him, calling him by many foul names, and threatening to hang him," according to Prickett.

Hudson's outburst against a man otherwise portrayed by Prickett as deeply loyal to the master was bizarre, considering how lightly Hudson had responded to Juet's bloody-minded insubordination. Staffe acquiesced and tried to build the cabin, but no use apparently was ever made of it.

Staffe then went off wandering the landscape without Hudson's knowledge or permission, possibly to hunt, or to seek help from any natives that might be in the area. He took Henry Greene with him. When Hudson learned of Staffe's unauthorized expedition, he turned against Greene, reclaiming the gunner's gown. When Greene objected, Hudson lit into him. "The master did so rile on Greene," wrote Prickett, "with so many words of disgrace, telling him, that all his friends would not trust him with twenty shillings, and why should he." According to Prickett, Hudson had promised to Greene the gown for as much as any other crewmember would pay, but also promised that he would arrange for him a position in the guard of the Prince of Wales, which would have come through Sir Thomas Challener. Hudson now threatened to deny Greene all promised benefits.

The overwintering had barely begun, and Hudson had worked himself into a position of profound isolation. Not only was he frozen into a distant recess of North America: the second group of financiers in as many Hudson voyages likely had gathered to wonder what had become of him after he failed to return as planned after a single summer of surveying. And aboard his ship, enemies were gathering. No insolent and unruly sea beggars were on hand this time. Hudson was creating adversaries from within the ranks of his closest allies.

WHEN SPRING ARRIVED, the entire crew (save the gunner) was still alive, but scurvy had begun to take hold, and fresh food was in short supply. Hudson had a stroke of good fortune. A single Cree visitor appeared at the *Discovery*. Hudson treated him well, and he returned pulling a sled of furs to trade. No European had ever visited James Bay, so far as anyone knows, but the Cree were linked through middlemen to the trade based on the St. Lawrence.

The Cree brought with him caribou skins and indicated he wanted an axe head for one skin. Hudson balked: he wanted two skins for the axe head. The Cree agreed, though not willingly. He indicated that there were settlements nearby and that he would return. But the man never did come back. He may have been deeply offended by Hudson's grasping behavior. For the price of a single caribou skin, Hudson's fate could have turned out much differently.

As Hudson had the *Discovery* prepared to sail with the breakup of ice in June, he made an extraordinary decision. He had the shallop assembled so that he could make a journey ostensibly in search of the Cree, to secure victuals, although Hudson assuredly had other things in mind. It would be his last chance to find a passage south out of the bay, as the crew would never have tolerated further explorations with the *Discovery* once under way. His decision to leave the *Discovery* as she was being prepared for departure was the strangest episode of an often strange career. It was as if Hudson had become the first ship's master to lead his own mutiny.

He disappeared with a crew of unknown composition for an unknown number of days. There was still too much ice for the *Discovery* to sail, which Hudson may have been counting on. He returned defeated, with no findings he was willing to share and, most importantly, no fresh supplies from the Cree. Whenever he approached land, Prickett would write, the Cree had set the trees alight, creating a flaming barricade of fear and hostility.

If only he had sailed directly home, as everyone aboard hoped. If only he had not given in to the temptation of further scheming. But Hudson was incapable of returning to London empty-handed. What he had discovered to date evidently was not enough, in his mind. He wanted to keep pushing, for a greater success, and so he began to manipulate the crew ranks in an effort to maintain absolute control of the *Discovery*'s itinerary.

Prickett's recounting of the departure from the overwintering bay is confused, but Hudson appears before leaving to have replaced William Wilson as mate with another sailor, Robert Bylot. At this time Hudson issued a "bill of return," in Prickett's description. It was probably a document that spelled out the command positions for the return voyage, including the order of succession, should Hudson perish. It also may have included language similar to the note he provided the crewmembers of the *Hopewell* in 1608, avowing that the decision to return to London was his alone and had not been made under duress. For as Prickett recounted, Hudson drafted it, "willing them to have that to show, if it pleased God that they came home; and he wept when he gave it to them."

But before the *Discovery* moved out of her overwintering bay, Hudson replaced Bylot as mate with John King, whom Prickett said could neither read nor write. Hudson further confiscated all navigational devices. If King truly was illiterate, that meant only Hudson was now capable of navigating the ship, which meant he alone knew where they were, and where they were going. The change in command may also have been intended to negate the succession orders of the bill of return, as his faith in Bylot's blind obedience could have been quickly tested prior to departure.

Hudson also had all the remaining food stores that didn't require cooking, the ship's biscuits and cheese, brought together and divided equally among the crewmembers. He wanted everyone to share alike, regardless of rank, and also to receive an equal portion of all the food, both good and spoiled, "that they should see they had no wrong done to them."

It was a well-meaning strategy, but it backfired badly, as some of the crew, Henry Greene included, wolfed down their personal store in a matter of days. When the *Discovery* encountered pack ice almost as soon as she set sail and was forced to anchor for about two weeks, Hudson's fate was set.

AROUND DAWN ON June 22, 1611, some twenty leagues north of the over-wintering place in James Bay, John King was lured into the hold to get him out of the way. Henry Hudson was seized and pinioned: his arms were held behind his back as a rod or pole was passed in front of his elbows and tied in place. Hudson, his son John, and seven other crewmembers of the *Discovery*, many of them ill, were directed into the shallop and were soon adrift, never to be seen again.

PRECISELY HOW THE mutiny unfolded, and who was responsible, cannot be firmly answered. The only version of events belonged to the survivors of the voyage home, and a more self-serving assemblage of depositions and narratives cannot be imagined.

Having survived the voyage, they then had to save their own necks as the horror of the mutiny became known. Their recollections (often contradic-tory, with some of the survivors even contradicting themselves) were care-fully tailored, and the very mutiny appears to have been engineered with foreknowledge of how the event would be received back home, if not in the court of public opinion then at least in the one that mattered, the High Court of the Admiralty.

The mutineers (and those who went along with them) intended to blame Henry Hudson for his own demise. But the apportioning of blame had evolved radically by the voyage's end, because none of the crewmembers identified as ringleaders by the survivors lived to see England again. Four of them, including Henry Greene and William Wilson, were killed in a skir-mish with the Inuit, in a trading encounter that rapidly spun out of control. The last of the ringleaders was Robert Juet, the aging navigator who had proved to be so unexpectedly opposed to Hudson's agenda, and had finally acted on his promises to turn the voyage around in an uprising that was never bloody but certainly deadly. Juet's navigation failed to produce an an-ticipated landfall in Ireland as the food ran out: the crew had been reduced to eating bird bones fried in the grease of tallow candles. Juet expired "for mere want," according to Prickett, only days before the battered *Discovery* and her weak and famished crew drifted into the company of a fleet of English fishing boats off Dursey on Ireland's south coast.

Habakkuk Prickett assuredly deserves much of the credit for shaping the defense strategy, and even elements of the actual mutiny. By his own account he was in his berth, weakened by scurvy, when the ringleaders approached him the night before the mutiny and asked him, as the supercargo, to join them. True, his circumstances were dire. He was ill, and would avow that the conspirators would have put him in the shallop if he had not gone along with them. And Hudson's behavior was erratic and troubling. Even so, that did not justify abiding the dreadful abandonment that followed, achieved with his apparent collaboration, whatever he claimed otherwise. By saving the necks of these brutal men, Prickett could save his own. And while Prickett indeed lived to write about it, a shadow would remain over his conduct and reputation. "Well, Prickett," Luke Foxe wrote in 1635, "I am in great doubt of thy fidelity to Master Hudson."

The model the mutineers evidently adopted in justifying and shaping the action was the overthrow of Sir Edward Maria Wingfield at Jamestown in 1607, an insurrection led by Henry Hudson's friend Captain John Smith. The accusations the survivors leveled against Hudson were suspiciously similar: that he secretly hoarded food and shared it with a favored circle while others went starving. The evidence of this in Hudson's case was inconsistently presented and dubious in detail, and while there might have been genuine shortages of food aboard, an inventory of goods after the mutiny indicates that the biscuits and cheese were not the end of their supplies: they still had three quarters of their meal, for example. The allegations of a secret stash, and of Hudson liberally sharing aqua vitae with cronies (a charge that had been leveled at Wingfield), did not jibe with the picture that had otherwise emerged of Hudson as a conscientious mariner who was uncommonly skilled at keeping his men alive.

Especially interesting was the parallel with how Wingfield was handled by Smith and his fellow rebels. Wingfield was placed aboard a pinnace anchored in the river James while his accommodations were searched for evidence of hoarding. This was exactly the strategy pursued with Henry Hudson—at least, it was how the mutineers convinced Hudson and the others to take their seats in the shallop. Some of the crewmembers that went along with the mutiny (not to mention the people in the shallop) thought that these men would be allowed back aboard once the allegedly hidden food caches were uncovered. As it turned out, no search for food was even made before an unnamed mutineer cut the tow rope with the swing of an axe and sent Hudson and seven others to their unknowable ends.

HABAKKUK PRICKETT AND Robert Bylot visited with Sir Thomas Smythe as soon as they were back in London. They had either cooked up a defense themselves or were aided in part by Smythe. The loss of Henry Hudson and his companions was a tragedy and assuredly a crime of some sort, but Smythe and the other leading investors in the voyage were most interested in capitalizing on the geographic intelligence the survivors had brought home. All five men identified as ringleaders were conveniently dead. Beyond the fact that only the dead men, in this defense scenario, were guilty of anything, the survivors had decided the dead men were guilty of spoliation, or piracy. As we've seen, English maritime law for commercial shipping at the time did not recognize mutiny as a crime. The seizure of a ship, if it went beyond the mundane matter of a wage dispute and was intended to provide a platform for piracy, was in itself an act of piracy. Prickett not surprisingly recalled in a High Admiralty Court deposition how three conspirators, led by Greene, "had consult him together to turn pirates."

Soon after their return to London, the survivors—the core of whom were Prickett, Bylot (who had been elected acting master on the passage home), and the barber-surgeon, Wilson—were largely in the clear. They had brought back enough evidence, real or otherwise, of the promise of a Northwest Passage that the voyage's investors were eager to send them right back out again. The backers needed them alive and on board, not hanged from a gibbet, and the survivors knew it.

The High Court of the Admiralty commission that took depositions from six survivors in January 1612 was deeply compromised politically.* The

* The presiding judge, Dr. Richard Trevor, was the uncle of four influential brothers in naval affairs that enjoyed the patronage of either the Lord High Admiral, who had invested in the 1610–11 *Discovery* voyage, or other members of the powerful Howard family, who would appear in the investor ranks of the 1612 follow-up voyage. One especially noteworthy nephew of the judge was Sir John Trevor, a career parliamentarian who represented Welsh boroughs controlled by the Lord High Admiral. He was made surveyor of the navy in 1598 (naval

questions it posed, which would lead to any decision to lay criminal charges, were rarely probing and were more concerned with getting on with the passage search before an advantage was lost. The barber-surgeon was asked what he might know of any charts from the voyage having fallen into Dutch hands, and if he was aware of any plans by the Dutch to attempt the Northwest Passage. Wilson allowed that he had heard that English merchants had shown charts abroad in an effort to raise backing for a new voyage. As it happened, Hudson's cartography by this time probably was already in the hands of Hessel Gerritsz, who would publish the only map deriving directly from Hudson's lost cartography later that year.

Wilson thought the route "may be easily discovered if such may be employed as have been acquainted with the voyage and knoweth the manner of the ice." Wilson might as well have testified: keep us alive, take us along, and you will secure a new passage to the Orient that will make you wealthier than you can imagine. No criminal indictments resulted, and when the *Discovery* sailed again for the passage that spring, in a two-ship expedition under the command of Thomas Button that was backed by the usual leading figures of commerce and court, Prickett, Bylot, and Wilson were all along, and were even listed among the subscribers.

So LONG AS the quest to prove the Northwest Passage remained alive, the survivors of Hudson's last voyage were able to avoid being held to account for the loss of the eight people in the shallop. Bylot made three more voyages following the 1612–13 expedition, the last two with pilot William Baffin, on which he served as the *Discovery*'s master. The voyages were financed by a new venture, the North-West Company, of which Sir Thomas Smythe was governor. The final expedition, in 1616, searched the entire coast of Baffin Bay for the passage. Baffin declared the search hopeless, yet he and

---

affairs were infamously corrupt) and a gentleman of the privy chamber in 1608. Sir John was close to Henry, the Prince of Wales, advising the youth on the discovery of the Northwest Passage. The prince, of course, had served as the 1610–11 *Discovery* voyage's patron. Sir John had also been involved in the Virginia Company since the London wing was formed in 1606, and he would have known Sir Thomas Smythe and many other figures who both invested in the Jamestown colony and financed the 1610–11 *Discovery* voyage. For the full scope of the Admiralty court's compromised position, see my book *God's Mercies.*

Bylot had unwittingly discovered the entrance. The indention at latitude 74 that they named Lancaster's Sound was actually a strait. It would not be recognized as the eastern entrance to the Northwest Passage until 1819.

With the passage search considered at this point a protracted failure, any protections from prosecution enjoyed by the survivors of the 1611 *Discovery* mutiny had dissolved. New depositions were gathered by the High Court of the Admiralty in 1617, and the interrogations were more probing, and full of alarming allegations: that shots had been fired at the shallop by the mutineers, that Bylot had stolen a ring from Henry Hudson's finger, that there was actually plenty of food on board, including freshly killed game. There were suspicions that influential men had been shielding them from prosecution, and Prickett was compelled to answer several insinuating questions from the hostile commission. He swore he had no knowledge that the masters of Trinity House had said "they deserved to be hanged" on their return, and that "he made no means to hinder any proceedings that might have been taken against them. Neither knows who."

But suspicions were being cast on the role of Sir Thomas Smythe, who had headed the North-West Company and promoted Bylot to master of the *Discovery*. In a 1617 deposition, Bylot stated, "He told Sir Thomas Smith the manner how Hudson and the rest went from them, but what Sir Thomas said to their wives he knows not." A back channel of information apparently had opened between the widows and the court commission, and Bylot's statement indicates there was a discrepancy between the accounts previously given to the court and what the widows had learned privately from Smythe. No widow would have been more voluble in her agitations than Katherine Hudson, who had lost both a husband and a son. She had applied to the directors of the East India Company, a co-sponsor of the *Discovery* voyage, in 1614, asking for some consideration for her youngest son, Richard. The directors, led by Smythe, literally made their problem go away by finding the youth a position on a company ship called the *Samaritan*, giving him five pounds for "apparels and necessities," and sending him to Bantam. Richard Hudson would become the company's chief representative in the Bay of Bengal, while the indomitable Katherine traveled to India and entered the import-export business through the company.

Smythe's was the only investor's name to ever surface in a deposition, and by 1617 he was under extreme pressure within the Virginia Company, as a faction of rival investors began agitating for better governance and ultimately for his removal as treasurer. Two of Smythe's enemies in the Virginia venture, Sir Edwin Sandys and Henry Wriothesley, Earl of Southampton, had been investors in the 1610–11 *Discovery* voyage. They would have had the political muscle to successfully petition to reopen the *Discovery* case, as well as the motivation: to stain the reputation of Sir Thomas Smythe, by securing convictions of the men he had sheltered and exposing his role in doing so.

On July 24, 1618, four of the *Discovery*'s survivors, including Prickett and Wilson, appeared in court at St. Margaret's Hill in Southwark to answer a charge of murder in the deaths of Henry Hudson and the other castaways. An undated indictment for some of the accused had charged them with placing the men in the shallop "without food, drink, fire, clothing or any necessaries, and then maliciously abandoning them, so that they came thereby to their death and miserably perished." The indictment rejected the survivors' testimony that only the dead conspirators, bent on piracy, could be held responsible, or that the men in the shallop had been provided with food, cooking utensils, weapons, and all the clothing and bedding they wished to take with them.

At least two accused, including Robert Bylot, had fled. The four defendants appeared with their unnamed sureties, who had posted the bonds securing their liberty until the trial. We can imagine that these sureties were influential men and may have included Smythe. The bonds had saved them from being clapped up in the gloom and squalor of Marshalsea prison with the other defendants marched into court that day, as many as fourteen men who were facing piracy and related murder charges.

Trials in 1618 were nothing like today. Defense lawyers were not even permitted until the eighteenth century, and the proceedings were a whirlwind of charges read and pleas entered on all of the cases, with the jury then reading out the sentences in one great batch before the day was out.

The *Discovery*'s accused all pleaded not guilty to the murder charge, but if convicted they had one slender hope. In a case the previous week, a mother of a young man sentenced to death for theft successfully appealed to Sir Thomas Smythe to have the sentence commuted by agreeing to ship him to the Virginia colony. The *Discovery*'s accused might also end up in exile at Jamestown, if such an arrangement could be made in so serious and notorious a case.

An appeal to Smythe to intervene proved unnecessary. Whereas most of the accused pirates that day were found guilty and sentenced to hang, all four *Discovery* defendants were found not guilty and set free.

None of the accused (or any other survivors) were ever heard from again. And while Henry Hudson had vanished in the mutiny, he lived on through a Bligh-like legacy, thanks to the self-serving depositions and recollections of the survivors. They had crafted a portrait of him as a selfish, heartless tyrant who had hoarded food and gulped down aqua vitae with companions while the crew around him starved. Hudson's conduct had been far from exemplary, but the portrait was an outrage that would prove difficult to overcome. And in a few years, Dutch writers would begin their own reworking of his portrait, based on the 1609 *Half Moon* voyage. They were not trying to save their own skins but rather to preserve their claim to New Netherland, and their investments therein.

CHAPTER 29

A FTER HENRY HUDSON WAS ALLEGEDLY ordered not to sail for any country but his own in January 1610, wrote Emanuel Van Meteren, "it was then thought probable that the English themselves would send ships to Virginia, to explore the river found by Hudson."

In 1611, a third Virginia Company charter was granted by James I, extending its territory all the way south to latitude 30 (virtually to San Agustín) and north to latitude 41, thus including Delaware Bay and the Hudson River as far upstream as its widening into the Tappan Zee. But whatever interest Hudson and Juet might have stirred with reports of minerals and ores (and actual samples) from the Hudson River could not budge a ship from London's docks to investigate them. The plans reported by Van Meteren never produced a voyage to the river that would bear Hudson's name, at least not one that the exploration record preserves. The Virginia Company had all it could handle on the Chesapeake, where the Jamestown venture was still struggling. And unlike the French and the Dutch, the English were not particularly interested in the fur trade at this time. English investors were focused on the fishery and colonization, on the establishment of plantations.

At the same time, Hudson's *Discovery* voyage of 1610–11 had reignited interest in proving the Northwest Passage, with four voyages sent out between 1612 and 1616, backed by leading merchant adventurers. The moneymen were more fearful of the Dutch beating them to the Northwest Passage than to the resources and opportunities of Hudson's 1609 discoveries.

Samuel Argall did enter Delaware Bay in 1610, but it was an accidental find. Only in 1613 did an English ship finally appear in Upper New York Bay, and it was again Argall, who stayed briefly and never returned. Hudson's friend John Smith might have had his curiosity piqued by what Hudson had seen, but he was out of the picture. Injured in a gunpowder explosion and surrounded by factional rivals, he had withdrawn from Jamestown in September 1609. Hudson and Smith would have had time to meet and discuss Hudson's findings before Hudson embarked on the *Discovery* voyage. When Smith returned to the North American theater in 1614, however, it was to make a fresh investigation of Norumbega, to which he gave the name New England in anticipation of a renewed colonization effort. He coasted modern Maine and Massachusetts, going nowhere near Hudson's discoveries.

That the Dutch ended up exploiting Hudson's 1609 discoveries owed nothing to top-down planning, ambitions of the VOC, or visions of an overseas empire. Hessel Gerritsz thought little of Hudson's voyage. "All he did in the west in 1609 was to exchange his merchandise for furs in New France," Gerritsz dismissed in 1612, in a work remembered now as *Detectio Freti Hudsoni*, which was devoted to recent passage discoveries. Gerritsz's real interest was in Hudson's final, fatal voyage, and by employing unknown English source materials he produced for that book the only map known to show Hudson's discoveries in the Canadian north. And as ignorant as Gerritsz may have been of what Hudson had actually seen and done in 1609, the opinion belonged to a leading Dutch cartographer and promoter of passage-making discoveries closely associated with the VOC.

Yet Gerritsz was out of step with fresh ambitions toward North America in his own country. In 1611 two Dutch merchants, Ernest Van der Wal and Pieter Aertszoon de Jonge, mounted their two-ship expedition, consisting of the *Vos* (or *Vosje*) and the *Craen* (*Fox* and *Crane*). Both merchants went along as supercargoes. The expedition was an apparent effort by interests beyond the VOC to fact-check the fact-checker, to investigate all of Henry Hudson's voyages from 1607 to 1609. Thwarted off Spitsbergen and at Novaya Zemlya in an attempt to find a northern passage to the Orient, the ships then set out for eastern North America. They coasted from Nova Scotia to somewhere beyond Cape Cod, engaging in a bit of trade and losing six men, including de Jonge, to the native attack at La Have. Both ships then overwintered presumably somewhere in New England, and there is no evidence they made it as far as New York. In February 1612, the *Vos*, un-

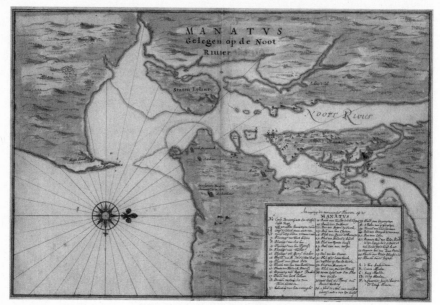

This hand-drawn map, Manatvs gelegen op de Noot Riuier, *made about 1670, is believed to be a copy of a lost original made in 1639. It depicts the Dutch settlements around present-day New York, with west being "up." It is often attributed (without firm evidence) to Joan Vinckeboons. (Library of Congress, Geography and Map Division.)*

der master Jan Corneliszoon May, sailed all the way back to the northeast, to try again (unsuccessfully) for a transpolar passage, while the *Craen* remained in eastern North America. The *Craen* arrived home in July, the *Vos* in October, to sneering commentary by Gerritsz, who opined that the slain de Jonge "by divine providence" had received "the reward of his folly." Gerritsz was forced to retract his libels.

The concerns of English merchant adventurers that the Dutch might beat them to exploiting Hudson's discoveries in the northwest proved to have merit. In 1613 the *Vos* was sent out under Pieter Franszoon by the Admiralty of Amsterdam and the merchants Jonas Witsen and Simon Willemszoon Nooms to examine the strait Hudson had explored in 1610–11. The only thing we know about this voyage is an annotation on a 1619 wall map published by Willem Janszoon Blaeu that indicates Franszoon got as far as the western end of Hudson Strait. The next year, the *Vos* was trading at the Hudson River.

By the time Hessel Gerritsz published his dismissal of Hudson's 1609

The Hessel Gerritsz map Tabula Nautica *(1612), depicting discoveries from Henry Hudson's fateful 1610–11 voyage, features this lively little illustration— one of the best portraits of ships from Hudson's time. (Note: this image was scanned from a nineteenth-century reprint of the map in the author's possession.)*

achievement in 1612, Dutch merchants had already moved into the Hudson River area. The men who followed in Hudson's wake were fur traders, not passage-seekers or land barons dreaming of plantations.

The record of the first Dutch voyages, which may have begun as early as 1610, is far from clear, as a swarm of operators appeared using either their own or chartered vessels. They were backed by merchant associations, called *voorcompagnieën*, which routinely operated in multiple business areas with partners in different countries, and tended to feature familiar faces in the directorships. A trading establishment of rude huts was on Manhattan by 1613, and a trading post upriver, at Castle Island on the Albany waterfront, was erected in 1613 or 1614. In 1614, Adriaen Block became the first European to investigate the East River and experience the tidal rip of Hell Gate, which he named. That introduced him to Long Island Sound, and his discoveries continued eastward, to include the Fresh River (Connecticut River), the elusive Port de Refugio (Newport Harbor in Narragansett Bay), and Block Island, whose name is self-evident. That same summer, Cornelis Jacobszoon May (or Mey), possibly a relative of the Jan Corneliszoon May who had commanded the *Vos*, visited the Hudson River and Delaware Bay, where he named both Cape May and Cape Henlopen.

Henry Hudson's 1609 discoveries were getting crowded, attracting at least one French trading vessel in addition to rival Dutch operations, and becoming much better known. In 1614, a posthumous edition of Emanuel Van Meteren's *History of the Netherland* was published (Van Meteren having died in 1613), which contained his authoritative, insider's perspective on the 1609 voyage.

In March 1614, the States-General passed an ordinance promising a limited trade monopoly to any discoverer of new lands. At the end of the year, rival Dutch merchant groups banded together as the United New Netherland Company. Effective January 1, 1615, it was granted a monopoly for four trading voyages within a period of three years for a territory called New Netherland, which was declared to extend from latitude 40 to latitude 45. A trading post was established on lower Manhattan in 1615, and a new Fort Nassau may have been built on Castle Island near Albany.

Further explorations in the summer of 1616 led the company to apply unsuccessfully for an extension of the monopoly to latitude 38 to include Delaware Bay and its tributaries. The monopoly expired in 1618, and the States-General rebuffed an appeal for an extension, although it allowed an exclusive right for a single trading voyage to Manhattan. Free trade returned to the Hudson River for three years.

Concerned about the impending expiration of the Twelve Year Truce and the possibility of fresh conflict with Spain and Portugal, the States-General created a powerful new enterprise, the Dutch West India Company (WIC), modeled on the VOC, with five investment chambers, armed merchant ships, and an array of monopoly territories. Chartered in 1621 as the truce expired, the WIC sphere included West Africa (for the slave trade) and the entirety of eastern North America and South America, including the Caribbean. New Netherland was granted the status of a province, with the WIC given exclusive control over the territory. Administration was assigned to the Amsterdam chamber, where most of the traders doing business on the Hudson either were from or were financed.

The WIC launched the most serious effort to make something of Hudson's 1609 discoveries. And as tentative as the start had been to New Netherland, Hudson had made possible the Dutch presence in America that his employer, the VOC, was never seeking. The *Half Moon* voyage was proving to be one of the transformative events of the continent's history.

The WIC was slow to start its New Netherland trade, and in the meantime other operators were permitted to secure furs there. Among the investors in independent trading voyages in the early 1620s was none other than Petrus Plancius. Approaching seventy years of age, Plancius had left the position of chief hydrographer of the VOC to Hessel Gerritsz in 1617 and was concentrating on his exhortations as a firebrand minister of the

Dutch Reformed Church. Never having wanted Hudson to go anywhere near eastern North America on the 1609 voyage, Plancius nevertheless was agreeable to profiting from trade in the lands Hudson had discovered in defying his sailing directions.

The WIC's charter required it to colonize New Netherland, and in 1624 the first settlers arrived in Upper New York Bay. A new stronghold, a simple blockhouse called Fort Amsterdam, was completed by 1625 on lower Manhattan.

That year, Johanne de Laet's *New World* was published, beginning a process of revision and reinvention of Henry Hudson's 1609 exploits. Much was at stake that depended on how New Netherland had been discovered and whether the Dutch could rightfully claim it. Asserting and strengthening that claim invited manipulations of the 1609 voyage record and the memory of Hudson. By the middle of the seventeenth century, Hudson would be transformed in Holland, with the *Half Moon* voyage's details reworked, his nationality tweaked, and incidents invented where required. The rewriting of the *Half Moon* story was at times as audacious and misleading as Hudson's own behavior had been while in command of her, and as self-serving as the accusations fabricated by the survivors of the *Discovery* voyage. Taken together, they would render Henry Hudson all but unrecognizable just a few decades after his disappearance.

ENGLISH OBJECTIONS TO the Dutch presence had surfaced early. In 1613, Samuel Argall had cruised the eastern seaboard looking for interlopers on the territorial claims of the Virginia Company and the English crown. He evicted the Jesuits from their new mission of St-Sauveur at Bar Harbor, Maine, and looted and burned Port Royal, the French outpost on the Annapolis Basin in Nova Scotia that had been revived by the Sieur de Poutrincourt in 1610. Then he made his visit to Manhattan, the first known English vessel to do so, to demand that Dutch traders swear allegiance to James I and recognize the Virginia Company's territorial rights. The trader on the receiving end of Argall's demands, Hendrick Christiaensen, is said to have complied, which he may have done only to make the irascible Englishman go away before he seized his ship and torched the simple huts the Dutch had built on lower Manhattan.

Although it has been suggested that Argall was enforcing a personal interest in the area that had been promised to him through the Virginia Company, neither he nor any other Englishman returned. The Dutch were left
alone on the Hudson River with their modest trading presence. For a few
years, anyway.

In 1619, an application was made to James I for a Charter of New England, with exclusive rights between latitudes 40 and 45. The result was a
new joint stock company in 1620, the Plymouth Council for New England.
Formed by Sir Ferdinando Gorges of Plymouth on the legal ashes of his old
Plymouth wing of the 1606 Virginia Company, it was granted an exclusive
right to the lands from latitude 40 all the way north to latitude 48. The
company immediately established the Plymouth colony of the Puritans,
who had been waiting in the Dutch Republic since 1608 for their chance to
settle a promised land.

English objections were voiced to the Dutch about the overlapping claim
granted to the WIC in 1621. Sir Dudley Carleton—the same Carleton who
traded in gossip about George Waymouth's dockside arrest in 1607—
delivered a formal protest as England's ambassador to The Hague in 1622.
The English came away with the impression that the Dutch had no actual
interest in colonization. But the Dutch believed that in accordance with the
Law of Nations a territorial claim could not be maintained without a permanent presence, and the English thus had forfeited any exclusive right to
the lands above the 1609 Virginia charter territory when the Sagadahoc
colony failed in 1608.

That position encouraged the WIC to get on with a colony of its own,
and to use Hudson's voyage to reinforce a claim to the territory. Papers
from the *Half Moon* voyage that had been lingering in the files of the VOC
were turned over to Johanne de Laet, who employed them in *New World* in
1625. As a leading WIC investor from Leiden, de Laet was one of two directors the city secured within its Amsterdam chamber. De Laet also sat on the
Amsterdam chamber committee that corresponded with the New Netherland colony. He was an early advocate for colonization, whereas other investors preferred to focus on the fur trade.

De Laet was able to contribute fresh and reputable observations on the
Half Moon voyage in *New World*, including paraphrases and direct quotes
from Hudson's journal, which is otherwise lost to us. Nevertheless, with de
Laet, the revisionism also began. De Laet stated that on his Atlantic cross-

ing Hudson "made land in latitude 41°43', which he supposed to be an island, and gave it the name of New Holland, but afterwards discovered it
was Cape Cod, and that according to his observation, it lay two hundred
and twenty-five miles to the west of its place on all the charts." The detec-
tion of a longitude error sounds plausible (as Juet had reported one for the
Faeroes), but Juet's journal (published for the first time in *Purchas His Pilgrimes*, the same year as de Laet's *New World*) makes clear Hudson well
knew they had found the cape named by the Gosnold expedition of 1602.

But if Hudson could be said to have claimed Cape Cod as New Holland,
the WIC had a geographic starting point for New Netherland. When de
Laet was writing, the WIC may already have begun to suspect that they
would not be able to defend a claim as far north as latitude 45, now that
New England was being colonized. Cape Cod would become the WIC's less
ambitious northerly limit of its claim, and Hudson would anchor it for
them.

DECADES PASSED BEFORE the serious rewriting of Hudson's legacy began.
In the meantime, New Netherland struggled. Settlement was proceeding
fitfully under the feudal patroon system introduced in 1629, in which
manors were established by private investors through direct land purchases from native tribes, while Manhattan (New Amsterdam) remained
the WIC's property. Political power was held by the WIC and the patroons,
which led to agitations for reform.

The legitimacy of the Dutch colony continued to grate in English circles,
and matters came to a head in 1632. New Netherland was deep in crisis, as
the WIC differed with the patroons over the right to trade with natives,
which the company insisted was its exclusive purview. Director-general Peter Minuit was recalled to Amsterdam that May, and on the way home his
ship, the *Union*, called at Plymouth, England. He had stopped in the power
base of Sir Ferdinando Gorges. The watchers of the coast were on the job:
the *Union* was seized, and its passengers, including Minuit, were detained
on the direction of Gorges's New England Company, for the offense of the
WIC having trespassed on its New World territory with the Dutch colony's
commercial activities.

A conciliatory WIC suggested that the territories below latitude 39, south
of the Delaware River, be assigned to the Virginia Company and those above

latitude 41, from around Cape Cod north, be reserved for the New England Company. The WIC would be content with the meat between these two slices of English bread. While Charles I agreed to release the *Union* and her passengers, he refused to surrender so much as an acre of eastern North America to the WIC.

For the time being, nothing further came of the dispute. The English Civil War helped, serving as a fairly pronounced distraction. But the territorial issue continued to fester, and the WIC came up with a novel solution: it would manufacture a Dutch claim prior to the claim attributed to Henry Hudson.

A company committee began a report on December 15, 1644, with the following statement: "New Netherland, situated in America, between English Virginia and New England, extending from the South [Delaware] river, lying in 38½ degrees to Cape Malabar [Cape Cod], in the latitude of 41½ degrees, was first frequented by the inhabitants of this country in the year 1598, and especially by those of the Greenland Company, but without making any fixed settlements, only as a shelter in the winter. For which they built on the North [Hudson] and the South [Delaware] rivers there two forts against the attacks of the Indians."

The company had conjured a prior claim to its territories that predated the *Half Moon* voyage by eleven years and featured trading posts on both the Hudson and Delaware rivers. These alleged trading points pushed back the presence of the Dutch at Manhattan by twenty-six years, and on the Delaware by thirty-three years.

By this time, the company was also striving to defend its claim on the Delaware over a Swedish presence that had appeared out of its own midst. After a Dutch colony failed there in 1631 (massacred by the Lenape), Sweden founded a settlement near present-day Wilmington in 1638. The expedition that brought the Swedish colonists was commanded by Peter Minuit, who had been recalled as New Netherland's director-general in 1632.

The Greenland Company cited in the 1644 WIC report doubtless was inspired by the Northern Company, a cartel of merchants that in 1614 had been awarded by the States-General a monopoly on northern whaling stretching from Davis Strait all the way to Novaya Zemlya. The resulting Dutch incursion led to the Muscovy Company's 1614 petition to the High Court of the Admiralty to protect its supposed monopoly against the Dutch startup—a petition that cited the 1608 explorations of the misnamed "William" Hudson at Novaya Zemlya.

The source of the WIC's 1598 fiction appears to have been a tangle of memories involving Cornelis Jacobszoon May. Some of the merchants behind the United New Netherland Company had already formed the Northern Company in 1614. May's 1614 voyage evidently was made in concert with the Northern Company cartel, as he managed both to find and name Jan Mayen Island and name Cape Henlopen at Delaware Bay for Tijmen Hinlopen, a director of the Northern Company. May was also master of the ship, *Nieu Nederlandt*, which delivered thirty Walloon families to Upper New York Bay in 1624, and he seems to have served as a provisional director-general of the colony. On his return to Amsterdam in 1624, he reported to the WIC that a new trading post, Fort Wilhelmus, had been established on the Delaware. Fort Orange had also been built at Albany in 1624, thus accounting for the creation of two forts on the two rivers in one year in accordance with the 1598 myth.*

No documentation could be produced to support the claim, which the English rejected. But one can find assertions in popular writing today that Dutch traders really were operating on the Hudson and the Delaware in 1598, more than a decade before Henry Hudson got there.

THE MOST EGREGIOUS distortions where Henry Hudson is concerned were contributed by Adriaen Van der Donck, the New Netherland lawyer, promoter of immigration, and agitator for political reform in the colony. He inserted fictions of enduring influence into the *Half Moon* story in his

---

*The idea that Dutch trading posts had existed in 1598 had taken root in New Netherland before the WIC committee wrote its 1644 report. In 1642, the Jesuit priest Isaac Jogues was captured by the Mohawk while in New France. He was enduring a captivity of slow torture that was steadily robbing him of his fingers when Dutch traders at Fort Orange liberated him. Shipped downriver to New Amsterdam, he remained in the colony through most of 1643, arriving in Brittany on Christmas Day that year. (He was less fortunate in 1646, when after returning to New France he was captured again and tortured to death. He was canonized in 1930.)

In his account of his ordeals and time in New Netherland, Jogues remarked: "It is about fifty years since the Hollanders came to these parts. The fort [i.e., Fort Amsterdam] was begun in the year 1615; they began to settle about twenty years ago, and there is already some little commerce with Virginia and New England." Jogues's casual observation that the Dutch had appeared in the 1590s would be seized upon in some histories as corroboration of the idea that traders indeed were on the scene in 1598. If it is actually anything more than sloppy scholarship by Jogues, it suggests he was only repeating a notion alive in New Netherland two years before the WIC report was written.

A Description of New Netherland first published in 1655, although some of the ideas had already appeared in a pamphlet he published in 1650 calling for governance reforms. The book appeared only a year after the first Anglo-Dutch war (1652–54), which was fought entirely at sea.

Determined to smother any idea that someone other than the Dutch had been the first Europeans in New Netherland, Van der Donck dismissed native memories of an original Spanish visit and overlooked altogether the Verrazzano voyage. With those prior claims out of the way, he could rely exclusively on Hudson securing the lands from Delaware Bay to Cape Cod for the Dutch.

Van der Donck acknowledged that the *Half Moon* was in command of an Englishman, Henry Hudson, but an Englishmen only "by birth," as he asserted that Hudson "had resided many years in Holland, and was now in the employment of the East India Company." The first English translation of Van der Donck's work in 1841 would introduce his many falsehoods to a credulous new audience interested in Hudson's exploits. In time, and with enough rounding of factual corners, some writers would come to present Hudson as a Dutchman through and through, a notion that persists, particularly when his name, rendered as "Hendrick Hudson" in Dutch accounts and his VOC contract, is taken too literally.*

Having wrongly sent Hudson to the Canaries on his way to the New World, Van der Donck then had him take possession in the name of the States-General of "the south bay, near the cape, which they named Cape Henlopen." Van der Donck was referring to Delaware Bay. Beyond the highly disputable point that Hudson ever formally claimed anything for the Dutch, he did not claim (or name) Cape Henlopen, as he did not even set foot on it.

Van der Donck was writing when title to Delaware Bay and its main river continued to be in serious dispute. The Dutch of New Amsterdam built a

---

* It's possible that Hudson had spent some time in Holland, as many Englishmen did, before the *Half Moon* voyage, but the idea of his having lived much or most of his life there would be easier to accept if someone who knew him personally like Emanuel Van Meteren happened to note this. As Van der Donck proceeded to lob a series of pure inventions into the record, the idea that Hudson had lived most of his life in Holland or was in fact or at heart a Dutchman is without merit. Among the contemporary accounts by people who actually met him, the scheming VOC investor Isaac Lemaire called him an "English pilot" in his correspondence with Pierre Jeannin; Thomas Holland described him as "an Englishman late of London." The debate should end there.

trading post, Fort Casmir, at the present town of Newcastle, in 1651, and a force from the rival Swedish colony seized it in 1654. The following year, a naval force under New Netherland director-general Petrus Stuyvesant left New Amsterdam to subjugate the entire Swedish colonial presence.

Van der Donck asserted that Hudson's expedition named the Hudson River (which he acknowledged was what "the English . . . call it") the Mauritius, in honor of Prince Maurice of Nassau. But there's no corroboration of this. The Dutch who followed Hudson knew the river as the North (the name by which the lower Hudson is still known to New Yorkers), and the Delaware as the South. The name Mauritius first appears in Adriaen Block's chart used to secure the United New Netherland Company monopoly.

Van der Donck then claimed that on the way home, Hudson visited Cape Cod and called it New Holland, repeating the unlikely story related by de Laet, but now placing the visit to Cape Cod on the wrong leg of the voyage. Van der Donck may have been subtly agitating against the Hartford Boundary Treaty, which Stuyvesant had negotiated in 1650 to end tensions with the English colony of Connecticut. It surrendered two thirds of Long Island to the English, and on the mainland set the Anglo-Dutch boundary close to the modern state border of Connecticut on the sound and ran it north from there, approaching no closer than within ten miles of the Hudson River. Any opposition by Van der Donck to the treaty in the name of Henry Hudson was futile, as it was ratified by the States-General in 1656. And all arguments over the legitimacy of the Dutch claim to the rest of New Netherland were settled in August 1664, when four English frigates appeared in the Narrows.

CHAPTER 30

BEFORE THE ENGLISH AND DUTCH formally went to war again in 1665, fighting had already broken out in 1663 between their mercantile interests over the West Africa slave trade, which had delivered the first of hundreds of slaves to New Amsterdam as early as 1626. The preconflict conflict moved to America in 1664. On March 12,* Charles II, who had been crowned the new English monarch in 1661, thus launching the Restoration that followed Cromwell's rule, awarded his younger brother James title to an enormous amount of American territory.

Charles had spent some of his exile years in the Dutch Republic but was disinclined to express his gratitude by conceding to the Dutch any claim to the New World. The tract he signed over to his brother stretched from the modern Maine–New Brunswick border to Delaware Bay and included Long Island, Nantucket, and Martha's Vineyard. The grant made specific mention of "Hudson's river," a finger in the eye to anyone who thought it should be called the Mauritius. (The river had already been called "Hudson's" in *The Planters' Plea*, published in London in 1630.) James, the thirty-one-year-old Duke of York and Albany (who would become James II after

---

*To minimize confusion with the documentary record, I have preserved the dates as originally recorded in this section. England was still using the old Julian calendar, and was at this time 10 days out of step with the Gregorian one used by the Dutch. Thus the awarding of the territory by Charles II to his brother James could be reported instead as March 22. The hoisting of the English colors at Fort Amsterdam on August 29, 1664, as reported here, is often transposed to the Gregorian date of September 8 as the day English rule began.

his older brother failed to produce a male heir), was also Lord High Admiral, and about to command the Royal Navy in the Second Anglo-Dutch War, of 1665–67.

Colonel Richard Nicoll led a flotilla of four warships to the colonies to proclaim the Duke of York and Albany's domain. Nicoll was prepared to take New Amsterdam by force, but an assault proved unnecessary. On August 27, the articles of capitulation were signed at the plantation, or *bouwery*, of the colony's director-general, Petrus Stuyvesant. Two days later, the English flag was hoisted at Fort Amsterdam.

With the change in management, New Amsterdam became New York, and Fort Amsterdam became Fort James. Up the Hudson, Fort Orange became Albany, in honor of James's dukedom in Scotland. Delaware, too, became an English possession.

Nine years later, the Dutch were back. In July 1673, during the third Anglo-Dutch War, a twenty-ship fleet entered New York's harbor, landed an invasion force on Manhattan, and demanded the surrender of Fort James. The vastly outnumbered English complied on August 9. The new governor, Anthony Colve, set about renaming (or un-renaming) everything: New York became New Orange, Fort James became Fort Willem Henrik, and the province of New Netherland was reinstituted.

Six months later, the Dutch and the English signed the Treaty of Westminster. Much swapping of global real estate was involved. The Dutch had previously captured Surinam and had decided to hold on to it in the 1667 Treaty of Breda while allowing the English to retain New Netherland. Now, in 1673, the Dutch decided they still wanted Surinam but also wanted back several Caribbean islands they had just lost to the English: Tobago, Sint Eustatius, Tortola, and Saba. In return, the Dutch were willing to return New Netherland. Fort Willem Henrik became Fort James again. New Orange was back to being New York.

Once New Netherland was unequivocally English, and then unequivocally American, there was little practical reason to continue the various fictions about Henry Hudson's nationality or what lands he claimed for whom and the names he gave them. But Adriaen Van der Donck had set a documentary precedent that has been difficult to displace.

N. C. Lambrechtsen van Ritthem's eight-volume *History of New Netherland*, published in 1818, perpetuated the notions that Hudson was quasi-Dutch and had lived there for some time, and that he laid explicit claim to

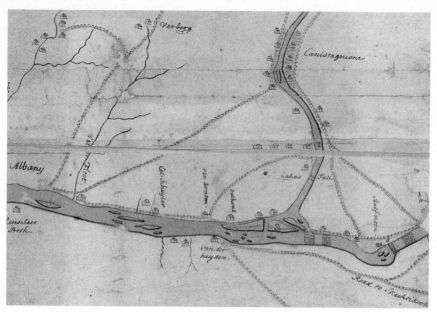

This detail from Map of the northern parts of New York, *a hand-drawn sketch of properties circa 1758, shows the Hudson River from Albany (on the left) north to the confluence with the Mohawk River. (West is "up.") Cohoe Falls is indicated (as "Cahos falls"). Note as well the village of Half Moon, just north of the confluence, named in honor of Hudson's voyage. The Hudson River above the confluence is marked with several sections of rapids, casting doubt on the assertion in Robert Juet's journal that the ship's boat managed to progress eight or nine leagues upriver from the anchorage around Albany—a single-day round-trip of some fifty nautical miles. (Library of Congress, Geography and Map Division.)*

New World landfalls in the name of the States-General: "This industrious navigator felt (although born in England) so sensibly his relation to the Holland East India Company, who had employed him in discoveries, that he could not have hesitated a moment to give the name of his adopted fatherland to this newly discovered country. He called it New Holland." Lambrechtsen also claimed that Cape Henlopen was probably named for the family of whoever on board the *Half Moon* saw it first, and that "North River" originated with sailors aboard the *Half Moon*.

By then the dispute wasn't even academic. It had become a point of national pride: that New York had once been New Amsterdam, and that it had been Dutch from the very beginning. Hudson was recruited as a Dutchman at heart if not by blood, and it became common for him to be referred to as Hendrick, not Henry.

WE CAN REASONABLY ask what eastern North America would have been like had Henry Hudson not explored in 1609 the river named for him. It requires no stretch of the imagination to say that somebody from Europe inevitably, eventually, would have found it (again). The preponderance of coastal activity heavily favored the honor going to the English. In a few years, someone like Samuel Argall would have gotten around to finding it.

What the English then would have done with it is another matter, and a reasonable answer is: not much. Because fundamentally, once Hudson visited the Hudson River estuary and carried the news aboard the *Half Moon* to Dartmouth, the English *had* discovered it in 1609, and proceeded to do nothing about it. Perhaps the momentum of history was unstoppable: when a new source of furs was identified here at some point by someone in the early seventeenth century, Dutch traders would have been on the scene in a heartbeat, just as they were after Hudson's voyage.

The fur trade invited trading posts, and establishing them had quickly pressed the Dutch presence to the very end of Hudson's discoveries, at present-day Albany. As humble as the original Fort Nassau might have been, it became a beacon radiating a signal of change deep into the hinterland, which only grew stronger as New Netherland expanded.

It was also through trade that the geopolitical significance of the Hudson-Champlain corridor emerged. When Thomas Pownall came on the scene in the mid-eighteenth century, the corridor was becoming infested with French and English forts on the eve of the Seven Years' (French and Indian) War, which broke out in the very year of his book's publication. The French built St-Frédéric and Carillon, which the English captured, turning Carillon into Ticonderoga. William Henry was built by the English and fell to the French. After conquering French Canada in 1760, the English secured all of the forts along the corridor and erected one at Crown Point as well. The corridor would prove to be strategically vital during the American Revolution and the War of 1812. Both Henry Hudson and Samuel de Champlain had grasped at the significance of this route between the Atlantic and the upper St. Lawrence, but neither had quite been able to close his hands around it as each found key components in the very same year.

The story of the seventeenth-century fur trade and the overlapping wars between native groups and the French, Anglo-Americans, and Dutch that led to the upheavals of the eighteenth century is far too complex to relate here. Still, the geopolitics of northeastern North America would have been a more straightforward (if that word is even appropriate) struggle between France and England and native allies for colonial dominance had not the Dutch entered the picture through Hudson's discoveries.

It would be ridiculous and myopic to blame the Dutch for the massive destabilization and destruction of native societies that ensued, because there was enough blame to go around, involving all of the European powers. But the WIC's presence had unique consequences, as the company (as well as patroons who believed they too had the right to trade with natives) readily exchanged guns and alcohol for furs.

The policy was in marked contrast to that of their chief trading rivals, the French on the St. Lawrence. Champlain saw the effects of liquor early enough that he demanded no alcohol be traded with natives for furs on the St. Lawrence, although he could not control the volumes reaching the Naskapi along the lower St. Lawrence from independent traders beyond his control. The French under Champlain and his administrative successors following his death at Québec in 1635, strongly influenced by Jesuit missionaries, were determined to prevent alcohol from being provided to natives.

As we've seen, plying natives with strong drink was a tactic employed by Henry Hudson, as well as whoever that European was in John Heckewelder's first-contact oral history, dressed resplendently in red. Native guests never seemed to be offered a beer, as Sebastian Cabot had suggested. The newcomers decanted the hard stuff, the 80 to 100 proof firewater, that went down burning in a single gulp and had immediate consequences.

Brandy became the opium of the seventeenth century in eastern North America. The traders created a demand for it, and hard liquor was so much more profitable than weaker beer. The ratio of intoxication to cargo volume was extremely efficient. Put crudely, one could get a lot more Indians drunk with a ship full of brandy than a ship full of beer, and that meant a correspondingly high return in furs. When the leading patroon Kiliaen Van Rensselaer, an Amsterdam pearl and diamond merchant (and Dutch West India Company director), promoted trading brandy for furs in 1634, not only at Fort Orange but all along the shore of New Netherland, he surely grasped the dark genius of creating and servicing a demand the French would not satisfy, as well as the efficiencies of hauling distilled spirits, rather than beer (which also didn't preserve as well), especially 150 miles up the river that flowed both ways. It was also a drug made for the canoe, compact and potent, and it laid waste to lives, families, clans, and villages.

The first still for making brandy locally (which might have been the first still in North America) went into operation on Staten Island in 1640. In 1642, an enraged native who had been swindled out of his furs by traders who had gotten him drunk randomly murdered an Englishman living on Staten Island in vengeance. A delegation of chiefs to Fort Amsterdam asked the Dutch to stop supplying natives with brandy but was ignored. Writing in 1655, Adriaen Van der Donck assured his readers that natives could handle their liquor as well as any Dutchman once they'd become used to it, but that the colony had decided to no longer permit it as a trade good, as it was blamed for fueling native attacks on settlers. But the tap could never be turned off entirely. In the coming late seventeenth-century trade struggle between the French and the English who took over New Netherland in 1664, natives would prefer the brandy offered by the French over the cut-rate brandy and gin available from the English.

The demand on the French by native traders for muskets was much harder to deflect than any craving for alcohol, particularly when the Dutch began arming the Mohawk and other members of the Five Nations confederacy of the Iroquois. But the French still resisted, reserving guns for Christian converts and even limiting the amount of ammunition supplied. The military advantage gained by the Iroquois, who acquired all the weaponry and ammunition they could afford from the Dutch, was decisive. By the late 1640s the Iroquois had employed Dutch firepower to scatter the Algonquin of the Ottawa River and destroy the once powerful Huron.

The WIC's decision to settle New Netherland rapidly (and at no expense to itself) by introducing the feudal patroon system in 1629 also had significant consequences for the native peoples Henry Hudson had met. The charter that introduced this plan had not even been formally adopted by the company when the land grab began by company insiders.

In 1630, the Van Rensselaer investment group (to which Johanne de Laet belonged) began to assemble a feudal holding around Fort Orange at present-day Albany. Its purchases from the Mahican stretched about twenty-four miles south from the confluence with the Mohawk to Coey-man's Landing on the west side and included lands on the east side as well. The patroon of Rensselaerswyck totaled more than 1,100 square miles and is represented today by Albany County on the west side of the river and Rensselaer County and part of Columbia County on the east side. The acquisition costs were a pittance. One tract was acquired for "certain quantities of duffels, axes, knives and wampum."

Patroons and their agents rapidly swallowed up the best agricultural land of the Hudson River Valley, and all of the waterfront locations around greater New York, displacing in a few short years the peoples who had lived there probably since the last ice age. They did so by outright purchase, a process of sovereignty-by-checkbook (or trade items, as it happened) objected to by the English.

The WIC's policy of land purchase might at first glance seem to have been an enlightened approach to native sovereignty, as it held that the aboriginals were free subjects, not under the rule of any European monarch or state and entitled to do whatever they saw fit with their land, up to and including selling all of it to strangers. In considering Dutch protests over the seizure of the *Union* in 1632, Charles I and the Lords Commissioners of England dismissed the legitimacy of such land purchases, denying that "the savages were possessors *bonae fidei*, of those countries, so as to be able to dispose thereof either by sale or gift, their habitations being changeable, (*mouvantes,*) uncertain, and only in common."

The English maintained that natives could not sell something they did not occupy in recognizably European terms. And it was certainly to the advantage of the Dutch to arrange these purchases and then order natives off the land (or make them rent it back). There was no concept of real estate, whether collectively or privately owned, in these cultures that meshed with a notion of its barter value and permanent loss of use. There was also no system of governance, in otherwise sophisticated societies that operated on consensus and without imperial rulers or nobles, that would permit a chief of any description, however elevated he might be declared in European eyes, to unload the land of his people for trade goods. Indeed, Charles I and his Lords Commissioners had further rejected the Dutch principle of acquiring territory by purchase on the reasonable ground that "it cannot be proved, *de facto*, that all the natives of said countries were parties to the said pretended sale."

Relations between Dutch settlers and natives whose land they purchased were often harmonious. But some tribes, like the Esopus in the 1650s, fought back against the incursion of settlers. Others were reeling under too many other blows—pandemics, conflicts with rival native groups over trade, the social devastation of alcohol—to do much about it.

The shame of the destruction of so many natives, individuals as well as tribes and nations, is not an exclusive historic burden to the Dutch of the WIC. But the company's role in fueling the Amerindian arms race and the complex conflicts over territory and trade made a considerable difference in the lives of tens of thousands, natives and Europeans alike.

Henry Hudson did not make the first deal for native land in the Hudson River estuary. But he served the first liquor (in at least several generations), conducted the first kidnappings, and led the men who were the first to kill with muskets. Some of his crew assuredly returned with Dutch traders to exploit the river's potential. Hudson was as well intentioned as one can expect of a man of his time, but intentions could not stem history's flow. It was a flood without an ebb.

HENRY HUDSON HAD listened to Mahican elders describe to him the surrounding countryside, with sketches by them likely being the source of the blue lines in the Velasco Map showing a waterway beyond the great river that would bear his name. In 1825, the Erie Canal was completed, linking the Hudson River at Albany with Lake Erie at Buffalo. Other locks and canals extended shipping to Lake Ontario, and further up the Hudson to Lake Champlain.

The promise of a passage westward had been realized. Even if it was not directly to the Orient, it proved to be incredibly lucrative. Through an extended reach by ships and rail, the Hudson River and its canals made New York the premier gateway into a continent that was no longer merely an impediment to be overcome, as Menéndez, Hayes, Champlain, and very likely Hudson himself had imagined. By the mid-nineteenth century, New York was the largest port on the eastern seaboard of North America.

In 1909, the city and state of New York were gripped by a trifecta of anniversaries. It had been three hundred years since Henry Hudson had arrived in the *Half Moon* and Samuel de Champlain had discovered Lake Champlain, and 102 years since Robert Fulton had introduced steamboat service between New York and Albany. Champlain's feat received its own festivities, while the other achievements were combined by civic leaders into the two-week Hudson-Fulton Celebration.

The anniversary inspired an effort to properly memorialize the English navigator who had sailed in the service of the Dutch. In 1904, the city of New York began planning the "Hendrick Hudson Memorial Bridge," which would span Spuyten Duyvil Creek and link Manhattan's Inwood district with the Bronx. On one side of the span, a statue of Hudson, sixteen feet tall, would top a hundred-foot marble column, allowing the mariner to gaze upon the river named for him as it flowed back and forth with the tide on the west side of Manhattan.

Lands were donated for the park that would contain the monument, and funds were raised to pay for it. The renowned sculptor Karl Bitter was secured, and he created a plaster model of Hudson. The Doric column was in place by 1912, but the money ran out, and Bitter was killed in a car accident in 1915 while leaving an opera performance. Henry Hudson was left with a soaring column in a field of weeds as a legacy. And there was no bridge. An original plan for a single steel arch design similar to the nearby bridge spanning the Hudson River at Washington Heights (formerly Jeffery's Hook, where Juet's falconet had blown apart Lenape archers) was rejected by the city's Municipal Arts Committee, which felt that it was unsuited to the natural setting of the creek.

Decades passed, with no progress made on either the bridge or the monument. In 1930, both initiatives were revived by the commissioner of city parks, Robert Moses, as part of a new arterial plan that included the Hudson River Parkway. After much haggling over design and financing, construction on what was now called the Henry Hudson Bridge began in 1935. The 840-foot main span was the longest steel arch in the world at the time, and its single four-lane deck, completed in 1936, gained a second deck of three lanes in 1938.

Meanwhile, work resumed on the monument. Bitter's design had been used to create souvenirs before the statue failed to materialize, and they show that he had been inspired by *The Last Voyage of Henry Hudson*, an 1881 oil painting by John Maler Collier, an academic painter whose output ranged from portraits of Charles Darwin and Thomas Huxley to racy Pre-Raphaelite nudes. Collier's depiction of Hudson's final days would be his most famous work. The castaway Hudson has a hundred-mile stare and a

Sculptor Karl Heinrich Gruppe in his studio with models for the Henry Hudson Memorial statue. (Peter A. Juley & Son Collection, Smithsonian American Art Museum, J0069070.)

menacing iceberg at his back. His left hand grips the tiller of the shallop while his right hand clutches the left of his son John, a mere child who sprawls helplessly at his feet and looks to him as beseechingly as a spaniel with a thorn in his paw.

Collier's Hudson was a quasi-medieval figure in a bulky robe and a long beard. After almost twenty years of project inertia, Karl Bitter's three-dimensional version of the Collier portrait had truly aged, lacking the bold vigor expected of exploration heroes. A former student of Bitter's, Karl Heinrich Gruppe, who produced a number of public monuments for the city and completed Ritter's fountain for the Plaza Hotel after his mentor was killed, was retained to reimagine Hudson, as well as produce two bas-reliefs for the memorial base. One shows Hudson receiving his commission from the VOC, the other the first trading post on Manhattan.

Gruppe's Hudson was a more fitting rival for the swashbuckling Champlain statues that had been cropping up in eastern North America: a seafarer in pantaloons, with boots planted firmly as he stares ahead, not with the glazed doom of Collier's castaway but with sharp anticipation of uncharted landfalls. The bronze casting was set atop the long-empty column on January 6, 1938.

Henry Hudson would have appreciated the spectacular view. It would have told him that Manhattan was an island.

Acknowledgments

My thanks, in no particular order, go out to:

- Dean Cooke and Sally Harding of the Cooke Agency, for working so hard to help me craft the proposal for this book and then finding it such a good home.
- Peter Ginna, publisher and editorial director of Bloomsbury USA, for providing that home as well as cogent and enthusiastic input.
- Pete Beatty, assistant editor at Bloomsbury USA, for his careful reading and prompt assistance.
- India Cooper, for a relentlessly attentive copyedit.
- Conrad Heidenreich, professor emeritus at York University, a leading expert in the cartography and writings of Samuel de Champlain who has also lectured on the Hudson mutiny of 1611, for several years of encouragement, advice, and sharing. His contributions have been enormous.
- Janet Ritch, an academic expert in early Spanish and French, who has been working on a new annotated edition of Champlain's writings being overseen by Dr. Heidenreich, for agreeing to provide me with a prepublication look at her fresh treatment of *Des Sauvages*, which proved critical to my ideas on Champlain's knowledge of the midcontinental passage theory of Edward Hayes.
- Ed Dahl, retired head of map collections at the National Archives of Canada, for his directions.
- Gord Laco, a fellow member of the Midland Bay Sailing Club who also happens to be a professional consultant on historic sailing ships (a job that saw him disappear for months to work on the film *Master*

and Commander: The Far Side of the World), for explaining to me that "bilbows" were leg irons.

- Nick Burningham, a nautical archaeologist in Australia who played a leading role in the design and construction of the replica VOC jaght *Duyfken*, for engaging in a lengthy and enjoyable series of e-mail exchanges that fundamentally informed my impressions of the nature of the *Half Moon*, from design and layout to how she sailed, and for providing illustrations employed in this book.

- Steve Killing, my coauthor on *Yacht Design Explained*, for entertaining my persistent questions about the sailing capabilities of historic vessels.

- John Carter Brown Library of Providence, Rhode Island, for providing the high-resolution digital scan of Edward Wright's 1599 map.

- Editors Jeffrey S. Levinton and John R. Waldman, and the many contributors to *The Hudson River Estuary* (see bibliography). This book was an invaluable resource on the natural history of the river. Especially informative were the chapters "The Hudson River Valley: Geological History, Landforms, and Resources," by Les Sirkin and Henry Bokuniewicz; "The Physical Oceanography Processes in the Hudson River Estuary," by W. Rockwell Geyer and Robert Chant; and "Fisheries of the Hudson River Estuary," by Karin E. Limburg and others.

- The late David B. Quinn, a giant of scholarship in the early English exploration and colonization of North America. Without his annotated edits of primary documents and his own writings on this fascinating period (see bibliography), I would be profoundly in the dark about Henry Hudson's day and age, and would never have been able to propose connections between the midcontinental theory of Edward Hayes and the activities of Samuel de Champlain and early French colonizing and exploration in eastern North America. I regret never having met or spoken with him before he passed away in 2002, a year before I began serious research in an area of scholarship he so dominated.

- The champions around the world of placing historical texts and images in free online databases. Whether transcribed or preserved in digital facsimiles, this wealth of primary materials has made it possible for me to conduct research from a remote location in Canada at a breadth and depth that would have been unheard of less than a decade ago.

- The members of Chelsea Yacht Club and Shattemuc Yacht Club who were so accommodating in getting me sailing on the Hudson River. Sharon Herring, commodore of Chelsea Yacht Club, and Sandy Mace, commodore of Shattemuc Yacht Club, went out of their way to hook up a perfect stranger with one of their members. At Chelsea Yacht Club, Serge Cryvoff provided an afternoon of brisk sailing aboard his J-34C *Noteworthy*. At Shattemuc Yacht Club in Ossining, Bob Millstein took me for an extended romp on the Tappan Zee aboard his Tartan 31 *Pentimento*. Shoreside hospitality was above and beyond any call of duty, and I thank everyone for their warm welcome and assistance.
- My wife, Deb, for deftly navigating around a husband hard aground in the early seventeenth century. Again.

Bibliography

Alden, Chester, and E. Melvin Williams. *Courts and Lawyers of New York: A History, 1609–1925*. New York: American Historical Society, 1925.

Alfieri, J., and more. *The Lenapes: A Study of Hudson Valley Indians*. Hudson River Maritime Museum. www.hrmm.org/halfmoon/lenape/indexm.htm.

Allen, Elizabeth. "Cope, Sir Walter (1553?–1614)." *Oxford Dictionary of National Biography*, Oxford University Press, 2004.

Andrews, Kenneth R. *Ships, Money and Politics: Seafaring and Naval Enterprise in the Reign of Charles I*. Cambridge: Cambridge University Press, 1991.

———. *Trade, Plunder and Settlement: Maritime Enterprise and the Genesis of the British Empire, 1480–1630*. Cambridge: Cambridge University Press, 1984.

Asher, Georg Michael. *Henry Hudson the Navigator: The Original Documents in Which His Career Is Recorded*. London: Hakluyt Society, 1861.

Ashton, Robert. *Reformation and Revolution, 1558–1600*. London: Granada Publishing, 1984.

Baigent, Elizabeth. "Brereton, John (b. 1571/2?, d. in or after 1619?)." *Oxford Dictionary of National Biography*, Oxford University Press, 2004.

———. "Bylot, Robert (fl. 1610–1616)." *Oxford Dictionary of National Biography*, Oxford University Press, 2004.

Baldwin, R. C. D. "Argall, Sir Samuel (bap. 1580, d. 1626)." *Oxford Dictionary of National Biography*, Oxford University Press, 2004.

———. "Poole, Jonas (bap. 1566, d. 1612)." *Oxford Dictionary of National Biography*, Oxford University Press, 2004.

Barbour, Philip (ed.). *The Jamestown Voyages Under the First Charter, 1606–1609*. 2 vols. London: Cambridge University Press for the Hakluyt Society, 1969.

Biggar, H. P. (ed.). *The Voyages of Jacques Cartier*. Updated with introduction by Ramsay Cook. Toronto: University of Toronto Press, 1993.

———, (gen. ed.). *The Works of Samuel de Champlain*. 6 vols. Toronto: Champlain Society, 1922–36.

Black, Frederick R. *Jamaica Bay: A History*. Gateway National Recreation Area, New York, New Jersey. Cultural Resource Management Study No. 3. Washington: U.S. Department of Interior, 1981.

Blackstone, Sir William. *Commentaries on the Laws of England*. Oxford: Clarendon Press, 1765–69.

Blunt, Edmund M. *The American Coast Pilot*. 10th edition. New York: Edmund M. Blunt/William Hooker, 1822.

———. *The American Coast Pilot*. 18th edition. New York: Edmund and George W. Blunt, 1857.

Braat, J. "Dutch Activities in the North and the Arctic During the Sixteenth and Seventeenth Centuries." *Arctic* 37, no. 4 (December 1984): 473–80.

Brinton, Daniel G. *The Lenâpé and Their Legends; with the complete text and symbols of the Walum Olum, a new translation, and an inquiry into its authenticity.* Philadelphia: D. G. Brinton, 1885.

"The Building of the Half Moon." Chapter 7, *The Fourth Annual Report on the Hudson-Fulton Celebration Commission to the Legislature of the State of New York, May 20, 1910.* Transcribed online at www.hrmm.org/quad/1909hudsonfulton/chapter07.html.

Burningham, Nick. "Learning to Sail the *Duyfken* Replica." *International Journal of Nautical Archaeology* 30, no. 1 (2001): 74–85.

———. "A Scurvy Life: Life at Sea Circa 1600." *Signals: Quarterly Magazine of the Australian National Maritime Museum* 48 (1999): 6–9.

Burningham, Nick, and Adriaan de Jong. "The *Duyfken* Project: An Age of Discovery Ship Reconstruction as Experimental Archaeology." *International Journal of Nautical Archaeology* 26, no. 4 (1997): 277–92.

Calendar of State Papers Domestic: James I, 1603–10, and 1611–18. Great Britain: Public Record Office, 1857, 1858.

Calendar of State Papers Colonial, vol. 1 (America & West Indies), 1574–1660. Great Britain: Public Record Office, 1860.

Campbell, Lyall. "Sable Island's First People and Livestock." Published online at www.greenhorsesociety.com.

Clark, Charles E. "Gorges, Sir Ferdinando (1568–1647)." *Oxford Dictionary of National Biography,* Oxford University Press, 2004.

Crane, Nicholas. *Mercator: The Man Who Mapped the Planet.* London: Weidenfeld & Nicolson, 2002.

Croft, Pauline. "Cecil, Robert, first earl of Salisbury (1563–1612)." *Oxford Dictionary of National Biography,* Oxford University Press, 2004.

de Veer, Gerrit. *The Three Voyages of William Barents to the Arctic Regions.* Edited by Charles T. Beke. London: Hakluyt Society, 1876.

De Vries, Jan, and A. M. van der Woude. *The First Modern Economy: Success, Failure, and Perseverance of the Dutch Economy, 1500–1815.* Cambridge: Cambridge University Press, 1997.

Delâge, Denys. *Bitter Feast: Amerindians and Europeans in Northeastern North America, 1600–64.* Translated by Jane Brierley. Vancouver: UBC Press, 1993.

Dodd, Arthur Herbert. "Trevor Family." *Dictionary of Welsh Biography Online,* yba.llgc.org.uk.

Elliott, J. H. *The Old World and the New, 1492–1650.* Cambridge: Cambridge University Press, 1970.

Elting, Irving. *Dutch Village Communities on the Hudson River.* Baltimore: Johns Hopkins University, 1886.

Elton, G. R. *England Under the Tudors.* 3rd edition. London: Routledge, 1991.

Emmer, Pieter. "The Dutch Atlantic, 1600–1800: Expansion Without Empire." In H. Pietschmann (ed.), *Jahrbuch für Geschichte Lateinamericas,* 38 (2001): 31–48.

Ewen, C. L'Estrange. *The Northwest Passage: Light on the Murder of Henry Hudson from Unpublished Depositions.* Private monograph, 1938.

Finkelpearl, P. J. "Chamberlain, John (1553–1628)." *Oxford Dictionary of National Biography,* Oxford University Press, 2004.

Furlong, Lawrence. *The American Coast Pilot.* 1st edition. New York: Blunt and March, 1796.

Gardiner, Samuel Rawson. *History of England,* vols. 1, 1603–07; 2, 1607–16. London: Longmans, Green, 1900.

Gehring, Charles T. "The Dutch Among the People of the Long River." Annals of New Netherland. New York: New Netherland Institute, 2001.

———. "Privatizing Colonization: The Patroonship of Rensselaerswijck." Annals of New Netherland. New York: New Netherland Institute, 2000.

Gelderblom, Oscar, and Joost Jonker. "Completing a Financial Revolution: The Finance of the Dutch East India Trade and the Rise of the Amsterdam Capital Market, 1595–1612." *The Journal of Economic History* 64, no. 3 (September 2004): 641–72.

Gerritsz, Hessel. *Detectio Freti Hudsoni*. Translated by Fred John Millard. Amsterdam: Frederik Muller, 1878.

Griffiths, Sir Percival. *A Licence to Trade: The History of English Chartered Companies*. London and Tonbridge: Ernest Benn, 1974.

Grotius, Hugo. *The Freedom of the Seas* [1608]. Translated by Ralph Van Deman Magoffin. Edited by James Brown Scott. New York: Oxford University Press, 1916.

Hacquebord, Louwrens. "In Search of Het Behouden Huys." *Arctic* 48, no. 3 (September 1995): 248–56.

Hakluyt, Richard. *The Principall Navigations, Voiages, Traffiques and Discoveries of the English Nation*. 3 vols. London, 1598–1600. Modern edition: Goldsmid, Edmund, (ed.). Edinburgh: E. & G. Goldsmid, 1885–90.

Hampson, Thomas. "Hudson River School," in *I Hear America Singing*, www.pbs.org/wnet/ihas/icon/hudson.html.

Harris, John. *Navigantium atque itinerantium bibliotheca; or, A Compleat Collection of Voyages and Travels*. London, 1705.

Hayes, Derek. *Historical Atlas of Canada*. Vancouver: Douglas & McIntyre, 2002.

Heidenreich, Conrad. "Explorations and Mapping of Samuel de Champlain." *Cartographica* monograph no. 17, 1976.

"Henry Hudson Memorial Park." Lehman College Art Gallery, www.lehman.edu/vpadvance/artgallery/publicart/sites/hudson.html.

"Henry Hudson Monument." New York City Department of Parks and Recreation, www.nycgovparks.org/sub_your_park/historical_signs/hs_historical_sign.php?id=11789.

"Henry Hudson Parkway." Historic American Engineering Record NY-334. Washington: National Park Service, Department of the Interior, n.d.

Hicks, Michael. "Davis, John (*c.* 1550–1605)." *Oxford Dictionary of National Biography*, Oxford University Press, 2004.

Hodsdon, James. "Hoddesdon, Sir Christopher (1533/4–1611)." *Oxford Dictionary of National Biography*, Oxford University Press, 2004.

Holland, Thomas. Letter to Sir Robert Cecil. Cecil Papers: Letters and Documents, 1563–1610, Hatfield House Library and Archives, ARCHON Code 2173.

Hoxie, Frederick E. (ed.). *Encyclopedia of North American Indians*. New York: Houghton-Mifflin, 1996.

Hunter, Douglas. *God's Mercies: Rivalry, Betrayal, and the Dream of Discovery*. Toronto: Doubleday Canada, 2007.

———. "Was New France Born in England?" *Beaver* 86, no. 6 (December 2006/January 2007): 39–44.

Jacobs, Jaap. *New Netherland: A Dutch Colony in Seventeenth-Century America*. Leiden and Boston: Brill, 2005.

James, Bartlett Burleigh (ed.). *Journal of Jasper Danckaerts, 1679–1680*. New York: Charles Scribner's Sons, 1913.

Jameson, Franklin (ed.). *Narratives of New Netherland, 1609–1664*. New York: Charles Scribner's Sons, 1909.

Janvier, Thomas A. *Henry Hudson: A Brief Statement of His Aims and his Achievements*. Private monograph, 1909.

Jenkins, Elizabeth. *Elizabeth the Great*. New York: Time, 1964.

Johnson, Donald S. *Charting the Sea of Darkness: The Four Voyages of Henry Hudson*. Camden, Maine: International Marine, 1993.

Kenny, Robert W. *Elizabeth's Admiral: The Political Career of Charles Howard, Earl of Nottingham, 1536–1624*. Baltimore: John Hopkins Press, 1970.

La Rocco, Barbara (ed.). *Going Coastal New York City*. New York: Going Coastal, 2004.

Laughton, J. K. "Wolstenholme, Sir John (1562–1639)," rev. H. V. Bowen. *Oxford Dictionary of National Biography*, Oxford University Press, 2004.

Le Blant, Robert, and René Baudry (eds.). *Nouveaux documents sur Champlain et son époque*, vol. 1, *1560–1622*. Ottawa: National Archives of Canada, 1967.

Lesger, Clé. *The Rise of the Amsterdam Market and Information Exchange: Merchants, Commercial Expansion and Change in the Spatial Economy of the Low Countries, c. 1550–1630*. Translated by J. C. Grayson. Burlington, Vt.: Ashgate Publishing, 2006.

Levinton, Jeffrey S., and John R. Waldman (eds.). *The Hudson River Estuary*. New York: Cambridge University Press, 2006.

Lewis, Clifford M., and Albert J. Loomie (eds.). *The Spanish Jesuit Mission in Virginia, 1570–1572*. Chapel Hill: University of North Carolina Press for the Virginia Historical Society, 1953.

Litalien, Raymonde, and Denis Vaugeois (eds.). *Champlain: The Birth of French America*. Montréal: McGill-Queen's/Septentrion, 2004.

Louis Berger Group. "Proposed New South Ferry Terminal, Lower Manhattan, New York, New York: Phase IA Archaeological Assessment." Prepared for New York City Transit, July 2003.

MacBeath, George. "Du Gua de Monts, Pierre." *Dictionary of Canadian Biography*, vol. 1, University of Toronto/Université Laval, 2000.

Marsden, Reginald Godfrey. "English Ships in the Reign of James I." *Transactions of the Royal Historical Society*, new ser. 19 (1905); 309–42.

Markham, Clements R. (ed.). *The Voyages of Sir James Lancaster, Knight, to the East Indies, with Abstracts of Journals of Voyages to the East Indies, During the Seventeenth Century, Preserved in the India Office; and the Voyage of Captain John Knight (1606), to Seek the Northwest Passage*. London: The Hakluyt Society, 1877.

McConnell, Anita. "Hondius, Jodocus (1563–1612)." *Oxford Dictionary of National Biography*, Oxford University Press, 2004.

McDermott, James. "Hudson, Henry (d. 1611)." *Oxford Dictionary of National Biography*, Oxford University Press, 2004.

Mitchell, Dr. Samuel. *An Essay on the Geology of the Hudson River and the Adjacent Regions*. New York: A. T. Goodrich, 1820.

Morgan, Basil. "Smythe, Sir Thomas (c. 1558–1625)." *Oxford Dictionary of National Biography*, Oxford University Press, 2004.

Morison, Samuel Eliot. *The European Discovery of America*, vol. 1, *The Northern Voyages, A.D. 500–1600*. Oxford and New York: Oxford University Press, 1971.

Morley, William F. E. "Verrazzano, Giovanni da." *Dictionary of Canadian Biography*, vol. 1, University of Toronto/Université Laval, 2000.

Motley, John Lothrop. *History of the United Netherlands, from the Death of William the Silent to the Twelve Year Truce*. 4 vols. New York: Harper & Bros., 1870–71.

MTA New York City Transit. Chapter 11, "Cultural Resources," in *Draft Environmental Impact Statement for Emergency Ventilation Plant for the 8th Avenue and 7th Avenue Subways*, 2008.

Murphy, Henry Cruise. *Henry Hudson in Holland*. Private monograph, 1859; New York: Burt Franklin, 1972.

———. *Journal of a Voyage to New York and a Tour in Several of the American Colonies in 1679–80, by Jasper Dankers and Peter Sluyter*. Brooklyn: Long Island Historical Society, 1867.

Nicholls, Mark, and Penry Williams. "Ralegh, Sir Walter (1554–1618)." *Oxford Dictionary of National Biography*, Oxford University Press, 2004.

Nichols, John. *The Progresses, Processions, and Magnificent Festivities of King James the First*. London: J. B. Nichols, 1828.

O'Callaghan, E. B. *Documents Relative to the Colonial History of the State of New-York, Procured in Holland, England and France*, vol. 2. Albany: State of New York, 1858.

———. *History of New Netherland; or, New-York Under the Dutch*, vol. 1. New York: D. Appleton, 1848.

Ohio History Central. "John G. Heckewelder." Online encyclopedia of the Ohio Historical Society, www.ohiohistorycentral.org/entry.php?rec=184.

Payne, Anthony. "Hakluyt, Richard (1552?–1616)." *Oxford Dictionary of National Biography*, Oxford University Press, 2004.

Porathe, Thomas, and Gary Svensson. "From Portolan Charts to Virtual Beacons: An Historic Overview of Mediated Communication at Sea." Presented at the International Visual Literacy Association's conference in Newport, Rhode Island, October 1–4, 2003.

Pownall, Thomas. *A topographical description of such parts of North America as are contained in the (annexed) map of the middle British colonies, &c. in North America*. Philadelphia: 1755.

Powys, Llewelyn. *Henry Hudson*. New York: Harper & Bros., 1928.

Quinn, David B. *England and the Discovery of America, 1481–1620*. London: George Allen & Unwin, 1974.

———. *New American World: A Documentary history of North America to 1612*. 5 vols. New York: Arno Press and Hector Bye, 1979.

———. *North America from Earliest Discovery to First Settlements: The Norse Voyages to 1612*. New York: Harper & Row, 1977.

Quinn, David B., and Alison M. Quinn (eds.). *The English New England Voyages, 1602–1608*. London: Hakluyt Society, 1983.

Purchas, Samuel. *Purchas His Pilgrimes (Hakluytus posthumus)*. London, 1625. Digital facsimile accessed online at the Kraus Collection of Sir Francis Drake, Library of Congress.

Rabb, Theodore K. "Sandys, Sir Edwin (1561–1629)." *Oxford Dictionary of National Biography*, Oxford University Press, 2004.

Rapple, Rory. "Gilbert, Sir Humphrey (1537–1583)." *Oxford Dictionary of National Biography*, Oxford University Press, 2004.

Ransome, David R. "Gosnold, Bartholomew (d. 1607)." *Oxford Dictionary of National Biography*, Oxford University Press, 2004.

———. "Newport, Christopher (bap. 1561, d. 1617)." *Oxford Dictionary of National Biography*, Oxford University Press, 2004.

———. "Waymouth, George (fl. 1587–1611)." *Oxford Dictionary of National Biography*, Oxford University Press, 2004.

———. "West, Francis (1586–1633/4)." *Oxford Dictionary of National Biography*, Oxford University Press, 2004.

Read, John Meredith, Jr. *A Historical Inquiry Concerning Henry Hudson, His Friends, Relatives, and Early Life, His Connection with the Muscovy Company, and Discovery of Delaware Bay*. Albany: Joel Munsell, 1866.

Reeve, L. J. "Carleton, Dudley, Viscount Dorchester (1574–1632)." *Oxford Dictionary of National Biography*, Oxford University Press, 2004.

Richter, Daniel K., and James Hart Merrell (eds.). *Beyond the Covenant Chain: The Iroquois and Their Neighbors in Indian North America, 1600–1800*. University Park: Penn State University Press, 2003.

Rosenberg, Jakob, Seymour Silva, and E. H. ter Kuile. *The Pelican History of Art: Dutch Art and Architecture, 1600–1800*. 3rd edition. New York: Penguin Books, 1977.

Rundall, Thomas (ed.). *Narratives of Voyages towards the North-West, in Search of a Passage to Cathay and India, 1496 to 1631*. London: Hakluyt Society, 1849.

Sanderson, Eric, and Marianne Brown. "Mannahatta: An Ecological First Look at the Manhattan Landscape Prior to Henry Hudson." *Northeastern Naturalist* 14, no. 4 (2007): 545–70.

Schilder, Gunter. "Development and Achievements of Dutch Northern and Arctic Cartography in the Sixteenth and Seventeenth Centuries." *Arctic* 37, no. 4 (December 1984): 493–514.

Schlesinger, Roger, and Arthur P. Stabler (eds.). *André Thevet's North America: A Sixteenth-Century view*. Montréal: McGill-Queen's, 1986.

Seaman, David, and others. "Gateway Between River and Mountains: Historic Catskill Point." Exhibition text for Historic Catskill Point Visitors' Center, Catskill, New York, exhibition opened May 2000.

Stewart, Alan. *The Cradle King: A life of James VI & I*. London: Chatto & Windus, 2003.

Stow, John. *A Survey of London*. Edited by Charles Lethbridge Kingsford. 1603 edition collated with the first edition of 1598. Oxford: Clarendon Press, 1908.

Sullivan, James (ed.). *The History of New York State, Book 1*. New York: Lewis Historical Publishing, 1927.

Symons, Thomas H. B. (ed.). *Meta Incognita: A Discourse of Discovery—Martin Frobisher's Arctic Expeditions, 1576–1578*. 2 vols. Ottawa: Canadian Museum of Civilization, 1999.

Tarrow, Susan. Translation of the Cellere Codex, pp. 133–43, in Lawrence C. Wroth, *The Voyages of Giovanni da Verrazzano, 1524–28*. New Haven: Yale University Press for the Pierpont Morgan Library, 1970.

Thrush, Andrew. "Button, Sir Thomas (c. 1575–1634)." *Oxford Dictionary of National Biography*, Oxford University Press, 2004.

———. "Mansell, Sir Robert (1570/71–1652)." *Oxford Dictionary of National Biography*, Oxford University Press, 2004.

Tillyard, E. M. W. *The Elizabethan World Picture*. London: Chatto & Windus, 1943.

Trigger, Bruce. *Natives and Newcomers: Canada's "Heroic Age" Reconsidered*. Montréal: McGill-Queen's, 1985.

——— (ed.). *The Handbook of North American Indians*, vol. 15, *Northeast*. Washington: Smithsonian Institution, 1978.

Van der Donck, Adriaen. *A Description of the New Netherlands*. Amsterdam, 1656. Translated by Jeremiah Johnson. New York: New-York Historical Society, 1841.

Van Dillen, J. G., and Geoffrey Poitras and Asha Majithia. "Isaac Le Maire and the Early Trading in Dutch East India Company Shares." *Pioneers Of Financial Economics*, vol. 1. Cheltenham and Northampton: Edward Elgar Publishing, 2006.

Vigneras, L.-A. "Gomes, Estevão." *Dictionary of Canadian Biography*, vol. 1. University of Toronto/Université Laval, 2000.

Waters, D. W. *The Art of Navigation in England in Elizabethan and Early Stuart Times*. New Haven: Yale University Press, 1958.

Wheatley, Henry Benjamin. *London, Past and Present: Its History, Associations, and Traditions*. London: J. Murray, 1891.

Wilkinson, Robert. *Londina Illustrata: Graphic and Historic Memorials [etc.]*. London: R. Wilkinson, 1819–25.

Wilson, James Grant. *The Memorial History of the City of New York, from Its First Settlement to the Year 1892*, vol. 1. New York: New York History, 1892.

Winton, John. *An Illustrated History of the Royal Navy, in Association with the Royal Naval Museum, Portsmouth*. London: Salamander Books, 2000.

Yates, John, and Joseph Moulton, *History of the State of New-York, Including Its Aboriginal and Colonial Annals*, vol. 1. New York: A. T. Goodrich, 1824.

INTERNET RESOURCES

Admiralty EasyTide. easytide.ukho.gov.uk

American Journeys. www.americanjourneys.org

The Avalon Project, Yale Law School. avalon.law.yale.edu/default.asp

British History Online. www.british-history.ac.uk

The Champlain Society. www.champlainsociety.ca

David Rumsey Map Collection. www.davidrumsey.com

Delaware Indians of Pennsylvania. www.delawareindians.com

Dictionary of Canadian Biography Online. www.biographi.ca

Duyfken 1606 Replica Foundation. www.duyfken.com

Early Canadiana Online. www.canadiana.org

Hudson River Maritime Museum. www.hrmm.org

Institute of Historical Research. www.history.ac.uk

The Internet Archive. www.archive.org

The Jesuit Relations and Allied Documents (Thwaites edition). puffin.creighton.edu/jesuit/relations

The Kraus Collection of Sir Francis Drake. international.loc.gov/intldl/drakehtml/rbdkhome.html

Library of Congress. www.loc.gov/index.html

Library and Archives Canada. www.collectionscanada.gc.ca

The Mannahatta Project. www.wcs.org/sw-high_tech_tools/landscapeecology/mannahatta

The Map of Early Modern London. mapoflondon.uvic.ca

National Oceanographic and Atmospheric Administration:
    Charting and Geodesy. www.noaa.gov/charts.html
    Historical Maps and Charts. www.nauticalcharts.noaa.gov/csdl/ctp/abstract.htm
    Historical Coast Pilots. www.nauticalcharts.noaa.gov/nsd/hcp.htm
    Tides and Currents. tidesandcurrents.noaa.gov/index.shtml

The Natural History of Nova Scotia, vol. 1. museum.gov.ns.ca/mnh/nature/nhns

New Netherland Institute/New Netherland Project. www.nnp.org

New Netherland Museum and the Half Moon. www.newnetherland.org

New York City Department of Parks and Recreation. www.nycgovparks.org

New York Public Library Digital Gallery. digitalgallery.nypl.org

New York State Historical Maps. www.sunysb.edu/libmap/nymaps.htm

Online Library of Liberty. oll.libertyfund.org

Oxford Dictionary of National Biography. www.oxforddnb.com

Project Gutenberg. www.gutenberg.org/wiki/Main_Page

Sable Island Green Horse Society. www.greenhorsesociety.com

She-philospher.com (studies in the history of science and culture). www.she-philosopher.com

The Society of Colonial Wars in the State of Connecticut. www.colonialwarsct.org

U.S. Geological Survey Historic Topographic Maps. historical.mytopo.com

University of Toronto Libraries. main.library.utoronto.ca

Virtual Jamestown. www.virtualjamestown.org

Index

A page number with the suffix "fn" denotes a footnote reference.
Numbers in italics refer to illustrations or their captions.

A Note on the Author

Douglas Hunter is the author of the acclaimed *God's Mercies: Rivalry, Betrayal, and the Dream of Discovery*, about the rivalry of Henry Hudson and Samuel de Champlain. An experienced sailor, he has written about the history of exploration as well as the early economic history of North America. His other works include a biography of the brewing baron John Molson, a standard reference on yacht design (coauthored with Steve Killing), and an exploration of the tech stock bubble. He lives in Port McNicoll, Ontario, Canada.